JAPANESE GRAMMAR SELF-TAUGHT

MARLBOROUGH'S SELF-TAUGHT SERIES. NO. 18

JAPANESE GRAMMAR SELF-TAUGHT

(IN ROMAN CHARACTER)

BY

H. J. WEINTZ.

SECOND EDITION.

GYAN

Published by

GYAN

Gyan Publishing House
5, Ansari Road
Daryaganj, New Delhi-110002
Phone: 011-47034999, 9811692060
E-mail: books@gyanbooks.com

Distribution Network
gyanbooks.com
India, USA, Canada, UK, Australia, France

ISBN : 978-81-212-4435-0 (PB)
First Published, 1907

2nd Impression 2020

Printed at: Gyan Press, Delhi.

The book at your disposal is the edition of an old book originally published long back. The Text quality of this book may not be at par as compared to our other books but many readers approached us to reprint this important book so that it could satiate their hunger. We request all the readers of this book to help us to improve its quality by providing the necessary text of those pages which are not properly visible. Your valuable support in this case will be highly appreciated and acknowledged and our future readers will be benefitted immensely.

MARLBOROUGH'S SELF-TAUGHT SERIES.—No. 18.—JAPANESE GRAMMAR.

Japanese Grammar Self-Taught.

(IN ROMAN CHARACTER.)

CONTENTS.

I.—GRAMMAR AND SYNTAX. With Pronunciation, Native Japanese Characters, etc.

II.—EXERCISES AND EXTRACTS.
1. Exercises for translation, with Key.
2. Reading Exercises, with Pronunciation and Translation.
3. Japanese Extracts, with Key.

III.—VOCABULARIES: Japanese-English. English-Japanese.

MONEY, WEIGHTS AND MEASURES.

BY

H. J. WEINTZ.

SECOND EDITION.

LONDON:
E. MARLBOROUGH & CO., 51, OLD BAILEY, E.C.
1907.

NOTE TO SECOND EDITION.

The proposal to issue a second volume of Japanese under the title of "Japanese Self-Taught," referred to in the Preface of this book—see opposite page—has now become an accomplished fact, and in the new volume the Publishers have carried out the idea of issuing a conversational phrase-book, consisting of the classified sentences in English and Japanese comprising Part II. of the first edition of "Japanese Grammar Self-Taught," together with a large number of classified Vocabularies. Throughout the work the pronunciation of the Japanese words has been added in accordance with Marlborough's well-known and popular system of phonetics, so that each page is arranged in three columns, viz., the English, Japanese (romanized) and the phonetic pronunciation respectively.

The space thus set at liberty in the Grammar has been filled by inserting three new sections of useful Exercises, as follows:—

A. Exercises for translation, in English and Japanese alternately, with Key.

B. Reading Exercises, interlined with the English phonetic pronunciation, and with Key.

C. Additional Extracts (short) from Japanese works, with translation.

The Exercises for translation (section A) consist of conversational sentences of a most practical and useful character, and both the Exercises proper and the Key may be used for translation, each forming the key to the other.

For this new matter the Publishers are indebted to Mr. J. Fife Mortimer, who for many years has made a special study of the Japanese language and literature.

The two works now form "a very comprehensive and "useful manual of the Japanese language, for students, "commercial men and traders, missionaries, travellers and "tourists." (See Preface, "Japanese Self-Taught.") They may be obtained bound together in one volume, entitled "Japanese Self-Taught and Grammar."

London, 1907.

PREFACE.

The scheme of this work is to provide a **complete manual of the Japanese language** rather than a phrase-book for travellers and others temporarily visiting Japan. Such visitors have not been overlooked, however, for a large number of **Conversational Phrases and Sentences**, conveniently classified, have been added, (including many of those running through the SELF-TAUGHT SERIES), together with full Vocabularies alphabetically arranged. The Publishers propose to develop these sections for issue under the title of "Japanese Self-Taught."*

The Japanese people, by their intelligence, energy, and enterprise—so remarkably displayed of late years—have raised their country to a prominent position amongst the Nations of the World, both politically and *commercially*. A great and growing interest, fostered by our recent alliance with its government, is being manifested towards "THE BRITAIN OF THE PACIFIC," and there is a **growing necessity** for a simple and inexpensive hand-book of the Japanese Language, which the present volume is designed to meet.

The work is carried out in the ROMAN CHARACTER, as for all practical purposes of international communication the Roman alphabet is being steadily adopted by the Japanese themselves. The native characters are however given, together with the rules of transliteration and a number of illustrative examples, so that the student may possess himself of the key to native literature.

Japanese is usually looked upon by Europeans as being terribly difficult to learn, but in reality it is *extremely easy*

* See "Note to Second Edition" on preceding page.

when studied in the Roman character; the want of a really practical grammar on modern lines has probably given rise to the idea referred to. The Syntax certainly *is* formidable to a European, as it is quite different from anything met with in Western languages, but Syntax is of very minor importance in Japanese—at least as regards making one's-self understood. A Japanese would be quite intelligible in England if he said "I to shop went, a book to buy," and *vice versâ* an Englishman would convey his meaning equally well by a similar distortion of a Japanese sentence, especially as the language itself is highly elliptical, thus accustoming Japanese people to readily infer meanings from context, &c.

The **simplicity of the language** is shown by such facts as that there is only one person in each tense—no *concord* (cf. French, and especially German)—no long lists of exceptions to rules,—only two irregular verbs of common occurrence,—and that it is *purely phonetic* (a most important point). The Author speaks advisedly in stating that one can make himself perfectly understood after far less time spent in study than is necessary in the case of any European language. Of course, to attain anything approaching syntactical accuracy, a much longer course of study is necessary than for obtaining an equal degree of proficiency in French, German or Spanish.

The **Grammar** has been compiled from the Author's notes, accumulated during many years' experience in preparing candidates for examinations, etc., and much of the matter introduced has been suggested by the questions and the difficulties of pupils. No attempt has been made to discuss verb-roots, archaic forms, and other matters interesting to philologists, but of no value to anyone taking up the study for practical purposes. The **Vocabularies** and **Conversational Phrases** are the outcome of a very great amount of time and care, bestowed on them with the object of ensuring completeness and accuracy in supplying the **words**

and phrases in actual use. The sentences are not mere literal translations from the English, but are those which would be used by a Japanese under similar circumstances. They are, in fact, not English-Japanese, but *Japanese-Japanese,* and in compiling them the Author has had the advantage of the co-operation of native linguists and others. The **literal translation** of Japanese sentences, in numerous instances throughout the book, will afford valuable assistance in synthetical construction, and will be found to lend considerable interest to the study of the language, by revealing the quaint and primitive nature of the native manner of putting ideas together.

The whole structure of the language is quite alien to anything found in Europe. In German, French and Spanish, for example, the equivalents for "give me," viz., *Geben Sie mir*, *donnez-moi*, and *déme*, respectively, may be taken as models, or forms which hold good for any noun which may be affixed. Not so in Japanese; an equivalent for "give me" cannot be isolated as it forms part of the context, and similarly with other expressions.

The **greatest care** has been taken to ensure that all the words found in the vocabularies are strictly conversational, so that the student will learn to employ the words in ordinary use, and will not be led into treating his Japanese hearers to such comicalities as "Condescend to demonstrate the route to —," instead of "Please tell me the way —." Many dialects are spoken in Japan, as in most countries, and yet the standard language is everywhere understood and spoken also, and anyone who carefully studies and masters the contents of this book, may rest assured that he can travel anywhere in Japan and make himself understood wherever he may go.

With regard to **pronunciation**, romanized Japanese is so purely phonetic that it has not been found necessary to introduce a third and phonetic column in the Conversations and Vocabularies in this volume (*see* Parts II. and III.), but with the few simple rules of pronunciation stated and exemplified in the early pages, and bearing in mind that, with few exceptions, **each letter has only one sound,** that **that sound never varies,** and that **every letter in each word must be distinctly sounded,** the student will readily acquire facility of speech in the language. Out of the 2,000 words (about) in the vocabularies, there are only four which present any divergency from the rules, and only two in the whole of the phrases, and in these cases I have noted the deviation and supplied an imitated pronunciation.

The short **extracts from Japanese authors** which are included, with literal and free translations, seem commonplace and puerile to English eyes, but they are thoroughly typical of the matter found in the few novels in the language. Fiction is beneath the notice of educated readers and writers, but there are signs indicating that it will be cultivated in the near future, and that a call will be made for translations of the leading English novels.

Students, Naval*, Military, and other Professional and Commercial men, Travellers and Tourists, will find this Manual of the greatest service, whether as a practical guide to the Language, or as a Conversational Phrase-book for every-day needs.

H. J. WEINTZ.

Shipley, 1904.

* The **Admiralty** offer special privileges and inducements to officers in the Royal Navy to STUDY JAPANESE.

CONTENTS.

PART I.

GRAMMAR, SYNTAX, etc.

(Pages 9 to 102.)

PART II.

EXERCISES AND EXTRACTS.

(Pages 103 to 128.)

PART III.

VOCABULARIES. (ALPHABETICAL.)

(Pages 129 to 178.)

JAPANESE GRAMMAR SELF-TAUGHT

Part I. GRAMMAR, SYNTAX, Etc.

The Syllabary, Pronunciation, Accent.

THE SYLLABARY.

The native characters used for writing the Japanese language are comprised in two alphabets termed "Syllabaries,"—the *Katakana*, which consists of the remnants of forty-seven Chinese square characters, and the *Hiragana*, which is composed of a number of cursive forms of Chinese symbols. Both of them differ entirely from any European alphabet and mode of writing, so that their acquisition at the commencement of the study of the language would really prove a hindrance to the student's progress. It is quite possible to obtain a thorough knowledge of the spoken language through the medium of the Roman characters, and, having gained an insight into the grammatical peculiarities, the student can easily transpose the Romanized characters into either of the two native Syllabaries, which may then be memorized in a few hours.*

In Japanese there are no separate *letters*, as these are understood in European languages, each of the characters of the syllabaries virtually representing a *syllable*; **n** final, which has a symbol to itself, forming the one exception.

Each syllable is composed of a vowel preceded by one of the consonants—*k* (or *g*, see p. 10), *s*, (*z* or *j*), *t* (*d*), *n*, *h* (*b* or *p*), *m*, *y*, *r*, *w*. Thus, every syllable is supposed to terminate with a vowel, and usually does so; e.g., *ka-ga*, *ga-ku*, *i-ka-nga-shi-i*. The exceptions occur principally in foreign words, or are produced by contractions.

The following table exhibits the syllables of the Japanese language in the Roman character, and arranged according to what is termed the *Go-jiu-on*, or "fifty sounds."

* For the Syllabaries in the native character see pages 96, 97.

THE SYLLABARY.

Vowel Syllables.

a	i	u	e	o

Consonant Syllables.

ka *ga*	ki *gi*	ku *gu*	ke *ge*	ko *go*
sa *za*	shi *ji*	su *zu*	se *ze*	so *zo*
ta *da*	chi *ji*	tsu *dzu*	te *de*	to *do*
na	ni	nu	ne	no
ha *ba* *pa*	hi *bi* *pi*	fu *bu* *pu*	he *be* *pe*	ho *bo* *po*
ma	mi	mu	me	mo
ya	i	yu	ye	yo
ra	ri	ru	re	ro
wa	i	u	ye	wo

By learning the nine consonants *k*, *s*, *t*, *n*, *h*, *m*, *y*, *r*, and *w*, together with the five consonantal softenings *g*, *z*, *d*, *b*, and *p*, the Syllabary is readily committed to memory.

PRONUNCIATION.

1. The Vowel Syllabics.

These are pronounced as pure vowels, having much the same sounds as in Spanish, Italian, &c., but are always short unless marked with the usual diacritic sign (*ō*, *ū*, &c.).

Character.		Sound represented.	Phonetic sign.*
ā	approximately as	*a* in *father*	*ah*
ī (ii)	,,	*i* ,, *machine*	*ee*
ū	,,	*oo* ,, *food*	*oo*
ē	,,	*a* ,, *date*	*eh*
ō	,,	*o* ,, *sore*	*oh*
a	,,	*a* ,, *man*	ah
i	,,	*i* ,, *tin*	ee
u	,,	*oo* ,, *foot*	oo†
e	,,	*e* ,, *bed*	e (*or* eh)
o	,,	*o* ,, *polo*	oh

* As used on pages 14 and 15. † Not dwelt on.

I and *u* are frequently cut so short as to become nearly inaudible. In such instances they are written throughout this book *ĭ*, *ŭ*. Thus, *shĭta*, with one of its meanings, is usually pronounced as if written *sh'ta*; *matsŭ*, with one signification, is pronounced *mats'*.

In the combinations *ai, au, ae, ao, ui, ei, oi,* each vowel is distinctly sounded. They read as follows:—*ah-ee* (= the English diphthong represented by *i* in *mile* or *y* in *my*—phonetic sign *i* or ah-ee), *ah-oo* (like *ow* in *how*), *ah-eh*, *ah-oh*, *oo-ee*, *eh-ee* (like *ay* in *gay*), *oh-ee* (like *oy* in *boy*).

2. The Consonant Syllabics.

These are pronounced by combining the consonants and the vowels.

It will be observed that the Syllabary contains certain repetitions and irregularities. Thus we find *shi* where we should expect *si*, *fu* for *hu*, *i* for *yi*, *i* for *wi*; and so on. These anomalies are due to the inability of the Japanese to pronounce the sounds for which the above irregularities are substituted.

Note.—This peculiarity considerably modifies the conjugation of verbs, and should therefore be carefully borne in mind by the student.

The consonants have the same, or nearly the same, sounds respectively as in English, with the exception of the following:—

R, r.—In the syllabic *ri*, the *r* is pronounced somewhat like the English *d*; that is, in its articulation the tip of the tongue touches the roof of the mouth at the same point as in pronouncing the letter *r* itself, but with the substitution of the *d* sound. In the other syllabics *r* more resembles the English *r*, but in none of them is the trill so decided as in, say, Scotch, French, or German.

H, h, and **F, f,** are regarded as identical in Japanese, and their pronunciation is somewhat similar. In pronouncing *f*, the lower lip does not quite come in contact with the upper teeth, but remains at about the same distance from them as in pronouncing *wh* in the word *when*.

G, g, at the commencement of a word has the hard sound of *g* in the English *go*, *gain*, or *gum*; in all other positions like *ng* in *singer*. [Phonetic sign "ng" in Roman type; see p. 15.]

T, t, and **D, d,** are pronounced as in Italian; that is, the tip of the tongue is brought into contact with the upper teeth, instead of touching the front part of the roof of the mouth. With the majority of Japanese speakers no perceptible difference is made between *zu* and *dzu*.

Ye.—In this syllable the *y* is mute in most words, and is sometimes omitted in the Roman character. In some words y is used as a vowel in place of i (ee).

N at the end of syllables and words is like the French nasal *n*, i.e., somewhat similar to *ng* in the English *thing* or the *n* in *bank*.

The syllabics *ga*, *za*, *da*, &c., printed in italics in the Syllabary, all commence with *softened* consonants, and are regarded by the Japanese merely as modifications of the syllabics commencing with hard consonants in the lines immediately preceding them, and not as different syllables.

NOTE.—In the native characters this distinction is represented by placing a diacritic sign by the side of the hard-consonant symbol; thus *ka* accompanied by the sign is read *ga*, *shi* is read *ji*, and so on.

The modification of a hard into the corresponding soft consonant often occurs in the formation of derivatives and compounds, so that this change (which with the diacritic sign, is termed *nigori*, or impurity), should be carefully noted.

When a letter is doubled it must be fully sounded twice, as *onna* (pronounced *ohn-nah*) ; *katta* (*kaht-tah*).

ACCENT.

The accentuation of Japanese words is much less prominent than that of English, the various syllables of the same word having an almost uniform degree of emphasis. Quickened, or silenced, vowel sounds frequently render prominent the other portions of the word, but, as a general rule, the stress is laid about equally on each syllable. The sound of the word *gozarimasu*, for example, is almost evenly emphasized—*go-za-ri-mas'*, the terminal *u* being nearly inaudible, and the syllable *masu* receiving but a very slight accent, the emphasis over and above the stress laid on the other three syllables being barely perceptible.

(*a*) In words of *two syllables* the accent is, as a rule, on the *first syllable*, as *hi'ro, tsu'ru.*

Exceptions.—When the vowel sound of the first syllable is short *i* or *u*, and when a long or double vowel sound occurs in the last syllable, the accent is laid on the last syllable, as *shĭka', tsŭki', hirō, musū.*

(*b*) In words of *three syllables* the accent is, as a rule, on the *second syllable*, as *ara'shi, moto'mŭ.*

Exception.—When the second syllable is short, as ĭ or ŭ, the first syllable bears the accent, unless the final syllable has a double (long) vowel sound ; in which case the primary accent is laid on the last syllable, and a secondary (subordinate) accent on the first, as *ta''ĭra', a''tsŭku'* ; *chi'kŭ-shō'', bo'kŭ-tō''.*

(*c*) In *polysyllables* the accent is on the *last syllable but one*, as *Hakoda'te, Yokoha'ma.*

Exception.—If the last syllable but one contains ĭ or ŭ, the accent is thrown back upon the preceding syllable, as *asa'gĭta, Shimo'tsŭke.*

N.B.—Bear in mind that in *all* words accent goes to long syllables, and whenever two such long syllables come together they are pronounced with equal stress. Examples: *Kanā'gawa, aimashō', hō-bō, shō-sō.*

NOTE.—In a very few instances of words written exactly alike, but with different meanings, there are differences in pronunciation which cannot be brought under a general rule, but must be learned by experience. These difficulties, however, need not trouble the student, and the preceding rules will suffice for all ordinary needs.

Examples of Phonetic Pronunciation,

illustrating the preceding rules.

English.	Japanese.	Pronunciation.
Oh!	*mā*	m*ah*
old lady	*obāsan*	oh-b*ah*'sahn
is good	*yoroshī*	yoh-roh-sh*ee*'
good	*ii*	*ee*
listening	*kiite*	k*ee*'teh
province	*shū*	sh*oo*
mother-in-law	*shūtome*	sh*oo*'tohmeh
interpreter	*tsūji*	ts*oo*'jee
(an interjection)	*nē!*	n*eh*
Miss	*nēsan*	n*eh*'sahn
already	*mō*	m*oh*
suitable	*sōtō*	s*oh*-t*oh*
chopsticks	*hashi*	hah'shee
new	*atarashĭki*	ah-tah-rah'sh'kee *or* ah-tah-rahsh'kee
one	*ichi*	ee'chee
melon	*uri*	oo'ree
a little	*sŭkoshi*	s'koh'shee
two	*fŭtatsu*	f'tah'-tsoo
sailor	*sendō*	sehn-d*oh*
harp	*koto*	koh'toh
adversity	*wazawai*	wahzahwah'ee
perilous	*ayaushi*	ah-yah-oo'shee
not returning	*kaerazu*	kah-eh-rah'dzoo
mending (*verb*)	*naosŭ*	nah'oh's'
firebrand	*moyekui*	moh-yeh-koo'ee
politeness	*rei*	ray (reh'ee)

English.	Japanese.	Pronunciation.
a little	*choito*	choh'eetoh *or* choy'toh
very	*goku*	goh'koo
a kind of palanquin	*kago*	kah'ngoh
two (in enumeration)	*fū*	foo
argument	*ron*	rohn
flying (*verb*)	*tonde*	tohn'deh
noisy	*sōzōshī*	s*oh*-z*oh*-sh*ee*
nun	*ama*	ah'mah
shampooer	*amma**	ahm'mah
hole	*ana*	ah'na [ah(n)'nah]
such	*anna**	ahn'nah
a sound	*oto*	oh'toh
a husband	*otto*	oht'toh

Parts of Speech.

The Japanese language, which is probably related to Mongol and to Manchu, differs entirely in composition and method of use from any European tongue.

The classification of Japanese words differs materially from that adopted by Western grammarians in dealing with their languages, but the components of Japanese sentences do duty for what are usually termed *Nouns*, *Pronouns*, *Numerals*, *Adverbs*, *Prepositions*, *Conjunctions*, and *Interjections*. The great majority of these words are *uninflected*, and are divided by native grammarians into two broad classes according to their importance, namely (1) *Na*, (2) *Teniwoha*.

(1) *Na* are the *name-words* proper.

(2) The *Teniwoha* consist of the suffixed syllables or particles, which correspond to the *Prepositions*, *Conjunctions*, and *Interjections* of the English and allied languages. They also serve as terminal inflections for Adjectives and Verbs.

The Japanese also make use of words which correspond with the *Verbs* and *Adjectives* of Western speech, and are termed *Kotoba*, i.e., "words," or *Hataraki-kotoba*, i.e.,

* *Amma* and *anna* are respectively contractions of *amuma* (a-mu-ma) and *anuna* (a-nu-na), their original forms, and thus illustrate the rule stated on p. 9 (3rd par.).

"working-words," so named on account of their activity in assuming continual change of form. They are inflected to express mood, tense, &c.

It will be seen, then, that in Japanese there are in reality but two classes of words: (i.) *Uninflected words*, including Na and Teniwoha, and (ii.) *Inflected words*, Hataraki-kotoba; and it must be borne in mind by the student that the classification according to European methods—i.e., into nouns, pronouns, adverbs, &c.—adopted in this work, is for his own convenience in study, and is not the native mode of dealing with the language.

THE ARTICLE.

The Japanese language has no Article, definite or indefinite; thus, *otoko* signifies indifferently "the man," "a man," "man."

Definiteness may, however, be expressed by periphrasis. Thus, whilst in English "the letter" signifies a particular object which has been the subject of conversation previously, to express the same idea in Japanese it is necessary to use some such periphrase as "letter *just mentioned*," "letter *I wrote*," "letter *brought now*."

THE NOUN.

The Noun has no inflection to mark gender, number, or case. In other words, there is no declension.

Gender.

(1) Names of inanimate objects are neuter, as in English.

(2) In general no distinction is made between the masculine and feminine. Thus, *mŭma* signifies indifferently "horse" or "mare"; *dori*, "cock" or "hen"; and the sex must be inferred from the context.

In a very few cases, however, difference in gender is indicated by the use of different words, as

otoko, man;	*onna*, woman;
musuko, son, boy;	*musŭme*, daughter, girl;
chichi, father;	*haha*, mother.

In some instances, gender is distinguished by prefixing *o* or *on* for the masculine, *me* or *men* for the feminine; as

on dori, a cock;	*men dori*, a hen;
o ushi, a bull;	*me ushi*, a cow.

Similarly:

otoko no ko, a male child (*literally*, man-child);
onna no ko, a female child (*lit.*, woman-child).

Number.

Number is indicated by the addition of prefixes and suffixes. Thus, if it be desired to specify only one particular thing, the numeral for "one," *hito, hitotsu*, or *ichi*, is added to the name of the thing either as prefix or suffix; as

hito-hako, one box = a box;
hon-hitotsu, one book = a book.

Ordinarily the plural is not distinguished from the singular, but plurality can be expressed when necessary by adding *particles* such as *domo*, *ra*, *gata*, *shū (shiu)*, or *tachi* to the singular, as

ninsoku domo, coolies; *kodomo ra*, children;
yakunin gata, officials; *tomo dachi*, friends;
hyakushō shū, farmers; *danna shiu*, masters.
yakunin tachi, officers;

NOTE.—*Gata* and *tachi* are used to show respect, whilst *ra* is generally employed in speaking to coolies and menial servants.

Plurality is sometimes expressed by repeating the noun, as

tokoro, a place;	*tokoro-dokoro**, places;
shina, an object;	*shina-jina**, all kinds of objects;
kuni, a country;	*kuni-guni**, all countries;
kusuri, a medicine;	*kusuri-gusuri**, all kinds of medicines.

* In most instances the second half of the word takes the *nigori*, i.e., its initial consonant is softened. (See p. 13.)

Case.

Case is expressed in Japanese by means of certain terminations, called "postpositions," added to the noun. These postpositions, so far as they extend, answer the same purpose as the English *prepositions*, or the case-endings of a Latin noun.

Example:—

Nom.	*Tori*, or *tori ga*,	a bird.
Gen.	*tori no*, or *tori ga*,	of a bird, *or* a bird's.
Dat.	*tori ni*, or *tori ye*,	to a bird.
Acc.	*tori*, or *tori wo*,	a bird.

Voc.	*tori*, or *tori yo*,	O bird!
Abl.	*tori kara*, or *tori yori*,	from a bird.
Loc.	*tori ni*,	at, to, *or* in a bird.
Agent	*tori de*,	with, *or* by means of, a bird.

N.B.—The plural terminations are placed between the noun and the postpositions, as

Yakunin gata ni kippu wo misemashita.	I showed my ticket to the officers.

(*Literally*,* Officers...to ticket showed.)

Classes of Nouns.

As in most European languages, nouns may be divided into *Primitive*, *Derivative*, and *Compound*.

I. Primitive Nouns.

These are nouns which cannot be referred to any root—being roots in themselves—that is, they are undecomposable; as *inu*, dog; *te*, hand; *kaze*, wind; *yama*, mountain.

II. Derivative Nouns.

These are formed from other nouns, and also from adjectives and other parts of speech, by means of prefixes and suffixes. They are divided into Abstract, Augmentative, Diminutive, Concrete, and Verbal Nouns.

1. *Abstract Nouns.*—These are formed chiefly from adjectives by adding to the stem *-sa*, which is equivalent to the English *-ness* in *brightness*, *happiness*, &c. Thus, from *takai*, high, is formed the abstract noun *takasa*, height; *wakasa*, youthfulness (from *wakai*, young); *omosa*, weight (from *omoi*, heavy).

True adjectives and some verbal forms, followed by *koto* (thing, fact), are also used as compound abstract nouns, as

takai koto height (*lit.*, high thing);
komaru koto, anxiety (*lit.*, trouble thing).

2. *Concrete Nouns.*—Compound concrete nouns may be formed by adding the word *mono*, thing, to adjectives and to some verbal forms. Thus, *umai mono*, delicacy, is formed from *umai*, delicious, and thing; *ao mono*, vegetables, from

* In the literal translations the Particles have not been included. Their significations will be found in the section on Particles. (See p. 69.)

aoi, green, and thing; *mono-shiri*, a learned man, from *shiru*, to know.

3. *Augmentative Nouns.*—The prefix *ō*, great, is used as an augmentative to other nouns, as

ō arashi, great storm (*i.e.*, tempest);
ō gurai, great eater (*i.e.*, glutton);
ō bune, great boat (*i.e.*, ship, vessel, &c.).

4. *Diminutive Nouns.*—These are formed by prefixing to other nouns the syllable *ko*, little; as

ko yama, little mountain (*i.e.*, hill);
ko inu, little dog (*i.e.*, puppy).

5. *Verbal Nouns.*—A large number of these are merely the unaltered stems of verbs, as

warai, laughter,	from	*warau*, to laugh;
nokori, remainder	,,	*nokoru*, to be left over;
soshiri, evil-speaking	,,	*soshiru*, to speak evil;
kakushi, pocket	,,	*kakusu*, to hide;
hikari, brightness	,,	*hikaru*, to shine.

III. Compound Nouns.

These nouns, which are very numerous, are formed in many ways, of which the principal are:—

(*a*) A noun + a noun, as

honya, a bookseller, from *hon*, a book, and *ya*, house;
kusuri-ya, a druggist's, from *kusuri*, medicine, and *ya*, house;
hanazono, a flower-garden, from *hana*, flower, and *sono*, garden.

(*b*) The stem of an adjective + a noun, as

yasu-mono, cheap article, from *yasui*, cheap, and *mono*, thing;
aka-gane, copper, from *akai*, red, and *kane*, metal;
waru-kuchi, evil-speaking, from *warui*, bad, and *kuchi*, mouth.

(*c*) A verbal form + a noun, as

urimono, an article for sale, from *uri* (stem of *uru*, to sell) and *mono*, thing;
nusubito, a thief, from *nusumu*, to steal, and *hito*, person;
moyekui, a firebrand, from *moyasu*, to burn, and *kui*, stake.

(*d*) A noun + a verbal form, as

hito-goroshi, a murder *or* murderer, from *hito*, person, and *korosu*, to kill;

ki-chigai, a lunatic, from *ki*, spirit, and *chigau*, to be wrong.

(*e*) A verbal form + a verbal form, as

kigaye, a change of clothing, from *kiru*, to wear, and *kayeru*, to change;

nukigaki, a synopsis, from *nuku*, to draw out, and *kaku*, to write down.

NOTE.—(1) In compound nouns the second component usually receives the *nigori* (see p. 13). Thus, the *h* of *hito* is changed into *b* in the compound *nusubito*; the *k* of *koroshi* into *g* in *hito-goroshi*; the *k* of *kaki* into *g* in *nuki-gaki*. (See *c*, *d*, and *e*, above.)

(2) The final vowel of the first component of a compound noun is often changed. This change is most common in connection with the letter *e*, which is replaced by *a*, as

sakate, drink-money, from *sake*, beer, and *te*, hand;
saka-oke, a sake (beer) vat, from *sake* and *oke*;
kaza-deppō, an air-gun, from *kaze* and *teppō*.

(3) As will be seen subsequently, certain parts of verbs and adjectives are, for purposes of syntax, regarded as nouns.

THE PRONOUN.

Pronouns in Japanese are for the most part merely nouns which have in process of time become pronominal. They are grouped together in various classes for the different degrees of respect and politeness which form so prominent a part of the general culture of the country.

The pronouns may be classified as *Personal*, *Possessive*, *Demonstrative*, *Interrogative*, *Indefinite*, *Relative*, *Reflexive*.

Personal Pronouns.

1. SINGULAR.

(*a*) *First Person.*

Watakŭshi, I, is the ordinary polite word for the pronoun of the first person.

Temaye is used in token of humility by the lower classes to their superiors. It is also employed for the second person.

Watashi and *washi* are used by intimate friends.

Boku serves for soldiers and students.

Ore is used with a lesser degree of respect, and is employed generally by servants, &c., to each other.

Examples:—

Watakŭshi wa kajiya de gozarimasŭ, [*lit.*, I...blacksmith...am]	I am the blacksmith.
Ore mo ikō, [*lit.*, I too will go]	I will go too.
Boku wa gakkō ye kaeru tokoro da, [*lit.*, I...school to return place am]	I am on the way back to school.

(*b*) *Second Person.*

Anata (= *ano kata*, that side) is really a pronoun of the *third* person which has gradually come to be employed for the *second*, like the German *Sie*. It is a polite form used to address equals or superiors, and is sometimes used as a noun as in *kono anata*, this gentleman.

Omaye (*omae*) *san* is nearly identical with *anata*, but more familiar, and is used principally by women.

[N.B.—The above will be found to suffice for Europeans.]

Kimi serves for students and soldiers.

Kisama and *temaye* show the least degree of respect, and are used to address people of the lowest class.

Sensei is employed to address professors and learned men in general.

Danna (master), *danna-san*, or *danna-sama* is used by an employé in addressing his principal.

Other words in use for the second person are:—*O nushi* (very familiar), *sokka* (formal), *sochi* (to inferiors), *ware* (among country people), and *unu* (abusive).

Examples:—

Omaye koko ni matte ore, [*lit.*, you here waiting remain.]	You wait here.
Anata ni o hanashi moshitai koto ga gozarimasu, [*lit.*, you...talk wish to, thing there is]	There is something I wish to tell you:
Kimi wa doko ye iku ka? [*lit.*. you...where to go...?	Where are you off to?
Unu berabō me,	You impertinent fellow!

(c) *Third Person.*

Are. This is used indifferently for "he" or "she," and is often replaced by the more respectful forms *ano hito*, that man, that woman; *ano o kata*, that gentleman, that lady; or *ano onna*, that woman.

Tō-nin, "the person in question," is often used for "he."

Aitsu is a contemptuous equivalent for *are*.

Examples:—

Ano o kata Tōkyo no akindo ja nai ka,	Is he not a Tokio merchant?

[*lit.*, ...Tokio...merchant is (he) not?]

Are wa mō Hiōgo ni tsukimashĭtarō,	He (she, it) has probably arrived in Hiogo by now.

[*lit.*, ...already Hiogo...has-probably-arrived]

2. Plural.

The plurals are formed from the singular, as in nouns, by adding *domo, gata, ra, shiu* (*shū*), and *tachi* (see p. 17). Thus, *watakŭshi*, I—*watakŭshi domo*, we; *ore, orera, are*, he, she, it—*arera*, they; *omaye, omaye gata*, you (thou), you; &c.

The grammar of the personal pronouns is like that of nouns, and particles (see pages 69–77) are affixed in the same manner as with nouns. It must be observed, however, that, with the pronouns of the first and second persons, the employment of plural particles, when two (or more) persons are intended, is much more frequent than in the case of nouns, and a Japanese often uses *watakŭshidomo* (we) for "I."

As in Latin and Spanish, personal pronouns are usually omitted unless they are used *emphatically*, or in cases where ambiguity would arise from their omission. Thus, "I never saw that woman before," would be rendered, *Are wa sen ni miyenakatta onna da*, unless the person addressed might be in doubt as to whether the speaker were referring to himself or to another person, in which case *watakŭshi* would be employed. In such sentences as "*I* am going home, but *you* had better remain here," the pronouns should be inserted because the significance depends on the emphasis laid on them.

Possessive Pronouns.

The Possessive Pronouns are simply personal pronouns with the possessive particle, *no* or *ga*, added to them, as

watakŭshi no,	my;	*anata no* / *omaye no*	your;
watakŭshi domo no,	our;	*ano hito no,*	his.

Mine, yours, his, hers, theirs, are also rendered by *watakŭshi no, anata no,* &c., but they can readily be distinguished from *my, your,* &c., by observing the particles used with them or by examining the context.

Examples:—

Anata no gakkō wa dochira desŭ? [*lit.*, your school...whereabouts is?]	Whereabouts is your school?
Watakŭshi no wa atarashiu gozarimasŭ; anata no wa furŭ gozarimasŭ, [*lit.*, mine...new is; yours...old is]	Mine is new; yours is old.
Ano hito no iye wa yohodo tōi, [*lit.*, that man's house...very much is far]	His house is a long distance away.

Demonstrative and Interrogative Pronouns.

NOTE.—With these pronouns are given several words closely allied to them in derivation and meaning, and which may be treated advantageously at the present stage.

1. THIS. Root, Ko or Ka.

kore (noun);	*konna*, this kind of;	*kayō*, this manner;
kono (adj.);	*konnani* (adv.);	*kahodo*, this much;
konata (pron.);	*koitsu*, this fellow;	*kaku*, or *ko*, thus.

Ko, ka. The root appears only in the compounds given in the above table; in *ko-toshi*, this year; and in a few other words of very rare occurrence.

Kore (plural, *korera*), this. *Kore* is a noun meaning "this one" when the object is near or in the possession of the speaker, and more rarely "this person"; as

Kore wa ikura desu ka?	As to this thing, how much is it?
Kore wa nani da?	What is this?

Kono, this, these, is an adjective corresponding to the French *ce, cette, ces*; as

kono michi, this road; *kono hako*, this box.

Konata (for *kono kata*), this side, is in reality a pronoun of the first person, and is often used for "I," but it is more frequently employed for the second person.

Konna, konnani; this kind of, in this kind of way. *Konna* is for *kore naru*, being this; *konnani* for *kore naru ni*, in being this.

Koitsu, this fellow, is also applied to inanimate objects. It is a contraction from *ko-yatsu* (*yatsu* = fellow), and is a very contemptuous expression.

Kono yō ni, in this manner, and *kono yō na*, this kind of, are almost synonymous with *kayō* and *kayō na*, and occur more frequently.

Kahodo, this much. *Kore hodo* is also used with a very similar signification, as

Korehodo osoroshĭkatta koto wa gozarimasenŭ,	I was never so afraid in my life.

[*lit.*, this-much frightened-was thing...is not]

Kaku, kō, thus. *Ko* is much more frequently used than *kaku*, but the latter is sometimes met with in certain expressions, such as *to mo kaku mo*, even so, even thus (= at all events, however).

2. That (2nd person). Root, So or Sa.

sore (noun);	*sonna*, that kind of;	*sayō*, that manner;
sono (adj.);	*sonnani* (adv.);	*sahodo*, that much;
sonata (pro.);	*soitsu*, that fellow;	*shika*, *so* or *sō*, so.

Sore is a noun meaning "that one," when the object is near or in the possession of the person spoken to, as

Sore wa kinodoku na koto de gozarimasŭ,	That is a sad thing.

[*lit.*, that...sad...thing is]

Sono is an adjective, and is joined to nouns, as

Sono hako,	That box ("near you," perhaps "your box").
Doko de sono mŭma wo o kai nasatta?	Where did you buy that horse?

[*lit.*, where...that horse...buy did]

Note.—The remarks with reference to the words under "This" (above) apply also to the corresponding ones in this table.

Examples:—

Sore wa chodō yoi,	As for that one (it is) just right.
Sore wa kinodoku na koto de gozarimasŭ,	That is a sorry affair.
Ame ga furi sō mo nai, [*lit.*, rain...fall...even is not]	It does not seem likely to rain.
Sō da sō yo, [*lit.*, that is appearance]	So it would seem.
Dare ga so iimashĭta? [*lit.*, who...so said]	Who said so?

3. THAT (3rd person). Root, A.

are (noun);	*anna*, that kind of;	*aitsu*, that fellow;
ano (adj.);	*annani* (adv.);	*ā*, in that way, so.
anata (pro.);		

Are is a noun meaning "that one," when the object is far away, not in possession of the speaker, or out of sight; as

Are wa nan desu?	As for that (yonder), what is it?

Ano is an adjective, also referring to something far away, not in possession of the speaker, or out of sight; as

*Ano kajiya wa kita ka?** [*lit.*, that blacksmith...come]	Has that blacksmith come?

Are and *sore*, *ano* and *sono*, must not be regarded as interchangeable. *Kore* may be termed the demonstrative pronoun of the first person, *sore* of the second person, and *are* of the third. *Sore* and *sono* are connected with the present subject of conversation, whilst *are* and *ano* are employed when a new topic is introduced. Thus, *sono kura* means "that saddle" (near or in the possession of the listener); *ano kura*, "that saddle" (you had yesterday, &c.).

NOTE.—The Japanese often commence a sentence with the word *ano* as serving merely to attract the attention of the person addressed, something like the English "'Er" or "I say!" in the phrases "'Er, would you kindly tell me the way to...?" and "I say, just take hold of this!"

Example:—*Ano, Kanda san,* I say! Mr. Kanda.

The words *konata* (for *kono kata*), this side, *sonata* (for *sono kata*), that side, and *anata* (for *ano kata*), that side, when employed as pronouns, ought really to signify "I," "you,"

* See remarks on Interrogation, p. 85.

"he," "she," "it," respectively, and *konata* often does stand for "I," but generally, by a peculiar anomaly, they are employed for the second person.

Ayō and *ahodo* are not in use, the expressions *ano yō* and *are hodo* being employed instead.

Examples:—

A iu hanashi wa mettani kikimasenŭ,	It is seldom we hear a story of that kind.
[*lit.*, that-way called story...seldom hear]	
Are wa, dare no uchi desŭ?	Whose is that house (yonder)?
[*lit.*, that as-for, who of house is-it?]	
A iu fūzetsu wa ate ni naranai,	One cannot depend on reports of that kind.
[*lit.*, that-kind report...dependence do not become]	
Are wa nan' da?	What is that?
[*lit.*, that...what is]	

4. That (3rd person). Root, Ka.

kare (noun); *kano* (adjective); *kyatsu*, that fellow.

Examples:—

Kare kore hiru desŭ,	It is just about noon (*hiru*).
Nani ya ka ya,	Anything whatever.

Note.—These expressions are not in very common use, except by the upper classes. Their meanings are similar to those in the columns under "That" on the preceding page.

Kano is sometimes employed with the meaning "a certain."

5. Who. Root, Da.

dare (noun).

Examples:—

Dare ga sō itta?	Who said so? (*familiar*).
Dare ni kane wo yatta? [*lit.*, ...to, money...gave]	To whom did he give the money?

Note.—The places of the words not appearing under this head are supplied by the derivatives of *do*, which (see No. 6, following).

6. Which. Root, Do.

dore (noun); *donata* (pron.); *dō*, how;
dono (adj.); *donnani*, what kind of; *donna* (adv.).

Dore is an old form of *idzure*, which is still employed with the meanings "at any rate," "however." *Idzure* is an abbreviation of *idzure ni mo*, which signifies literally "in whichever case."

Examples :—

Dore ga ichiban ii ka ?	Which is the best ? (*familiar*).
Dore wa yoroshiu gozarimasŭ ? [*lit.*, which...good is]	Which do you like best ?

Donata is employed as a polite substitute for *dare*, a still more respectful phrase being *donata sama*. Thus, *Donata desu ?* who is it ? (who is there ?)

Dōka, somehow, and *dōzō*, somehow or other, are formed from *dō*, and both may be used to translate the English "please"; as

Dōka o negai mōshimasu, [*lit.*, somehow...beg...]	Please do !

Examples :—

Dono gurai yoroshiu gozarimasŭ, [*lit.*, what quantity good is]	How much do you require ?
Do shĭyō ? [*lit.*, how shall do]	What shall we do ?
Donnani ureshi ka shiremasenŭ, [*lit.*, how much joyful, cannot know]	I cannot tell you how pleased I am.

7. What. Root, Na.

nani (pron.) ; *nanihodo*, how much ; *naze*, why.

Nani is employed for inanimate objects only. No adjective form exists, *nanno*, *nani no*, or *dono* being used instead.

Examples :—

Nani go yō de gozarimasu? [*lit.*, what honourable business is there]	What can I do for you ?
Nani shi ni kata ? [*lit.*, what do to have come]	What has brought you here?
Nanno go yō desŭ ka ? [*lit.*, what...business is]	What is your business ?

Naze is an abbreviation of *na-zo-ye*, which is composed of the root *na*, the emphatic *zo*, and the ejaculatory particle *ye*. (See Particles, pages 69–77.) Thus, *Naze hayaku konai !*—why do you not come quickly ? (*lit.*, why quickly not come?).

Examples :—

Nani to ka shiyō wa arimasumai ka ? [*lit.*, ...do manner will not be]	Can nothing be done ?
Kono mono wa nanda ? [*lit.*, this object...what is]	What is this object ?

Sono mŭma wa nan to iu? [*lit.*, that horse...what is called]	What is that horse called?

Indefinite Pronouns.

There are certain phrases which, employed pronominally to signify *number*, *comparison*, *quantity*, &c., may be regarded as INDEFINITE PRONOUNS. These locutions are formed by adding to the Interrogative Pronouns the particles *ka*, *mo*, *demo*, and *zo*. Thus:

dare ka, somebody;
dare mo, anybody, somebody;
dare de mo, anybody;
nani ka, something, anything;
nani de mo, anything, something;
dore ka, some one thing;
dore mo, any one thing;
dore de mo, anything whatever;
nani mo, anything at all;
nani zo, *nanzo*, something or another, any.

Interrogative *adverbs* may in a similar manner become indefinite, as *doko*, where: *doko demo*, anywhere; *dokka* (for *doko ka*), somewhere.

Dare mo, *dore mo*, and *nani mo* are ordinarily employed with negative verbs, and are equivalent to the English words "nobody" and "nothing."

The respectful forms for *dare* are:—

donata ka, somebody;
donata de mo, anybody;
donata mo, everybody.

Examples:—

Dare ka shĭta ni matte oru, [*lit.*, ...below...waiting remains]	Somebody is waiting below.
Dare ka sō itta, [*lit.*, someone so said]	Someone said so.
Dore mo shiranŭ,	Nobody knows.
Dare mo shitte imasen,	Nobody knows it.
Dare de mo yoroshiu gozarimasŭ, [*lit.*, ...good is]	Anyone whatever will do.
Dare de mo shitte imasu,	Everyone knows it.
Donata mo ikaremasen,	No one can go.
Kyūji ni nani ka o yari nasare, [*lit.*, waiter to, ...give, do please]	Give something to the waiter.

Kono hako no naka ni nani ka haitte iru ka?	Is there anything in this box?
[*lit.*, ... box ... inside ... having entered is]	
Nani ka chōdai,	Please give me something.
[*lit.*, ...please-give]	
Nani mo gozarimasenŭ,	There is nothing at all.
Donata de mo ikareru,	Anyone can go.
Dore de mo chōdai,	Please give me any one of them.
Dore mo ikemasen ka?	Will not one of these suit you?
Nani mo arimasen,	I have nothing at all.
Doko ka de mita yō ni omoimasŭ,	I think I have seen (him) somewhere.
[*lit.*, ... seen manner ... think]	

Relative Pronouns.

The Relative Pronoun proper does not exist in Japanese, and reference or relation to another noun or pronoun in the sentence is expressed by employing the *verb* of the relative clause as an *adjective*, placing it before the word to which the relative pronoun refers. Thus, for "the robber who ran away" we may say, "the run-away robber," which is exactly equivalent to the phrase *nigeta dorobo.*

Examples :—

Anata go o uri nasatta inu,	The dog which you sold.
[*lit.*, ... sell did dog]	
Kareta matsu,	The pine which withered.
[*lit.*, the withered pine]	
Nihon go wakaranŭ hito,	A man who does not know Japanese.
[*lit.*, Japanese language not-understand man]	
Kanda to iū hito,	The man who is called Kanda.
[*lit.*, Kanda, that-called person]	

Reflexive Pronouns.

jibun, self ; *jibun no, waga,* one's own ;
tagai ni, each other, one another.

Jibun is often replaced by *jishin* or *onore.*

Waga only occurs in the expressions *waga kuni,* one's own country ; *waga ko,* one's own child ; *waga kiōdai,* one's own brothers and sisters ; and a few others.

Tagai ni is really an adverb, meaning "mutually."

Examples :—

Jibun ga warui, [*lit.*, himself...is bad]	It is his own fault.
Tagai ni tasŭkeru,	They help each other.
Jibun de dekinai kara te-tsŭdatte kudasare, [*lit.*, ... cannot because, lending hand give]	Help me, please, because I cannot do it myself.

THE NUMERAL.

Cardinal Numerals.

In Japanese the employment of Numerals is very intricate, but as they are in frequent use the student should become acquainted with their names and uses.

The words employed for numbering up to *ten*, and those which stand for *one hundred*, *one thousand*, and *ten thousand*, form the basis of all the others.

From *one* to *ten* the numbers are indicated by two groups of words, one group consisting of words whose origin is purely Japanese, whilst the other is composed of words of Chinese origin. The Japanese series for the numbers above *ten* has now fallen into disuse, its place being taken by a continuation of the Chinese scale.

In Japanese, therefore, the elements of cardinal enumeration are as follow :—

		Japanese.	Chinese.
一	1.	*hĭtotsŭ.*	*ichi.*
二	2.	*fŭtatsŭ.*	*ni.*
三	3.	*mitsŭ.*	*san.*
四	4.	*yotsŭ.*	*shi.*
五	5.	*itsutsŭ.*	*go.*
六	6.	*mutsŭ.*	*roku.*
七	7.	*nanatsŭ.*	*shichi.*
八	8.	*yatsŭ.*	*hachi.*
九	9.	*kokonotsŭ.*	*ku.*
十	10.	*tō.*	*jiu.*
十一	11.		*jiu ichi.*
十二	12.		*jiu ni.*
十三	13.		*jiu san.*
二十	20.		*ni jiu.*

		Chinese.
二十一	21.	*ni jiu ichi.*
	30.	*san jiu.*
	40.	*shi jiu.*
	60.	*roku jiu.*
	80.	*hachi jiu.*
百	100.	*hiaku.*
	200.	*ni hiaku.*
	300.	*sam biaku*.*
	600.	*rop piaku*.*
	800.	*hap piaku.*
千	1,000.	*sen.*
	2,000.	*ni sen.*
萬	10,000.	*man.*

* The letter changes which occur will be understood from the examples appearing under *Auxiliary Numerals* (see p. 32).

NOTE.—(1) It will be observed that combinations from the Chinese series are employed between *one* and *one hundred*; such as *ten-one* = 11, *ten-two* = 12, *ten-three* = 13, *two-ten* = 20, *two-ten-one* = 21, &c.

(2) Above *one hundred* a like combination of the lower numerals occurs; thus, *two hundred* is represented as in English, *two-hundred*, &c.

(3) For *ten thousand*, however, a separate word is used—*man*, and numbers beyond this are expressed by its multiples. Thus, 150,000 is *jiu go man*; 1,000,000, *hiaku man*.

(4) Consecutive numerals are arranged as in English, thus:
150 is *hiaku go jiu*; 1128, *sen hiaku nijiu hachi*;
1868, *sen hap piaku rokujiu hachi*;
1904, *sen ku hiaku shi*.

(5) *Riō*, both, is frequently employed instead of *ni*, two; as
Riō san nin, two or three persons.

(6) *Shichi jiu*, seventy, is sometimes replaced by *nana jiu*; as
Nana jissen, seventy cents.

The following rules must be observed in the use of the numerals:—

1. The *Chinese* numerals below eleven must be employed only when standing *alone*, or when preceding monosyllabic or uncompounded nouns derived from the *Chinese*; as
ku nin, nine men; *jiu go kin*, fifteen katties;
rop piaku, (for *roku hiaku*), six hundred.

2. When employed with nouns of purely Japanese origin the terminal *tsŭ* of the Japanese numerals is dropped, as
mi hako, three boxes; *fŭta hiro*, two fathoms;
yo tsutsumi, four parcels.

Notice also that*—

(1) The numeral may stand alone, as

Ikutsŭ aru?	How many are there?
Nanatsŭ gozarimasŭ,	There are seven.

(2) The numeral is frequently placed *after* the noun, as *mikan mitsŭ*, three oranges.

(3) The possessive particle *no* is often introduced after a numeral, when the latter *precedes* the noun, as *mitsŭ no mono*, three things. (*Mono* = thing.)

* No satisfactory rule can be given for these customary and arbitrary practices, and the same remark will apply to other usages mentioned in the succeeding pages of this work.

Auxiliary Numerals.

In Japanese, objects are usually enumerated as so many things of a certain class or species, by the medium of what are termed Auxiliary Numerals, somewhat corresponding with the English expressions, "eight head of cattle," "three sets of harness," "four brace of partridges," &c. The noun is placed first, the numeral and class following; the numeral is seldom joined immediately to the noun.

Examples:—*Kami ichi mai*, one sheet of paper.
[*lit.*, paper, one, flat (object)]
Sara jiu mai, ten plates.
[*lit.*, plate, ten, flat (objects)]
Kodomo jiu ichi nin, eleven children.
[*lit.*, children, eleven (human objects)]
Fude go hon, five pencils.
[*lit.*, pencil, five (sticks or cylindrical objects)]

Note.—The majority of these auxiliaries are of Chinese origin, and come under Rule 1 of the preceding section (p. 31), but several of them are native words, and come under Rule 2; as *kura mi tomai*, three go-downs.*

The following are the most commonly used of these numerals, and they will be found to suffice for all ordinary needs:—

Nin is applied to *human beings*.

1, *ichi nin*, or *hĭtori*;	6, *roku nin*;
2, *ni nin*, or *fŭtari*;	7, *shichi nin*;
3, *san nin*;	8, *hachi nin*;
4, *yottari*, or *yo*† *nin*;	9, *ku nin*;
5, *go nin*;	10, *jiu nin*; &c.

Examples:—*Onna roku nin*, six women.
[*lit.*, woman, six persons]
Ninsoku ni nin, or *ninsoku fŭtari*, two coolies.

Hiki for *animals*, a *draught* of a net, *pieces* of silk, &c.; as 1, *ip piki*; 2, *ni hiki*; &c.

Examples:—*Kinu ippiki*, one piece of silk.
Ushi nambiki? how many head of cattle?

* "Go-down" is a common term for a warehouse or store throughout the East. It is a corruption of the Malay *gādong*, warehouse.

† In many expressions the Japanese substitute *yo* for *shi*, *nana* for *shichi*, and *kyu* for *ku*, in order to avoid certain ambiguities of sound, and also an unpleasant suggestion of the word *shinin* (dead person) by the expression *shi nin* (four persons).

Wa helps to count *birds* and *bundles*, as 3, *sam ba*; 4, *shi wa*.

Examples:—*Tsuru shi wa*, four storks.
Maki sam ba, three bundles of wood.

Hon is used in connection with *sticks*, *cylinders*, *long* and *round articles*, such as pencils, masts, poles, bottles, trees, &c.; as 5, *go hon*; 6, *rop pon*.

Examples:—*Kasa go hon*, five umbrellas.
Ki rop pon, six trees.

Mai is used for *broad*, *flat objects*, like sheets of paper, plates, coin, clothing, &c.; as 7, *shichi mai*; 8, *hachi mai*.

Examples:—*Kimono shichi mai*, seven garments.
Ketto hachi mai, eight blankets.

Ken is used for *houses* and *buildings in general*, as 9, *ku ken*; 10, *jik ken*; &c.

Example:—*Tera jik ken*, ten churches.

So is applied to *ships*, *boats*, &c.; as 1, *is sō*; 3, *san zō*; &c.

Example:—*Gunkan san zō*, three men-of-war.

Hai is used for so many "fills" of a *cup*, *bowl*, *glass*, &c.; as 5, *go hai*; 7, *shichi hai*; &c.

Example:—*Koppu ip pai no mizu*, a cupful of water.

Soku helps to count *shoes*, *socks*, *sandals*, &c.; as 2, *ni soku*; 4, *shi soku*; &c.

Examples:—*Waraji ni soku*, two pairs of straw sandals.
Kutsu shi soku, four pairs of boots.

Cho for *objects with handles*, such as *jinrikisha*, *palanquins*; also for guns, cannon, tools, candles, sticks of ink, and utensils; as 6, *roku chō*; 8, *hat chō*; &c.

Examples:—*Jinriki hat chō*, eight jinrikishas.
Rōsoku roku chō, six candles.

Fuku for *doses of medicine*, "smokes" of *tobacco*, and the like.

Examples:—*Kusuri ni fuki*, two doses of medicine.
Tabako ip puku, a "smoke."

NOTE.—Another *fuku* is employed for *pictures* and *maps*.

Jo is for *mats*, which cover the floor in Japanese dwellings; it designates the *areas of compartments*.

Satsu is used for *volumes of books*. For *complete copies* of a work, irrespective of the number of volumes in it, *bu* is employed.

Example:—*Jibiki is satsu*, one dictionary.

Other numeral auxiliaries are: *Suji* for extended objects, such as rivers, roads; *dai* for things supported by a base; *mune* for ridge-like things or houses; *tsū* for letters, documents; *kumi* for sets of objects such as suits of clothing, toys; *men* for looking-glasses; *tsutsumi* for packages; and many others.

Ordinal Numerals.

The order of objects in a series is sometimes indicated by using the cardinal numbers with the addition of the syllable *me* as a suffix, but the most usual method is by prefixing the word *dai* (*lit.*, order), or suffixing *ban* (*lit.*, number) or *bamme* (= *ban* + *me*) to the cardinals.

Examples:—*Hitotsu me*, or *ichi ban*, or *dai ichi*, first.
Ni ban, or *dai ni*, second.
Sam ban, third.
Dai go, fifth.

Rules.—(1) When the ordinal numbers precede the noun the particle *no* is placed between them, just as with the cardinals in like circumstances. (See p. 31.)

(2) If there be a specification with reference to *place, time, kind*, or *quantity* in enumeration, the name of the thing specified is usually placed between the cardinal and the syllable *me* to indicate ordinal enumeration.

Examples:—

Dai ichi no yakunin,	The first (chief) officer.
Sam ban no kisha,	The third train.
Ni ban no fune, or, *Ni ban me no fune*,	The second ship.
Go mai me,	The fifth page.
Yo nin me,	The fourth man.

Interrogations as to Number and Quantity.

1. Number.

In interrogations as to the number of persons or things the numeral auxiliary indicating the object asked about is employed with the adverbial *iku?* (what number?—*i.e.*, how many?)

The interrogation *ikutsu?* is sometimes heard, though less frequently.

Examples :—

Iku nin? or *iku tari?* in enquiring "how many men (women, children)?"

Fude wa iku hon?—how many pencils?

Ikutsu gozarimasu?—how many (of anything) are there?

2. Quantity.

Interrogations with reference to quantity are introduced by the adverbial *dore? ika?* or *nani?*—which? or what?—followed by *hodo*, degree of quantity. *Dono kurai*—which grade?—is also used, and all these phrases are used to translate the English *how much?*

In enquiring the price of anything the interrogative *ikura?*—about how much?—is generally employed.

Examples :—

Kore wa ikura?	What is the price of this?
Ika hodo arimasu ka?	What quantity is there?
Dono kurai irimasu ka?	How much do you require?
Dore hodo hairi masu?	What quantity will it hold?

Fractional Numbers.

The method of expressing these will be readily understood from the following observations and examples.

Thirty-one hundredths (31-100ths) is *hiaku bun no san jiu ichi*, which is, literally, of one hundred parts thirty-one (*bun* = part). The particle *no* is usually omitted, in which case *bun* is replaced by *bu.**

Example :—

Sam bun no ichi, or *sam bu ichi*, One-third.

N.B.—When no denominator is expressed, *tenths* are to be understood; thus, *hachi bu*, eight-tenths.

One-half is represented by *han*, or *ham bun*; one-third, *mitsŭ ichi*; and one-fourth, *yotsŭ ichi*. These forms are in very common use, but this mode of using Japanese and Chinese numbers in combination is contrary to strict grammatical rules.

* See footnote. p. 31.

The following miscellaneous locutions should be noted:

Ni-do, twice	*San-do*, thrice
Ni-do-me, the second time	*San-do-me*, the third time
Ni-bu, two per cent.	*Sam-bu*, three per cent.
Shi-bu, four „	*Go-bu*, five „
Ichi-wari, ten „	*Ni-wari*, twenty „
Ni-bai, two-fold; double	*Sam-bai*, three-fold; treble
Fŭtatsu zutsu, two at a time	*Mitsu zutsu*, three at a time
Dai ni mi, in the second place; secondly	*Dai san ni*, in the third place; thirdly
Hĭtotsu oki, every other one; alternate	*Ichi-nichi oki*, every other day
Fŭtari-mae, portions for two	*San-nin mae*, portions for three

Examples of the use of Numerals:—

Kore yori nan' ri hodo aru? [*lit.*, this from what...quantity is?]	How many *ri* is it from here?
Shichi hachi ri hoka (or *shika*) *wa gozarimasenŭ* [*lit.*, seven eight other...is not]	It is not more than seven or eight *ri*.
Shichi bu sam bu ni wakete o kuro,	Divide it into sevenths and tenths.
Kado kara, san-gen-me, [*lit.*, corner from, third house.]	The third house from the corner.
Iku iro arimasŭ ka? [*lit.*, how many colours are?]	How many kinds are there?
Sōtai de kokono iro gozarimasŭ. [*lit.*, all in, nine colours there are]	There are, in all, nine kinds.
Mina de ikutsŭ? [*lit.*, altogether, how many?]	How many altogether?
Nanatsŭ gozarimasŭ,	There are seven.
Budōshu ip pai kudasai,	Give me a glass of wine.
Hito tsutsumi ni hiaku mai dzutsu haitte imasŭ,	There are one hundred (coins, or other flat objects) in each parcel.
Ni san gen,	Two or three houses.
Nan' doki desŭ, or *Nan' ji desŭ,*	What is the time?
Kare kore yoji de gozarimasŭ,	It is about four o'clock.
Shi go nichi,	Four or five days.

Divisions of Time.

Years.

In Japan there are two methods of reckoning years. The first is by means of a cycle of twelve years named according to the signs of the Japanese zodiac. These signs are:—

Year.	Sign.	Year.	Sign.
1888,	*Ne*, the rat.	1894,	*Mŭma*, the horse,
1889,	*Ushi*, the bull.	1895,	*Hitsuji*, the goat.
1890,	*Tora*, the tiger.	1896,	*Saru*, the monkey.
1891,	*U* (for *Usagi*), the hare.	1897,	*Tori*, the cock.
1892,	*Tatsu*, the dragon.	1898,	*Inu*, the dog.
1893,	*Mi*, the serpent.	1899,	*I*, the wild boar.

For 1900 the sign *Ne* is again used, and so on.

Except for referring to the year of one's birth, this mode of reckoning has now gone out of use.

The second method is by periods of uncertain length, distinguished by a special name, *nengō* (*lit.*, year-name). Formerly these periods were appointed arbitrarily, but it has been arranged that for the future they will coincide with the Emperors' reigns.

Thus, formerly, if a *great fire* occurred, for instance, the Japanese would adopt a fresh *nengō* and call it, perhaps, "sainan" (calamity); an event occurring in the following year would then be spoken of as taking place on, say, *14th April*, 2, *Sainan*—and so on. The present period is termed "*Meiji*" (lit. *Enlightened Government*) and began in 1868, so that the current year (1904) is known in Japan as "year 37, Meiji."

Months.

The Gregorian Calendar has for some years been in use for the months as well as for the years. January is termed *shō gatsŭ* (*lit.*, the chief month), and the rest are formed by affixing *gatsŭ* (month) to the Chinese numerals.

Thus, the names of the months are:—

Shō gatsŭ,		January.	*Hachi gatsŭ*,	August.
Ni	,,	February.	*Ku* ,,	September.
San	,,	March.	*Jiu* ,,	October.
Shi	,,	April.	*Jiu ichi* ,,	
Go	,,	May.	or *Shimotsuki*,	November.
Roku	,,	June.	*Jiu ni gatsŭ*,	
Shichi	,,	July.	or *Shiwasŭ*,	December.

For expressing "one month," "two months," &c., the word *tsŭki* (month) is employed with the Japanese numerals. Thus, *hĭto tsŭki*, one month; *fŭta tsŭki*, two months, &c.

Sometimes *ik-ka-getsŭ* (contraction for *ichi-ka-getsŭ*), one month, *ni-ka-getsŭ*, two months, &c., are used.

Days.

The days of the month are:—

1st,	*Tsuitachi.*	17th,	*Jiu shichi nichi.*
2nd,	*Futsŭka.*	18th,	,, *hachi nichi.*
3rd,	*Mikka.*	19th,	,, *ku nichi.*
4th,	*Yokka.*	20th,	*Hatsŭka.*
5th,	*Itsŭka.*	21st,	*Ni jiu ichi nichi.*
6th,	*Muika.*	22nd,	,, *ni nichi.*
7th,	*Nanuka.*	23rd,	,, *san nichi.*
8th,	*Yōka.*	24th,	,, *yokka.*
9th,	*Kokonoka.*	25th,	,, *go nichi.*
10th,	*Tōka.*	26th,	,, *roku nichi.*
11th,	*Jiu ichi nichi.*	27th,	,, *shichi nichi.*
12th,	,, *ni nichi.*	28th,	,, *hachi nichi.*
13th,	,, *san nichi.*	29th,	,, *ku nichi.*
14th,	,, *yokka.*	30th,	*San-jiu-nichi.*
15th,	,, *go nichi.*	31st,	,, *ichi-nichi.*
16th,	,, *roku nichi.*		

These numerals may also be employed to express a number of days as well as the days of the month, with the exception of the expression "one day," for which *tsuitachi* is not permitted, *ichi nichi* being the correct form. The last day of the month is termed *Misoka,* on whatever day it may happen to fall.

The days of the week are:—

Nichi yō bi,	Sunday.	*Moku yō bi,*	Thursday.
Getsu yō bi,	Monday.	*Kin yō bi,*	Friday.
Ka yō bi,	Tuesday.	*Do yō bi,*	Saturday.
Sui yō bi,	Wednesday.		

NOTE.—*Bi* (for *hi*), day, is sometimes dropped. Thus, for Sunday we may say *Nichi yō bi* or *Nichi yō.*

The months are also divided in three *jun* (*Chinese,* period of ten days); the first ten days being termed *jōjun,* the second ten *chiujun,* and the third ten *gejun.*

Hours.

The European division of the day has now been adopted in Japan. The "time of day" is expressed by affixing the

Chinese numerals to the Chinese word *ji* (time, hour); thus, one o'clock is expressed by *ichi ji*; two o'clock, *ni ji*; three o'clock, *san ji*. For four o'clock *yoji* is used, for the reason explained above. (See footnote †, p. 32).*

"One hour" is *ichi-ji-kan*; "two hours," *ni ji kan*, &c.

Minutes are termed *fun*, and seconds *biō*. Thus, *san ji go fun shichi biō* is "five minutes and seven seconds past three."

THE VERB.

Transitive and Intransitive.

In English it seldom happens that the same verbal root possesses separate words or forms for its transitive and intransitive applications. Thus, the words *stop*, *break*, *boil*, &c., are either transitive or intransitive, according to their applications.

In Japanese, however, there are usually two distinct verbs having roots in common. For example, *tateru*, to set up, is transitive, and *tatsu*, to stand, is intransitive.

It must be observed that the distinction does not rest upon this peculiarity, for some verbs have precisely the opposite formation and character; as, for instance, *neru*, to sleep (intrans.), and *nekasu*, to put to sleep (trans.).

No rule, therefore, can be formulated for distinguishing the two classes, and only by familiarity with their uses can the student know whether the various verbs are transitive or not.

Person and Number.

The verb has no forms to express person or number. *Taberu*, for instance, may mean "I, you, we, *or* they eat," or "he, she, *or* it eats," according to circumstances. This applies to all verbs in the language.

Distinction of *Person* is usually understood through the use of pronouns, and it is especially by the employment of "honorific" or "humble" verbs† that the speaker indicates whether he refers to himself or others.

Distinction of *Number* is generally made by the use of associated pronouns, numerals, or auxiliary words.

* See also "The Time," pp. 117, 118.

† See pages 79 and 83.

Tense.

The inflection of verbs to express the time or condition of an action is almost entirely confined to forms indicating *Present* or *Past* time, and as either probable or positive, so that in Japanese *there are virtually but four tenses*:—

1. The Certain Present.
2. The Probable Present.
3. The Certain Past.
4. The Probable Past.

Future time is expressed by the *present* tenses accompanied by particles, and in some cases by the Probable Present tense standing alone.

The verbs *kasu*, to lend, and *makeru*, to lose, for examples, have really by inflection but the following four tenses:—

1. *Certain Present.*

kasu, lend, *or* lends.* *makeru*, lose, *or* loses.

2. *Probable Present* (or *Future*).

kasō, probably lends, *or* will lend. *makeyō*, probably loses, *or* will lose.

3. *Certain Past.*

kashĭta, lent, *or* has lent. *maketa*, lost, *or* has lost.

4. *Probable Past.*

kashitarō, probably lent. *maketarō*, probably lost.

Alternative Form.

There is another tense inflection in Japanese, named the Alternative Form. Its function is to express *occasional action* or *alternation of action*; e.g.,

kashitari, sometimes lends, *or* at one time lending. *maketari*, sometimes loses, *or* at one time losing.

The termination *tari* is contracted from *te ari*, the Classical Past Tense of *aru*, to be.

* The student must bear in mind the fact that the verb in Japanese has no person—so that *kasu* may be used for any person and any number. In the types of verbs given later, where a pronoun (I, he, &c.) is introduced, any other pronoun might be substituted. (See "Person and Number," p. 39.)

The Alternative Form is usually accompanied by one or more verbs having the same inflection, as

Naitari warattari shĭte orimasŭ,	Sometimes I am crying and sometimes I am laughing.

[*lit.*, sometimes-crying, sometimes-laughing doing (I) am]

Mood.

The inflections for the purpose of expressing *Mood* consist of modifications showing simple *declaration*, *order* or *command*, and *doubt* or *contingency*. These forms correspond with those of the Indicative, Imperative, and Subjunctive Moods respectively, of English verbs.

The Subjunctive consists practically of two modifications:

1. The Conditional. 2. The Concessive.

These are employed according as the action implied is *dependent* or *concessive*.

Indicative Mood.

Present Tense.

kasu, lend, *or* lends. *makeru*, lose, *or* loses.

Past Tense.

kashĭta, lent, *or* has lent. *maketa*, lost, *or* has lost.

Imperative Mood.

kase, lend! *makero*, lose!

Subjunctive Mood.

(*a*) Conditional. *Present Tense.*

kaseba, if (he) lend. *makereba*, if (he) lose.

Past Tense.

kashitara, if (I) had lent. *maketara*, if (I) had lost.

(*b*) Concessive. *Present Tense.*

kasedo, though (he) lend. *makeredo*, though (he) lose.

Past Tense.

kashitaredo, though (he) lent. *maketaredo*, though (he) lost.

The termination *tara* is a contraction of *tareba*, which is the form given by some grammarians.

The Past Conditional may mean not only *if (I) had lent*, but also *if (I) lent*, *if (I) shall have lent*, *since (I) have lent*, *when (I) had lent*, *when (I) lent*, *when (I) shall have lent*.

Verbal-Adjective Forms.

Several other forms of the verb exist whose functions are somewhat allied to those of adjectives. These modifications are usually classed under the names (*a*) Past Participle, or Gerund, and (*b*) Desiderative Adjective, or Desiderative Form, and are as follows:—

Past Participle.

kashĭte, lending, *or* having lent. *makete*, losing, *or* having lost.

Desiderative Adjective.

kashĭtai, (he) wishes to lend. *maketai*, (he) wishes to lose.

NOTE.—The term "Past Participle" has been retained in preference to "Gerund" in conformity with the usage of the majority of grammarians, though it must frequently be treated as a present participle. Often, too, it has no reference to time, but simply describes the mode of the action involved in the verb following.

The Verb-Root; Inflection.

In the Japanese verb the *root* is often obscure, having become corrupted in the process of time. There are, however, certain developed modifications of the verb which can be treated as primary forms or bases, to which all further inflections or terminations have been added. These forms consist of the root slightly modified, and are commonly termed, respectively:

The STEM.
The NEGATIVE BASE.
The CERTAIN PRESENT BASE.
The CONDITIONAL BASE.

THE STEM.—This form is employed as a support for a larger number of inflections than any of the others, and ends with a syllabic in either *i* or *e*; as, for example,

With *shi* in *kashi* of the verb meaning to lend;
,, *be* ,, *tabe* ,, ,, to eat;
,, *ji* ,, *oji* ,, ,, to fear.

By adding to the stem various words and particles we obtain the several forms of the *Positive Past Tenses*, as well as the *Positive Alternative*, the *Positive Participle*, and the *Desiderative Adjective* form of all verbs. We also get all the inflections of the verbs of the *Second Conjugation*, and the moods and tenses of the polite forms of inflection.

There is an important rule of syntax in connection with the *Stem*, viz., If two or more consecutive clauses of a sentence contain verbs in the *same* mood and tense, the *final verb only* assumes the distinctive termination of the mood and tense, all the others taking the *Stem form.*

The Stem is frequently used as a *noun*, and also serves to form compounds with *nouns*, *adjectives*, and *other verbs.* Thus,

From the stem	of the verb	together with	is derived
mi	*miru*, to see,	*kurushi*, painful,	*migurushi*, ugly.
kashi	*kasu*, to lend,	*ya*, a house,	*kashiya*, a house to let.
ki	*kiru*, to dress,	*mono*, a thing,	*kimono*, clothes.
buchi	*butsu*, to thrash,	*korosu*, to kill,	*buchikorosu*, to beat to death.

THE NEGATIVE BASE.—This form follows the Stem in order of importance, and terminates in a syllabic in *a* for verbs of the First Conjugation, and in *e* or *i* for the Second. For example, *kasa* is the Negative Base of the verb meaning "to lend," *make* of the verb "to lose," and *oji* of the verb "to fear."

This base supports the majority of the affixes of the *Negative* Forms of the verbs in the First Conjugation, and also the *Probable Present* tense, the *Passive* or *Potential*, and the *Causative* inflections.

In the Second Conjugation the *Negative Base* and the Stem are identical; that is, the Negative Base in this conjugation is merely a name applied to the Stem for the sake of convenience in showing the verbal types.

THE CERTAIN PRESENT BASE.—This form when used without any inflection serves as the Certain Present *tense*, and plays but a minor part in the process of inflection, supporting the Negative Probable Present and the Negative Imperative terminations only.

Its ending, in the First Conjugation, is any syllabic in *u*, but in the Second the terminal is invariably *ru*, which is added to the Stem to form this base. For example: The Certain Present bases of the verbs, to lend, to lose, to fear, are respectively *kasu*, *makeru*, and *ojiru*, in the two latter of which will be recognised the stems terminating in *ru*.

The *Certain Present Base* is the form by which each verb is known, just as in English verbs are known by the Indefinite Infinitive (to go, to say, &c.)

Note.—The special grouping of the verbs in conjugations is determined by means of the Stem in connection with the Certain Present Base; and the latter, besides doing duty as a verb, serves also as a noun and as an adjective.

The Conditional Base.—This forms a support for the inflections of the two tenses of the Subjunctive—the *Present Conditional* and the *Present Concessive*, and is identical with the Imperative of the verbs in the First Conjugation. Its ending may be any syllabic in *e* in the First Conjugation, but in the Second the terminal is invariably the syllabic *re* added to the Stem. Thus, *se*, forming *kase* for the verb "to lend," and *re*, forming *makere* and *ojire* for the verbs "to lose" and "to fear," compose the Conditional Bases of those verbs.

The following Table forms a summary of the principal parts of the verbs discussed above:—

Verb.	Stem.	Neg. Base.	Certain Pres.	Cond. Base.
Kasu,	*kashi,*	*kasa,*	*kasu,*	*kase.*
Makeru,	*make,*	*make,*	*makeru,*	*makere.*
Ojiru,	*oji,*	*oji,*	*ojiru,*	*ojire.*

From these four primary forms are produced other forms in some degree corresponding to the moods and tenses of English verbs, all verbal inflection taking its start from one or another of them.

Conjugation.

In the spoken language the verbal forms divide themselves into two distinctly marked series, or *Conjugations*, the distinguishing characteristics of which are as follows:—

1. The First Conjugation.

This group is composed of all the verbs whose Stems terminate in an *i* syllabic, and whose Certain Present Bases end with the *u* syllabic of the same series as that of the Stem-ending. For example: If the Stem of a given verb end in *ki*, and the Certain Present in *ku*; or if the former end in *gi* and the other in *gu*, in *shi* and in *su*, *ji* and *zu*, and so on throughout the syllabary, then the verb may be regarded as belonging to the *First Conjugation*.

Every verb whose Stem and Certain Present Base are in conformity with the arrangement just illustrated follows one model during the process of inflection, euphonic variations of the primary forms excepted.

Illustrative Verbs.

	Stem.	Cert. Pres.		Stem.	Cert. Pres.
be,	*ari*,	*aru*.	know,	*shiri*,	*shiru*.
become,	*nari*,	*naru*.	lend,	*kashi*,	*kasu*.
buy,	*kai*,	*kau*.	look at,	*nozoki*,	*nozoku*.
call,	*yobi*,	*yobu*.	mend,	*naoshi*,	*naosu*.
climb,	*nobori*,	*noboru*.	pile up,	*tsumori*,	*tsumoru*.
come, *or* go,	*mairi*,	*mairu*.	pour,	*tsugi*,	*tsugu*.
draw back,	*hikkomi*,	*hikkomu*.	read,	*yomi*,	*yomu*.
end,	*shimai*,	*shimau*.	return,	*kaeri*,	*kaeru*.
enter,	*iri*,	*iru*.	shine,	*teri*,	*teru*.
fly,	*tobi*,	*tobu*.	smell,	*kagi*,	*kagu*.
give,	*yari*,	*yaru*.	take,	*tori*,	*toru*.
go,	*iki*,	*iku*.	twist,	*nai*,	*nau*.
hear,	*kiki*,	*kiku*.	wait,	*machi*,	*matsu*.
			win,	*kachi*,	*katsu*.

Euphonic Letter-changes.—The Stems of all verbs in the First Conjugation undergo various modifications during the process of inflection, especially in the Past Participle, in the Past Tenses, and in the Alternative Form.

(1) Stems ending with the ki syllabic drop the *k*, as

	Yaku, to burn.	Kiku, to hear.	Seku, to hurry.	Toku, to melt.
Stem ...	*yaki*,	*kiki*,	*seki*,	*toki*.
Past Part. ...	*yaite*,	*kiite*,	*seite*,	*toite*.
Cert. Past ...	*yaita*,	*kiita*,	*seita*,	*toita*.
Con. Past, &c.	*yaitara*,	*kiitara*,	*seitara*,	*toitara*.
Altern. Form	*yaitari*,	*kiitari*,	*seitari*,	*toitari*.

Exception.—Iku, to go (Stem *iki*), forms *itte* as Past Participle; *itta*, &c., *ittari*, Past Tenses and Alternative Form.

(2) Stems ending with the **gi** syllabic drop the *g*, and the *t* sound of the suffixes is changed into *d*, as

	Kagu, to smell.	Kogu, to row.	Hegu, to peel off.
Stem ...	*kagi*,	*kogi*,	*hegi*.
Past Part. ...	*kaide*,	*koide*,	*heide*.
Cert. Past ...	*kaida*,	*koida*,	*heida*.
Con. Past, &c.	*kaidara*,	*koidara*,	*heidara*.
Altern. Form	*kaidari*,	*koidari*,	*heidari*.

(3) Stems ending with the **bi** or **mi** syllabic drop the *i*; the *b* or *m* is changed into an *n* sound, and the *t* sound becomes the *d* sound in the suffixes; as

	Tobu, to fly.	Amu, to weave.	Hikkomu, to draw back.
Stem ...	*tobi*,	*ami*,	*hikkomi*.
Past Part. ...	*tonde*,	*ande*,	*hikkonde*.
Cert. Past ...	*tonda*,	*anda*,	*hikkonda*.
Con. Past, &c.	*tondara*,	*andara*,	*hikkondara*
Altern. Form	*tondari*,	*andari*,	*hikkondari*.

(4) Stems ending with a **chi** syllabic drop the *i*, and *ch*—or rather *tch*—is sounded as a double *t* with the suffixes; as

	Katsu, to win.	Motsu, to hold.	Butsu, to beat.
Stem ...	*kachi*,	*mochi*,	*buchi*.
Past Part. ...	*katti*,	*motte*,	*butte*.
Cert. Past ...	*katta*,	*motta*,	*butta*.
Con. Past, &c.	*kattara*,	*mottara*,	*buttara*.
Altern. Form	*kattari*,	*mottari*,	*buttari*.

(5) Stems ending with an **ri** syllabic drop the *i*, and the *r* element is sounded as a double *t* with the suffixes; as

	Toru, to take.	Naru, to become.	Aru, to be.	Yaru, to give.
Stem ...	*tori*,	*nari*,	*ari*,	*yari*.
Past Part. ...	*totte*,	*natte*,	*atte*,	*yatte*.
Cert. Past ...	*totta*,	*natta*,	*atta*,	*yatta*.
Con. Past, &c.	*tottara*,	*nattara*,	*attara*,	*yattara*.
Altern. Form	*tottari*,	*nattari*,	*attari*,	*yattari*.

(6) Stems ending with the syllabic i or hi drop the vowel syllable, and the consonant *t* of the suffixes is doubled; as

	NAU, to twist.	KAU, to buy.	IU, to say.	WARAU, to laugh.
Stem ...	*nai,*	*kai,*	*ii,*	*warai.*
Past Part. ...	*natte, nōte,*	*katte, kōte,*	*itte, iūte,*	*waratte.*
Cert. Past ...	*natta, nōta,*	*katta, kōta,*	*itta, iuta,*	*waratta.*
Con. Past, &c.	*nattara,* *nōtara,*	*kattara,* *kōtara,*	*ittara,* *iutara,*	*warattara.*
Altern. Form	*nattari,* *nōtari,*	*kattari,* *kōtari,*	*ittari,* *iutari,*	*warattari.*

NOTE.—The syllabic terminations of the verbs of this class belong really to the *h* or spirant series of syllabics, so that their euphonic modifications are in accordance with the modifications belonging to the syllables *ha, hi, fu, he, ho.*

It must be borne in mind that the Negative Base is *wa,* and not *a* or *ha.* Thus, *nau* (*nafu*) has the Negative Base *nawa* (*naha*), and not *naa*; *kau* (*kafu*) has *kawa*; *iu* (*ifu*), *iwa*; and similarly with other verbs.

2. THE SECOND CONJUGATION.

This group is composed of all the verbs whose Stems terminate in an e or i syllabic, and whose Certain Present Bases are formed by adding the syllabic ru to the Stem. For example, if the Stem of a given verb end in *ke* and the Certain Present in *keru,* or if the Stem end in *ki* and the Certain Present in *kiru,* in *se* and in *seru, ji* and *jiru,* and so on throughout the series of syllabics in *e* and *i,* then the verb may be regarded as belonging to the Second Conjugation.

Illustrative Verbs.

	Stem.	Cert. Pres.		Stem.	Cert. Pres.
bathe,	*abi,*	*abiru.*	get,	*e,*	*eru.*
be,	*i,*	*iru.*	go out,	*de,*	*deru.*
borrow,	*kari,*	*kariru.*	grow,	*hae,*	*haeru.*
break,	*ore,*	*oreru.*	lose,	*make,*	*makeru.*
can,	*deki,*	*dekiru.*	see,	*mi,*	*miru.*
cool,	*same,*	*sameru.*	sleep,	*ne,*	*neru.*
eat,	*tabe,*	*taberu.*	wear,	*ki,*	*kiru.*
fear,	*oji,*	*ojiru.*			

In the Second Conjugation the scheme of inflection separates the forms into two groups, distinguished from each other by the **e** or **i** syllabic of the Stem; otherwise they follow one model. There are thus two groups of inflections, known respectively as the First and Second Forms of the Second Conjugation.

Models of Inflection.

We have now seen that Japanese verbs are divided into two conjugations, and that their inflectional forms are joined to one of four primary parts. The following table shows the terminations of the principal parts of the two conjugations:—

	Stem.	Neg. Base.	Cert. Pres.	Cond. Base.
Conjugation I. ...	*i*,	*a*,	*u*,	*e*.
,, II. Form 1.	*e*,	*e*,	*eru*,	*ere*.
,, II. ,, 2.	*i*,	*i*,	*iru*,	*ire*.

The student will now be prepared to follow the process of inflection, and we therefore give the three verbs *kasu*, *makeru*, and *ojiru* as models.

The Stems of these verbs are respectively **kashi**, **make**, and **oji**.

The Stem.

This primary variation, as observed before, supports a larger number of inflections than any of the others. In some verbs it has the appearance of being identical with the Root, and in the Second Conjugation the Stem virtually serves to support all the inflections.

(*a*) First Conjugation: *Kasu*, to lend; Stem, **kashi**.

The following forms are derived from the Stem by the use of suffixes:—

Past Part. ...	*kashĭte*,	having lent, *or* lending.
Cert. Past ...	*kashita*,	(he*) lent, *or* has lent.
Con. Past ...	*kashitara*,	if (he) had lent.
Prob. Past ...	*kashitarō*,	(he) probably lent.
Concess. Past	*kashitaredo*,	though (he) lent.
Altern. Form.	*kashitari*,	at one time lending, *or* at times lending.
Desid. Adj....	*kashitai*,	(he) wishes to lend.

* See footnote, p. 40.

(*b*) Second Conjugation: *Makeru*, to lose; Stem, **make**. *Ojiru*, to fear; Stem, **oji**. From which are derived:—

Past Participle	*makete*	and	*ojite*.
Certain Past	*maketa*	,,	*ojita*.
Conditional Past	*maketara*	,,	*ojitara*.
Probable Past	*maketarō*	,,	*ojitarō*.
Concessive Past	*maketaredo*	,,	*ojitaredo*.
Alternative Form	*maketari*	,,	*ojitari*.
Desiderative Adj.	*maketai*	,,	*ojitai*.

NOTE.—As will be observed in the continuation of this process of inflection, the Stem not only supports the above inflections, but also the remainder of those in the Second Conjugation. The preceding list (Past Participle, Certain Past, &c.) is inserted merely for the sake of completeness, to show the correspondence of the inflections of the two conjugations.

THE NEGATIVE BASE.

This form differs from the Stem in the First Conjugation, but in the Second the Negative Base is only the Stem as appearing in the inflectional forms corresponding to those supported by the Negative Base of the First Conjugation.

(*a*) First Conjugation: *Kasu*, to lend; Neg. Base, **kasa**.

The following forms are derived from the Negative Base with the aid of suffixes:—

Probable Present.	*kasō*,	probably lend, *or* will lend.
Cert. Pres. (Neg.)	*kasanŭ*, *kasanai*	do not, shall not, lend.
Con. ,, ,,	*kasaneba*, *kasanakereba*	if (I) do not lend.
Conc. ,, ,,	*kasanedo*, *kasanakeredo*	though (he) does not lend.
Cert. Past ,,	*kasanakatta*, *kasananda*	(he) did not lend.
Prob. ,, ,,	*kasanakattarō*, *kasanandarō*	probably (he) did not lend.
Con. ,, ,,	*kasanakattara (ba)*, *kasanandara (ba)*	if (he) did not lend.
Conc. ,, ,,	*kasanandaredo (mo)*,	though (I) do not lend.
Altern. Form ,,	*kasanakattari*, *kasanandari*	at times not lending.
Past Part. ,,	*kasazu*, *kasanakute*	not lending, not having lent.

(*b*) Second Conjugation: *Makeru*, to lose; Neg. Base, **make**. *Ojiru*, to fear; Neg. Base, **oji**. From which are derived:—

Prob. Present ...	*makeyō*	and	*ojiyō*.
,, ,, (Neg.)	*makemai*	,,	*ojimai*.
Certain ,, ,,	*makenŭ*, *makenai*	,,	*ojinŭ*, *ojinai*.
Condit. ,, ,,	*makenakereba*	,,	*ojinakereba*.
Concess. ,, ,,	*makenakeredo*	,,	*ojinakeredo* (*mo*).
Certain Past ,,	*makenakatta*	,,	*ojinakatta*.
Prob. ,, ,,	*makenakattarō*	,,	*ojinakattarō*.
Condit. ,, ,,	*makenakattara* (*ba*)	,,	*ojinakattara* (*ba*).
Concess. ,, ,,	*makenakeredo* (*mo*)	,,	*ojinakeredo* (*mo*).
Altern. Form ,,	*makenakattari*	,,	*ojinakattari*.
Past Part. ,,	*makezu*	,,	*ojizu*.
Imperative (Pos.)	*makenakute*	,,	*ojinakute*.

NOTE. (1) *The Negative Base.*—This form has no signification when standing alone; thus, *kasa*, *make*, and *oji* are not in use as separate words.

(2) *The Certain Present* (*Negative*).—As with the other tenses in the Indicative, this tense may be either (*a*) a verb, (*b*) a noun, or (*c*) an adjective; thus,

(*a*) *Shiranŭ*,	I do not know.
Konai no darō, [*lit.*, comes-not fact probably-is]	He is probably not coming.
(*b*) *Shirimasenŭ de gozarimasŭ*, [*lit.*, not know is]	I don't know (used by inferiors to superiors).
(*c*) *Shiranŭ koto wa gozarimasenŭ*, [*lit.*, not-know thing is not]	He certainly knows.

The final *ŭ* of this form is usually dropped in conversation.

(3) *The Certain Past* (*Negative*).—For this tense, the negative of the present is sometimes used. Thus, in answer to the question, *O ide nasatta ka?* (did you go?), the reply may be *Ikimasenŭ*, instead of *ikemasenakatta* or *ikemasenanda*.

(4) *The Conditional Present* (*Negative*).—This form, in conjunction with the negative of *naru*, to become, is used as an equivalent of the English "must"; thus,

Te wo arawaneba naranŭ, [*lit.*, hand...if not wash]	I must wash my hands.

The final *ba* of this tense is sometimes sounded as *ya*.

THE CERTAIN PRESENT BASE.

This form plays but a minor part in inflectional processes. In the First Conjugation it is a verbal variation, and in the

Second it is an inflection of the Stem with the addition of the syllable *ru*.

(*a*) First Conjugation: *Kasu*, to lend; Cert. Pres. Base, **kasu**. This is inflected thus:—

Certain Present.	*kasu*,	(he) lends.
Improbable ,,	*kasumai*,	probably (I) do not, will not lend.
Imperat. (Neg.)	*kasuna*,	do not lend!

(*b*) Second Conjugation: *Makeru*, to lose; Cert. Pres. Base, **makeru**. *Ojiru*, to fear; Cert. Pres. Base, **ojiru**.

Certain Present.	*makeru*,	(I) lose, shall lose.	*ojiru*,	(I) fear, shall fear.
Imperat. (Neg.)	*makeruna*,	do not lose!	*ojiruna*,	do not fear!

NOTE. (1) *Certain Present.*—As observed above, all the tenses of the Indicative may be either verbs, nouns, or adjectives. The following examples show the use of this tense in each capacity.

(*a*) As a verb.

Hai ga taisō oru, There are a great number of flies.
[*lit.*, fly many abide]

Dare ka soto de matsŭ, Somebody is waiting outside.
[*lit.*, somebody...outside waits]

(*b*) As a noun.

Nani shi ni kita?* What have you come to do?
[*lit.*, what do to, have come]

(*c*) As an adjective.

Taberu mono ga nai, I have nothing to eat.
[*lit.*, eat thing...is not]

(2) *The Imperative (Negative).*—Examples of the use of this form are:

Sore wo taberuna! Do not eat that!
Ikuna! Do not go!

THE CONDITIONAL BASE.

In the First Conjugation this base is a primary variation, but in the Second it is produced by applying the suffix *re* to the Stem.

(*a*) First Conjugation. *Kasu*, to lend; Conditional Base, **kase**. It is thus inflected:

Conditional Pres.	*kaseba*,	if (I) lend.
Concess. ,,	*kasedo*,	though (he) lend.
Imperative (Pos.)	*kase!*	lend!

* It must be borne in mind that *ni* after the stem signifies "in order to."

(*b*) Second Conjugation: *Makeru*, to lose; Cond. Base, **makere.** *Ojiru*, to fear; Cond. Base, **ojire.**

Conditional Pres. *makereba* and *ojireba.*
Concess. „ *makeredo* „ *ojiredó.*

NOTE.—(1) The Conditional Base never stands alone except as the Imperative of the First Conjugation.

(2) *The Concessive Present.*—This is usually replaced, in conversation, by the Present Indicative followed by *keredo*, which may be employed in conjunction with all the tenses of the Indicative. *Keredo* is the Concessive of *keru*, the perfect tense of *kuru*, to come. The Concessive Forms frequently have the syllable *mo*, even, added to them.

Examples:—

To wo shimero! or *To wo shimete!*	Shut the door!
Kono hako wo akero! [*lit.*, this box, open]	Open this box!
Ii keredo, ne ga takai, [*lit.*, good though, price is high]	Though the article is good, it is too dear.
Tadzunemashĭta keredomo, gozarimasenŭ, [*lit.*, enquired although is not]	I enquired, but there was none.

Summary of Inflectional Forms.

First Conjugation ... **Kasu,** to lend.

INDICATIVE MOOD.

Certain Present.

Positive.		*Negative.*	
kasu,	(I) lend, will lend.	*kasa-nŭ, kasa-nai,*	(I) do not lend.

Probable Present.

kas-ō—(sa-u),	probably lend, *or* shall lend.	*kasu-mai,*	probably do, *or* shall not lend.

Certain Past.

kashi-ta,	(I) lent, (he) has lent.	*kasa-nakatta,* *kasa-nanda*	(he) did not lend.

Probable Past.

kashi-tarō,	(they) probably lent.	*kasa-nakattarō,* *kasa-nandaro*	(he) probably did not lend.

Alternative Form.

kashi-tari,	at times, *or* at one time lending.	*kasa-nakattari,* *kasa-nandari*	at times, &c., not lending.

Positive.		Negative.	
	Desiderative Adjective.		
kashi-tai,	(I) wish to lend.	*kashi-takunai*,	(I) do not wish to lend.
	Past Participle.		
kashi-te,	lending, having lent.	*kasa-zu*, *kasa-nakute*	not having lent, not lending.

IMPERATIVE MOOD.

Positive.		Negative.	
kase!	lend!	*kasu-na!*	do not lend!

SUBJUNCTIVE MOOD.

Certain Present. (*a*) *Conditional.*

Positive.		Negative.	
kase-ba,	if I lend.	*kasa-nakereba*, *kasa-neba*	(if) he does not lend.
	(*b*) *Concessive.*		
kase-do, *kasu-keredo*	though (I) lend.	*kasa-nakeredo*, *kasa-nedo*	though (I) do not lend.
	Certain Past. (*a*) *Conditional.*		
kashi-tara(*ba*),	if (he) had lent.	*kasa-nakattara*, *kasa-nandara*	if (he) had not lent.
	(*b*) *Concessive.*		
kashi-taredo, *kashi-ta-keredo*	though (he) has lent.	*kasa-nakattakeredo*, *kasa-nandakeredo*	though (I) have not lent.

Second Conjugation. First Form: **Makeru**, to lose.

INDICATIVE MOOD.

	Positive.	Negative.
Cert. Pres.	*make-ru.*	*make-nu, make-nai.*
Prob. Pres.	*make-yo.*	*make-mai.*
Cert. Past.	*make-ta.*	*make-nakatta, make-nanda.*
Prob. Past.	*make-taro.*	*make-nakattarō, make-nandaro.*
Alt. Form.	*make-tari.*	*make-nakattari, make-nandari.*
Desid. Adj.	*make-tai.*	*make-takunai.*
Past Part.	*make-te.*	*make-zu, make-nakute.*

IMPERATIVE MOOD.

Positive.	Negative.
make-ro!	*make-runa!*

SUBJUNCTIVE MOOD. (*a*) Conditional.

	Positive.	Negative.
Cert. Pres.	*make-reba.*	*make-nakereba, make-neba.*
Cert. Past.	*make-tara.*	*make-nakattara, make-nandara.*

(*b*) Concessive.

Cert. Pres.	*make-redo.*	*make-nakeredo, make-nedo.*
Cert. Past.	*make-taredo, make-takeredo.*	*make-nakattakeredo, make-nandaredo.*

Second Conjugation. Second Form: **Ojiru**, to fear.

INDICATIVE MOOD.

	Positive.	Negative.
Cert. Pres.	*oji-ru.*	*oji-nu, oji-nai.*
Prob. Pres.	*oji-yo.*	*oji-mai.*
Cert. Past.	*oji-ta.*	*oji-nakatta, oji-nanda.*
Prob. Past.	*oji-taro.*	*oji-nakattarō, oji-nandarō.*
Alt. Form.	*oji-tari.*	*oji-nakattari, oji-nandari.*
Desid. Adj.	*oji-tai.*	*oji-takunai.*
Past Part.	*oji-te.*	*oji-zu, oji-nakute.*

IMPERATIVE MOOD.

Positive.	Negative.
oji-ro!	*oji-runa!*

SUBJUNCTIVE MOOD. (*a*) Conditional.

	Positive.	Negative.
Cert. Pres.	*oji-reba.*	*oji-nakereba, oji-neba.*
Cert. Past.	*oji-tara.*	*oji-nakattara, oji-nandara.*

(*b*) Concessive.

Cert. Pres.	*oji-redo.*	*oji-nakeredo, oji-nedo.*
Cert. Past.	*oji-taredo, oji-takeredo.*	*oji-nakattakeredo, oji-nandaredo.*

Irregular Verbs.

In ordinary conversation there are several verbs of somewhat irregular conjugation, which are sometimes heard, and of these there are two which so frequently recur that their forms should be thoroughly learnt by the student. They are, *Kuru*, to come, and *Suru*, to do, their conjugations being as follows :—

Kuru, to come.

Stem, *ki*. Neg. Base, *ko*. Cert. Pres. Base, *kuru*.
Conditional Base, *kure*.

Indicative Mood.

Positive.		*Negative.*	
	Certain Present.		
ku-ru,	come, shall come.	*ko-nu*, *ko-nai*	not come, shall not come.
	Probable Present.		
ko-yo, *ki-yo*	probably come, shall come.	*ko-mai*, *ki-mai*	probably not come, shall not come.
	Certain Past.		
ki-ta,	came, has come.	*ko-nakatta*, *ko-nanda*	came not, has not come.
	Probable Past.		
ki-tarō,	probably came, *or* has come.	*ko-nakattarō*, *ko-nandarō*	probably did not come.

Imperative Mood.

Positive.		*Negative.*	
ko-i!	come!	*kuru-na!*	do not come!

Subjunctive Mood.

Positive.		*Negative.*	
	Conditional Present.		
kure-ba,	if (he) come.	*ko-nakereba*, *ko-neba*	if (he) does not come.
	Conditional Past.		
ki-tara(ba),	if (he) came.	*ko-nakatta*, *ko-nandara*	if (he) did not come.
	Concessive Present.		
kure-do,	though (I) come.	*ko-nakeredo*, *ko-nedo*	though (I) do not come.
	Concessive Past.		
ki-taredo,	though (I) came.	*ko-nakattakeredo*, *ko-nandaredo*	though (I) had not come

---

Alternative Form.

ki-tari,	at times coming.	*ko-nakattari*, *ko-nandari*	sometimes not coming.

Desiderative Adjective.

ki-tai,	(I) wish to come.	*ki-takunai,*	(I) do not wish to come.

Past Participle.

ki-te,	coming, having come.	*ko-zu,* *ko-nakute*	not coming, not having come.

Suru, to do.

Stem, *shi.* Neg. Base, *se.* Cert. Pres. Base, *suru.* Conditional Base, *sure.*

Indicative Mood.

Positive.		*Negative.*	
	Certain Present.		
su-ru,	do, (I) shall do.	*se-nu,* *shi-nai*	not do, (I) shall not do.
	Probable Present.		
shi-yō, *shō*	probably do, *or* (I) shall do.	*shi-mai,* *se-nai*	probably not do, *or* shall not do.
	Certain Past.		
shi-ta,	did, has done.	*shi-nakatta,* *se-nanda*	did not, has not done.
	Probable Past.		
shi-tarō,	probably did, *or* has done.	*shi-nakattaro,* *se-nandarō*	probably did not.

Imperative Mood.

Positive.		*Negative.*	
shi-ro!	do!	*suru-na!*	do not!

Subjunctive Mood.

Positive.		*Negative.*	
	Conditional Present.		
sure-ba,	if (he) do.	*shi-nakereba,* *se-neba*	if (he) do not.
	Conditional Past.		
shi-tara(ba),	if (he) did.	*shi-nakattara,* *se-nandara*	if (he) did not.
	Concessive Present.		
sure-do,	though (he) does	*shi-nakeredo,* *se-nedo*	though (I) do not.

Concessive Past.

shi-taredo,	though (he) did.	*shi-nakattakeredo,* *se-nanderedo,*	though (I) did not

---

Alternative Form.

shi-tari,	at times doing.	*shi-nakattari,* *se-nandari*	sometimes not doing.

Desiderative Adjective.

shi-tai,	(I) wish to do.	*shi-takunai,*	(I) do not wish to do.

Past Participle.

shi-te,	doing, having done.	*se-zu,* *shi-nakute*	not doing, not having done.

Conjugation of Polite Forms of Speech.

Except among relatives and friends, and with one's own servants, verbal forms usually differ somewhat from those given above, Japanese verbs having a special form to express respect, politeness, or reverence. "Honorific" and "humble" forms of speech are fully dealt with later, but while on the subject of verbs it may be advisable, for the sake of completeness, to notice one important verb, which, as a suffix to the stems of other verbs, serves to relieve what would otherwise sound harsh and familiar to Japanese ears.

This verb is *Masŭ*, to be; its inflections, which constantly recur in conversation, are combined with other verbs to form polite tenses. *It always appears as* **a suffix**, *and is* **not** *now in use as* **a separate word**.

The conjugation of *masŭ* differs somewhat from that of any of the verbs previously noticed. Its Stem is *mashi*, its Negative Base *mase*, Certain Pres. Base *masŭ*, and its Cond. Base *masure*, there being no Desiderative Adjective. A part only of the inflections of *masŭ* are in common use, of which the following are those occurring most frequently:—

	Positive.	*Negative.*
Cert. Pres.	*masu,*	*mase-nu.*
Prob. Pres.	*ma-shō (seu).*	*masŭ-mai.*
Cert. Past.	*mashi-ta.*	—
Prob. Past.	*mashi-taro.*	—
Cond. Pres.	*mashi-tareba.*	*mase-nakattareba.*
Cond. Past.	*mashi-tara(ba).*	—
Alt. Form.	*mashi-tari.*	*mase-nakattari.*
Past Part.	*mashi-te.*	*mase-nakŭte.*

For the Negative Tenses of *masŭ*, its Certain Present, *masen(ŭ)* is conjoined with auxiliary forms such as *deshō*, *deshita*, and *deshitara*, which are contractions of the inflections of the verb *gozaru*, with the particle *de*; thus,

Cert. Past (Neg.)	...	*masen deshita.*
Prob. Past (Neg.)	...	*masen deshitarō.*
Cond. Past (Neg.)	...	*masen deshitara(ba).*

The substitute for the Desiderative Adjective is formed by changing *tai*, the termination of the usual Desiderative, into *to*• for the Positive, and into *taku* for the Negative, suffixing the polite verb *gozarimasŭ* (or *gozaimasŭ*), Positive or Negative; thus,

Desiderative Adj. (*Polite*).

	Positive.	*Negative.*
(*a*) **Kasu**:	*kashito-gozarimasŭ.*	*kashitaku-gozarimasen.*
(*b*) **Makeru**:	*maketō-gozaimasŭ.*	*maketaku-gozaimasen.*
(*c*) **Ojiru**:	*ojitō-gozaimasŭ.*	*ojitaku-gozaimasen.*

The Imperative is formed by the aid of certain auxiliaries, both with and without *masŭ*. Thus, *masŭ* combined with *nasaru* (please do), will exemplify this form; as,

IMPERATIVE MOOD (*Polite*).

Positive.	*Negative.*
nasaimase! or *nasaimashi!*	*nasaimasu na!* or *nasaimasura na!*

NOTE.—The honorific *o* is usually associated with the verb which is supported by *nasaimasu* as auxiliary.

Summary of Polite Forms.

N.B.—It must be remembered that the Polite Inflection for nearly all other verbs may be deduced by substituting the Stem of the verb "To be" conjugation for that of the Stem *kashi* in the following type of *kasu*:—

Kasu, to lend.

INDICATIVE MOOD.

	Positive.	*Negative.*
Cert. Pres.	*kashi-masŭ.*	*kashi-masen.*
Prob. Pres.	*kashi-mashō.*	*kashi-masumai.*
Cert. Past.	*kashi-mashita.*	*kashi-masen deshita.*
Prob. Past.	*kashi-mashitarō.*	*kashi-masen deshitarō.*

IMPERATIVE MOOD.

o kashi-nasaimase (shi).	*o kashi-nasai masuruna.*

SUBJUNCTIVE MOOD.

Cond. Pres.	*kashi-masureba.*	*kashi-masenakereba.*
Cond. Past.	*kashi-mashitara.*	*kashi-masen deshitara.*
Alt. Form.	*kashi-mashitari.*	*kashi-masenakattari.*
Past Part.	*kashi-mashite.*	*kashi-masenakute.*
Desid. Adj.	*kashi-tō gozaimasŭ.*	*kashi-taku gozaimasen.*

Derivative and Phrase-Verbs.

The Japanese language is very rich in combinations of words which perform the functions of single parts of speech, and especially in those which do duty for verbs. This latter class may be aptly termed *Phrase-Verbs*, inasmuch as they are composed of various primary forms of the verb conjoined with one or more auxiliary verbs, the whole combination in each case being subject to inflection in the same manner as simple verbs. These phrase-verbs serve to express *Voice* different from that of direct active relation, so that the language thus possesses equivalents for:

The Passive Voice.
„ Potential Voice *or* Mood.
„ Causative Voice.

THE PASSIVE VOICE.

In Japanese, the change from the active to the passive form is made by adding *reru* to the Negative Base in the First Conjugation, and *rareru* to the same base in the Second Conjugation. Thus, the verbs *shiru* (to know), *eru* (to obtain), and *miru* (to see) are made passive as follows :—

1st Conj. *Shiru,* to know ; Neg. Base, *shira.*
Passive Voice, *shirareru,* to be known.

2nd Conj. (Form I.). *Eru,* to obtain ; Neg. Base, *e.*
Passive Voice, *erareru,* to be obtained.

2nd Conj. (Form II.). *Miru,* to see ; Neg. Base, *mi.*
Passive Voice, *mirareru,* to be seen.

NOTE.—This voice is in much less frequent use than in English, and its types all follow the First Form of the Second Conjugation. *Ni* usually serves to render "by" after a passive verb.

Illustrative phrases:—

Doko wo miraremashita ka?	Where were you seen?
Hachijiu yen to iu taikin wo torareta (*toru*, to take),	He had the large amount of eighty yen taken from him.
Watakushi ni yoku shirareru,	He is well known to me.

The Potential Voice.

"Potentiality" is expressed by the same phrase-verbs as those employed with a passive signification. Examples:—

Miraremashĭta ka?	Could you see?
Korareru ka kiite mimasho,	I will ask him if he can come.
Mairaremasenŭ,	I cannot come.
Mairaremasen to iimashita,	He said, he couldn't come.

[*lit.*, "can not come"; that (was what) he said]

Note.—(1) The majority of the verbs of the First Conjugation possess an alternative potential form, which in most cases is formed by adding the syllable *ru* to the Conditional Base. Thus, *shirareru* and *shireru*, both meaning "may" or "can know," are the potentials of *shiru*, to know. Ordinarily, however, a slight distinction is drawn between the forms, *shirareru* being held to signify "may," i.e., authority or permission, and *shireru* to signify "can," i.e., positive ability or innate power, this distinction applying similarly to all verbs in *reru* and *ru* respectively.

(2) In the Second Conjugation there are two exceptional potentials. These are *mirareru*, may see, and *mieru*, can see, formed from the verb *miru*, to see.

The Causative Voice.

A large number of phrase-verbs express causing of action, as, e.g., "causing to finish," "causing to meet," &c.

These causative verbs are formed by adding *seru* to the Negative Base of verbs in the First Conjugation, and *saseru* to the same base in the Second Conjugation.

For example, the verbs *tsukuru* (to make), *eru* (to obtain), and *miru* (to see) assume the causative form thus:

1st Conj. *Tsukuru*, to make; Neg. Base, *tsukura*.
Causative Voice, *tsukuraseru*, to cause to make.

2nd Conj. (Form I.). *Eru*, to obtain; Neg. Base, *e*.
Causative Voice, *esaseru*, to cause to obtain.

2nd Conj. (Form II.). *Miru*, to see; Neg. Base, *mi*.
Causative Voice, *misaseru*, to cause to see.

All causative verbs follow the model of the First Form, Second Conjugation.

The irregular verbs *kuru*, to come, and *suru*, to do, form *kosaseru*, to cause to come, and *saseru*, to cause to do.

The causative verbs are often replaced colloquially by such phrases as *Iku yō ni suru*, go-manner-make, i.e., to make him to go.

Examples:—

Ima onna ni ii-tsŭkete, heya no sōji wo saseru ga ii,	You had better tell the woman to come and clean the room.
[*lit.*, now woman to, commanding, room of, cleaning cause-to-do is good]	
Sugu ni kikashite kudasai,*	Please let me know (hear) at once.
Mo ichido kikasete kudasare,	Please let hear once more.
[*lit.*, more once having made hear give]	

THE ADJECTIVE.

The Japanese equivalent for the Adjective differs materially from the latter in its construction and use. Thus, Japanese adjectives have no forms to express *gender* or *number*, and no inflections to indicate degree. This deficiency, however, is supplied by an inflection somewhat similar to that of verbs, and by the frequent use, as adjectives, of true verbs and adverbial words.

Inflection.

The primitive (simplest) form of the adjective is termed the STEM; by adding to it certain syllables, various adjectival words and phrases are obtained. These are simple adjectives, verbal adjectives, and adverbial adjectives, and by inflection they are made both affirmative and negative, as is the case with verbs.

(1) The syllable **i** added to the Stem forms the SIMPLE ADJECTIVE, which may be employed both attributively and predicatively.

For example, from the Stems *yo*, *naga*, and *yasu* are formed the simple adjectives *yoi*, good, *nagai*, long, and *yasui*, easy *or* cheap; and we may say *nagai nawa*, a long rope, or *nawa ga nagai*, the rope is long.

* The transitive verbs of the First Conjugation in *su* and the causatives are often used indiscriminately, e.g., *kikashite* being confounded with *kikasete*.

Examples:—

Yoi hĭto,	A good man.
Yasui hari,	A cheap needle.
Hari ga yasui,	The needle is cheap.
Warui onna,	A bad woman.

NOTE.—The particle *no* is sometimes used with this form of the adjective, being, in this connection, analogous to the English indefinite pronoun "one."

Examples:—

Shiroi no wa ikutsŭ arimasŭ? [*lit.*, white one, how many]	How many white ones are there?
Kuroi no bakari aru,	There are only black ones.
Kirei na no wo mitai,	I wish to see a pretty one.
Nagai no wo motte o ide,	Bring a long one.

(2) The syllable *ku* added to the Stem forms an adverbial adjective or adjectival adverb, which usually has a predicative force. It is followed by the verb, which it modifies when used adverbially. Thus, from the stem *naga* is formed *nagaku*, and from *yasu* is formed *yasuku*, which may be used as follows:—

Kono nawa ga nagaku gozaimasu, [*lit.*, this rope...long is]	This rope is long.
Yasuku dekimashita, [*lit.*, cheap made]	It is made cheaply.

NOTE.—Colloquially, the adverbial form of the adjective drops the *k* sound, and the *u* sound combines with the vowel element of the preceding syllabic. Thus, the form *hiro* is produced from *hiroku*, wide, by the elimination of the *k* sound, leaving *hirou*, which is pronounced as *hirō*. Similarly *nagaku* becomes *nago*, *yasuku* becomes *yasu*, and *furuku*, *furu*. *Shigeku*, dense, becomes *shigeu*, which then contracts into *shigyō*.

This contraction is especially employed before the polite verb *gozaru*, to be; so that in ordinary conversation the sentence, *Kono nawa ga nagaku gozaimasu*, would be rendered *Kono nawa ga nagō gozaimasu* (this rope is long).

Adverbial forms with terminal *iku* drop the *k*, but undergo no further contraction; thus, *yakamashiku*, noisy, becomes *yakamashiu*.

Examples:—

Kono hako wa goku tako gozaimasu, [*lit.*, this box...very (*goku*) dear is]	This box is very dear.
Yoku dekita,	It is well made.

The following Rule is of great importance, and should be carefully noted :—

> Whenever two or more adjectives are coupled together by the conjunction *and* in English, all but the final one must be rendered in Japanese *by the adverbial form.*

Examples :—

Kami no ke ga kuruku, me ga awoi musume, A girl with black hair and blue eyes.
[*lit.*, head of, hair...black, eyes...blue, girl]

Utsŭkushiku chisai musŭko, A boy both small and pretty.

(3) Besides these simple inflections for the formation of true adjectival and adverbial forms, adjectives *undergo conjugation* for mood and tense exactly like true verbs. This conjugation consists in adding certain forms of the verb *aru*, to be, positive and negative, to a modified form of the adjective.

Conjugation of the Adjective.

Furuki, or *furui*, old.

Stem, *furu* ; Adverbial Adjective, *furuku*, of old, anciently.
Polite Predicative Form, *furū gozaimasu*, is old.

Indicative Mood.

Certain Present.

Positive.		*Negative.*	
furui,	is old.	*furuku nai,*	is not old.

Probable Present.

furukaro,	probably is, *or* will be old.	*furuku nakarō,*	probably is not, *or* will not be old.

Certain Past.

furukatta,	was old.	*furuku nakatta,*	was not old.

Probable Past.

furukattarō,	was probably old.	*furuku nakattarō,*	was probably not old.

Subjunctive Mood.

Conditional Present.

furukereba,	if it is old.	*furuku nakereba,*	if it is not old.

Conditional Past.

furukattara(ba),	if it were old.	*furuku nakattara(ba),*	if it were not old.

Concessive.

furukeredo, though old. *furuku nakeredo,* though not old.

Alternative Form.

furukattari, being at times old. *furuku nakattari,* being at times not old.

Past Participle.

furukute, being old. *furuku nakute,* not being old.

Adjectival Words and Phrases.

A large number of adjectives are formed from other words by combining and associating with them suffixes and other additions.

Those most frequently used are derived as follows :—

(1) From Nouns, by adding *rashii,* are formed a number of adjectives corresponding with those in English terminating in "ish" or "ly," such as *foolish, childish,* &c.

Examples :—

Kodomo rashii, like a child, i.e., childish.
Baka rashii, like a fool, i.e., foolish.
Hontō rashii, like the truth, i.e., true-seeming.

Nouns followed by the particle *no,* and the contraction *na* (*naru,* to be), are sometimes employed as adjectives proper, as

Nippon no, of Japan, i.e., Japanese.
Kin no, of gold, i.e., golden.
Baka na, fool being, i.e., foolish.

A few adjectives proper employ the particle *na* as a termination to both the attributive form and the root, as *okī* or *ōkina,* large ; *chisai* or *chisana,* small.

(2) The present and past forms of Verbs are frequently used as adjectives ; thus, equivalents for "possible" and "impossible" are presented by *dekiru,* able to do, and *dekinai,* not able to do, whilst the English "open" is sometimes rendered by *aita,* the meaning of which is "has become open." Other examples are *osoroshī,* terrible, from *osoreru,* to fear ; *isogashi,* busy, from *isogu,* to be in a hurry.

Yasui, easy, *katai,* hard, and *nikui,* difficult, are added to the Stems of Verbs to form adjectives ; as in *koware-yasui,* easy to break, fragile ; *ii-nikui,* difficult to say.

The negative adjective *nai,* not, added to the Negative Base of Verbs, serves to form another important series of adjectives which constantly take the place of the negative forms of the verbs themselves.

Examples :—

Ashi ga hiete, tamaranai, I don't know what to do, my feet are so cold.

[*lit.*, feet...being-cold, (I) cannot-bear]

Wakaranai, I do not understand.

[*lit.*. it is unintelligible]

The Desiderative form of the verb, i.e., the Stem with the termination *tai* suffixed, is in frequent use as an adjective; as *ojitai*, desirous of fearing, i.e., anxious, timid; *naoshitai* (*naosu*, to mend or cure), desirous of mending or curing, i.e., kind, helpful.

(3) Several Adjectival Phrases are formed by compounding two or three words, as *ishi no ōi*, abounding in stone, i.e., stony; *ashi no hayai*, quick of foot, i.e., swift. When used predicatively, such phrases take *ga* in place of *no*, as *mimi ga toi* (for *mimi no toi*), distant of ear, i.e., deaf; *me ga chikai*, near of eye, i.e., short-sighted.

Comparison.

As previously remarked, the Japanese adjective has no inflection to express Comparison, which is made in the following manner :—

(*a*) The Comparative Degree.—This is expressed by the simple adjective with the particle *yori* (than) employed as in the sentence *Sakujitsŭ yori konnichi wa tenki ga yoroshi*, which means literally "than yesterday to-day the weather is good," i.e., the weather is finer to-day than yesterday. Similarly, "that is brighter than this" becomes in Japanese "this than, that bright is."

Examples :—

Watakŭshi yori anata o wakō gozarimasŭ, You are younger than I.

[*lit.*, I than, you young are]

Mime yori kokoro, The heart is more to be desired than the face.

[*lit.*, heart than, face (is better)]

In sentences like the first of the above, the first part is sometimes dropped when the meaning is sufficiently clear without it; as

Anata wa (or *anata no hō ga*) *o wakō yozarimasu,* You are the younger.

[*lit.*, your side is young]

The English "more" preceding adjectives is represented in Japanese by such words as *motto*, more, and *nao*, yet, or still, &c.; thus,

Motto nagai (more long), longer.
Nao yasui (yet cheap), cheaper.

(*b*) The Superlative Degree.—This is expressed either in the context or by using such words as *ichi ban*, number one, or *dai ichi no*, first, principal.

Examples:—

Ichi ban nagai nawa,	The longest rope.
Kore wa ichi ban takai, [*lit.*, this...number one is high]	This is the highest.

THE ADVERB.

(1) The Adverb proper is in Japanese the adjectival form in *ku*, as *nagaku*, long; *hayaku*, quickly; *atarashĭku*, newly (see p. 60). Words and phrases used adverbially are, however, very numerous, many of them being originally verbs, adjectives, and nouns, which are rendered adverbial with the aid of particles and combinations.

(2) Nouns which are employed as adjectives by adding *na* or *no*, are rendered *adverbial* by substituting the suffix *ni* for *no* or *na*; as

bakani, foolishly.	*makotoni*, truthfully, really.	*shizukani*, gently.
sakini, before.	*ōkini*, gently.	*teineini*, politely.
suguni, at once.	*shinsetsuni*, kindly.	*hokani*, in another way.
yōni, in the manner of.	*shimaini*, finally.	*daijini*, carefully.

(3) The Past Participles of numerous verbs are used adverbially, as

kaette, on the contrary	— from *kaeru*, to return.
hajimete, for the first time	,, *hajimeru*, to begin.
sadamete, probably	,, *sadameru*, to confirm.
damatte, silently	,, *damaru*, silent.
machigatte, wrong	,, *machigau*, to err.
yorokonde, gladly	,, *yorokobu*, glad.
subete, generally	,, *suberu*, to unite in one.
semete, at least	,, *semeru*, to treat with rigour.

(4) Many adverbial ideas are expressed in Japanese by the mere Repetition of words, the second member of the compound taking the *nigori* when susceptible of it, as

kaesu-gaesu, over and over again—from *kaesu*, to send back.
miru-miru, visibly „ *miru*, to see.
nichi-nichi, daily „ *nichi*, day.
iro-iro, various kinds „ *iro*, sort.
dan-dan, gradually „ *dan*, a step.

These are often followed by the particle *to*.

(5) Poetic Name-words are common in Japanese, and a large number of them are used adverbially. Most of them, however, are somewhat vulgar.

Examples :—

pon-pon, sound of guns.
para-para, sound of rain.
bara-bara, with a rattling noise.
gudzu-gudzu, loiteringly.
soro-soro, moving slowly.
patchiri, sudden breaking.
butsu-butsu, grumblingly.

Bara-bara to ochimashĭta, It fell with a rattling noise.
[*lit*., rattling noise with, it fell]

The following is a list of the adverbs most frequently heard :—

Adverbs of Time.

ashita, to-morrow.
ichi do, *hito tabi* } once.
itsu, when ?
itsudemo, always.
ni do, *fŭta tabi* } twice.
jikini, soon.
kio, to-day.
kinō, yesterday.
konnichi, to-day.
mada, not yet.
mettani (with neg.), seldom.
miōnichi, to-morrow.
mō, *mōhaya* } already.
nochihodo, by and by.
sakujitsŭ, yesterday.
sendatte, some days ago.
sudeni, already.
toki, when (relative).
tadaima, immediately.
tabi tabi, several times.

Adverbs of Place.

achi, *achira* } there, thither.
asuko, *asukoni* } there.
atode, behind.
dochi, *dochira* } where, whither.
doko, *dokoni* } where.
kochi, *kochira* } here, hither.
koko, *kokoni* } here.
sakini, before.
sakasama, upside down.
shĭtani, below.
soko, *sokoni* } there.
uyeni, above.
yokoni, across.

Adverbs of Manner.

chitto, slightly.
dō, how.
dōmo, howsoever.
goku, *hanahada* } very.
ikaga, how.
jōzu ni, cleverly.
kayōni, *kō* } in this way.
kitto, positively.
naze, why.
sappari, wholly.
sayōni, *sō*, in that way.
yoku, well.
zehi, positively.

Adverbs of Quantity.

amari, *yokeini* } too much.
bakari, only.
donokurai, *ikura* } how much.
ikutsŭ, how many.
jiubun, enough.
motto, more.
sukoshi, little.
takusan, *taisō*, much.

Adverbs of Affirmation and Negation.

The responses "Yes" and "No" have not, strictly speaking, exact equivalents in Japanese, and generally the reply to a question is a repetition of the verb used in putting the question. The negative answer *iye!* (*iiye*) is, however, almost equivalent to "No!" and the response *hei!* (*he*, *hai*) may signify "Yes!" but it often merely implies that the person addressed has heard, or is paying attention to, what the speaker is saying.

Examples:—

Mo kimashĭta ka?	Has he come yet?
Kimashĭta.	Yes, he has.
Kanda san wa orimasu ka?	Is Mr. Kanda in?
Iye mada mairimasen.	No! he has not come yet.
Tegami wo yaremashō ka?	Can I send a letter?
Yaremashō.	Yes! you can probably send it.

N.B.—The adverb invariably precedes the words which it modifies, as

Achira ye mate.	Wait there.
Mada ki ya shimasŭmai.	He cannot have come yet.
Doko ye itte kita?	Where has he been?
Kiō kita?	He came to-day.
Itsu shuppan shimashō ka?	When is she likely to sail?
Tokidoki o me mi kakarimasŭ.	I see you now and then.

THE PARTICLE.

There are a large number of words in Japanese named by native grammarians *Teniwoha*, from the four most important among them—*te, ni, wo, ha.* They serve instead of case and plural terminations, and also of prepositions, conjunctions, and interjections. Many of them are identical with terminations of verbs and adjectives previously dealt with.*

The particles are usually suffixes, and especially is this the case with those serving as the Japanese equivalents of *Prepositions.* As the latter, however, *follow* the noun instead of being placed before it as in English, they are usually termed by European grammarians "*Post*positions."

The following is a list of the particles most commonly used, arranged alphabetically to facilitate reference:—

De. This particle has varied uses, but primarily it corresponds with the English prepositions *by, with, at, in, of,* and *for*, and the phrases "by means of," "on account of," as

Hiogo de tokei wo kaimashō,	I shall buy a watch at Hiogo.
Heya wa hanahada fukutsu de komarimasŭ,	I am annoyed at the room being so dirty.
[*lit.*, room very dirty at, I am annoyed]	

De is also employed as a contraction for *nite,* and with the various equivalents of the verb "To be" it forms a series of abbreviations, as *da* (for *de aru*), *desŭ* (for *de arimasŭ*), *deshĭta* (for *de arimashĭta*), *datta* (for *de atta*), *darō* (for *de arō*), &c. *De wa* is replaced by the contraction *ja.*

A large number of compound tenses are formed by the Present Indicative followed by *de* and the verb *aru* (to be), and in this construction the Present Indicative is a noun, *de* being the sign of the predicate.

When the verb "To be" unites two nouns, the second noun takes *de* as an affix, as

Kono mushi wa ka desŭ,	This insect is a mosquito.
[*lit.*, ...insect...mosquito]	
Yoroshiu arimasenŭ d' atta,	It was not good.
[*lit.*, good is, not was]	
Konŭ d' atta,	He did not come.
[*lit.*, not come was]	

NOTE.—It will be seen from the last two sentences that the negative in this construction is placed with the principal verb.

* Thus for *te*, see *kashĭte*, p. 42. For *ha* see rule 10, p. 100, and *wa*, p. 74. For *ni* and *wo*, see below, pp. 72 and 75.

Demo is used to express the signification of *de* combined with that of *mo*, even, also, and may be translated "even"; as

Ato demo yoroshī, [*lit.*, after even is good]	It will do afterwards.
Kao demo o arai nasaru ka? [*lit*, face even honourably to-wash deign?]	Will you wash your face as well?

Ga. This particle was originally used to convey an idea of *appurtenance* or *possession*, and still retains this character in certain phrases, as *Waga kuni*, one's own country; *Koma-ga-take*, Colt's Peak (a mountain). It is now, however, regarded as the generic nominative sign, although the subject of the sentence is not necessarily conjoined with *ga*; for when a noun is followed by *mo* or *wa*, and in various other instances, *ga* is dropped entirely. Moreover, nouns may stand in the nominative relation unaccompanied by any particle at all.

After adjectival and verbal forms treated as nouns, *ga* serves the same purposes as when following nouns proper.

Examples:—

Natsu ga kimashita,	Summer has come.
Yūbe ame ga futta, [*lit.*, last night...rain fell]	It rained last night.
Massugu ga chikakatta, [*lit.*, straighter was near(est)]	It would have been nearer to go straight forward.
Iku ga yoroshi, [*lit.*, the going is good]	You had better go.

Ga is an equivalent for the adversative conjunction "but," when following verbs in the Indicative, or adjectives in the verbal form, as in the following examples:—

Arigatō gozaimasu ga ika-neba narimasen,	I thank you, but I must go.
Tori-naosō to omou ga, tori-naosenai,	I want to mend it, but I cannot.

Ka might almost be replaced by the mark of interrogation, being employed in most cases merely to denote a query or to express a doubt; as

Kita ka,	Has he come?
Sō desŭ ka, [*lit.*, so it-is (?)]	Is that so?

Ka may be omitted in sentences commencing with another interrogative word, as

Doko ye itte kita?	Where has he been?

Placed between two nouns, *ka* is an equivalent for the conjunction "or," and when occurring twice in a sentence it represents the correlatives "whether ... or"; as

Tōkyo ka Hiogo no uchi ni orimasu,	He lives in Tokio or Hiogo; I do not know which.
Inu ka kuma ka shirimasen,	I do not know whether it is a dog or a bear.

(For *ka* with interrogative pronouns see p. 23.)

Kara. When following nouns this particle may be rendered by "from" or "since," and by "because," "after," when occurring after verbs.

Examples:—

Yokohama kara Tōkyo made,	From Yokohama to Tokio.
Konnichi kara,	From to-day.
Sakujitsu kara,	Since yesterday.
Rusu datta kara shiranai,	I do not know, because I was absent.
Atsui kara,	Because it is hot.
Mukukashikŭ kaite aru kara watakŭshi-domo ni wa yomemasen.	I cannot read it because the writing is so difficult.

[*lit.*, difficutly writing is because, me to as-for, is unreadable]

Hiru-meshi wo tabete kara de nakŭcha ikimasenŭ,	I shall not go until I have had my mid-day repast.

[*lit.*, noon repast having eaten after if not do not go]

Made (compounded from *ma*, space, and *de*, with) may be translated by *to, up to, as far as, until, inclusive of*, &c.

Examples:—

Komban made machimasu,	I shall wait until this evening.
Hiogo kara Ikao made,	From Hiogo to Ikao.
Miōgonichi made ni deki-agarimasu,	It will be completed by the day after to-morrow.

[*lit.*, day-after-to-morrow by, ... is finished]

Mo may be translated by the copulatives *also, too, even*, when standing alone, but when repeated in affirmative phrases it signifies "both ... and." In negative phrases its English equivalents are the correlatives "neither ... nor."

Examples :—

Anata mo irasshai,	You come also.
Kono kura mo o kai nasare, [*lit.*, this saddle...buy, do]	Buy this saddle too.
Chitto mo kamaimasen, [*lit.*, a-little even matters-not]	It does not matter at all.
Hiogo mo Yokohama mo,	Both Hiogo and Yokohama.
Neko mo inu mo,	Both cats and dogs.
Saji mo sara mo uchi ni arimasen,	There is neither spoon nor plate in the house.

Ni. The uses of this particle are legion, the more important only of which are here noticed.

(*a*) With nouns it usually signifies *to, in, at, into, on* or *by.*

Examples :—

Kioto ni mairimasu, [*lit.*, Kioto, to go]	I go to Kioto.
Tokyo ni orimasŭ,	He lives in Tokio.
Dai ni oite kudasai,	Please put (it) on the table.
Inu wa neko ni kamereta,	The dog was bitten by the cat.
Gakkō ni haitta, [*lit.*, school into, he entered]	He went into the school.

(*b*) Used to couple together the names of several objects, *ni* means "and."

Example :—

Sake ni budō ni mikan ni sono hoka iro iro arimasu,	There are wine, grapes, and oranges, besides various other things.

(*c*) *Ni* is a component of many phrases used as postpositions. The following are those most frequently met with :—

no kawari ni, instead of.	*no tame ni,* for the sake of.
to issho ni, together with.	*no naka ni,* inside.
no soba ni, beside.	*nashi ni,* without.
no ue ni, upon.	*no mukō ni,* across.
no saki ni, beyond.	*no uchi ni,* among, within.
no mawari ni, around.	*no shita ni,* under.
no hoka ni, except.	*no aida ni,* between.
no ato ni, after.	*no ushiro ni,* behind.

No, signifying "of" is the ordinary sign of the genitive.

Examples:—

Hari no ana, [*lit.*, needle of, hole]	Needle's eye.
Me no maye de, [*lit.*, eye of, before at]	Before my eyes.
Wake no wakaranai koto, [*lit.*,reason of, understand-not-thing]	A thing I cannot understand at all.

When preceding the nouns they qualify, the cardinal numerals are generally followed by this particle; as

Mitsu no ishi,	Three stones.
Sannin no dorobō,	Three thieves.

The apposition of nouns may be shown by *no*, as

Taiwan no kuni,	The province Taiwan.
Bettō no Kōdzuke,	The groom Kōdzuke.

Shi. This serves for the copulative "and," when employed with verbs in the Indicative. It also signifies in some cases "and so ...," "not only ... but."

Examples:—

Yasui shina mo aru shi takai no mo aru,	There are cheap things and also dear ones.
Sewashī hi mo aru shi; hima na hi mo are,	I have busy days and days of leisure.
Kono yadoya wa, yama mo mieru shi, kawa mo mieru shi,	From this hotel, not only is the mountain visible, but also the river.

[*lit.*, this hotel as-for, mountain even is-visible..., river even is-visible...]

To, like *ni*, is very extensively employed. Its commonest uses are:—

(*a*) Between two nouns its meaning is "and." It is sometimes repeated after the second noun, as

Hone to kawe to ni natta, [*lit.*, bone and skin (he) has become]	He has become skin and bone.
Kōri to mizu to wo motte o ide,	Bring ice and water.

(*b*) *To* has the force of the conjunction "that" when introducing a statement with regard to a previous assertion, as

"*Kori to mizu*"; *to iimashĭta,*	He said, "Ice and water."

Taisō ni fŭkai desŭ to hĭto ga iimasu,	People say that it is extremely deep.

[*lit.*, "greatly deep is," *that* people...say]

N.B.—In such sentences as the latter, the conjunction "that" is often omitted in English. It must, however, always be expressed in Japanese (*cf.* the French and Spanish usages).

(*c*) *To* sometimes has the meaning of the preposition "with"; thus,

Ano hĭto to shibai ni ikimashita,	I accompanied him to the play-house.
Kono hĭto to issho no ike,	Go with this man.

[*lit.*, this man with, same place go]

(*d*) With nouns, *to* often has the signification of inverted commas expressing quotation, as

O namaye wa nan to iu?	What is your name?
Watakŭshi wa Tsunekichi to mōshimasŭ,	My name is "Tsunekichi."

Wa. This is the opposite of *mo*, and the full explanation of the latter word has been deferred so that the resemblance of function, but dissimilarity of meaning of the two words may be more clearly shown.

Wa means "this (only)," "this and nothing besides," and "this, if nothing further." It singles out or isolates one object from among others, or limits an assertion to the word preceding *wa*, the part of the sentence coming before the latter word being thus separated from the other part.

A just conception of what is meant by the singling out or isolation of a word or phrase may be obtained by reference to such a French expression as "Moi, je travaille; toi, tu ne fais rien" (as for) me, *I* work; (as for) *you*, you do nothing, in which "moi" and "tu" are, so to speak, withdrawn from the body of the sentence and relegated to positions to themselves. Thus the French *quant à* very nearly expresses the force of *wa*, and the nearest English equivalent is "as for," though in translating a Japanese sentence containing *wa* it is usually sufficient to place an emphasis on the word which *wa* accompanies, or by placing such word at the beginning of the sentence.

Examples:—

Sore wa, ichi-ban omoshirō gozaimashō,	*That* will perhaps be the most amusing of all.

[*lit.*, that as-for, number-one amusing will-probably-be]

Ima wa, te-sŭki de gozaimasŭ,	*Now* I am at liberty.

[*lit.*, now as-for, hand-free (I) am]

Kuwashiku wa zonjimasen,	I don't *quite* know.

[*lit.*, exactly as-for (I) know-not]

Mo, however, implies that the noun with which it is used is closely associated with some other thing. Thus, *mo* has the connective meanings *also*, *too*, *both*, &c.

[It must be observed that *wa* has often very little meaning, and might be omitted without interfering with the import of the sentence.]

Examples:—

Ano kurumaya wa ashi ga hayai,	As for that kurumaya, he is quick of foot.
Kuru koto wa, sŭkuno gozaimasŭ, [*lit.*, comes act as-for, few are]	They come but rarely.
Mina wa miemasen, [*lit.*, all as-for, appear-not]	I can't see them *all*.
Are wa warui; kore wa yoroshĭ,	That is bad; this is good.
Hiogo to Kioto to wa dochira ga suzushii deshō?	Which is cooler, Hiogo or Kioto?

Wo. This particle, like *ga*, is a true case sign, and signifies that the word with which it is employed is the object of the sentence, though a noun in the accusative is not necessarily followed by *wo*. The latter is not infrequently omitted before *suru* (or *itasu*), to do, and in other cases, and the accusative case governed by a preposition does not require it.

Examples:—

Michi wo oshiete kudasai, [*lit.*, road...teaching condescend]	Please tell me the way.
Daiku wa dai wo tsŭkuru, [*lit.*, carpenter...table...makes]	The carpenter makes a table.
Rika ni kammuri wo tadasaru,	Under a plum-tree, do not adjust your cap. —*Japanese Proverb.*
Kannin shĭte kudasare, [*lit.*, patience having done give]	Please have patience with me.

Wo is sometimes used in cases where no preposition appears in English; thus,

Senyen no kane wo torareta, [*lit.*, 1,000 yen...money of (*wo*) was robbed]	He had 1,000 yen stolen.

Ya is sometimes expressive of doubt, but often a mere ejaculation. As a conjunctive it translates "and."

Examples:—

Tora ya!	I say, Tora! (Tora—a person's name).
Nido ya sando,	(Some) two or three times.
Iko ya!	Let us go.
Hana ya chō ya,	The flowers and the butterflies.
Hon ya sumi ya fude ga arimasu,	There are books, ink and pen, and such (things).

Yara, which is a contraction of *ya* and *aran*, the old form of the future of *aru*, to be, is expressive of uncertainty and doubt; as

Kakemono to yara de gozaimasŭ gena,	I am told that it is a kakemono (if that is the right name).

[*lit.*, Kakemono (if-that-is-the-right-name), it-is, I-am-told]

Doko ye itta yara,	I wonder where he has gone.
Doko ni orimasŭ yara watakŭshi ni wa wakarimasenŭ,	I do not know where he lives.

[*lit.*, where...lives (?), me to, is not known]

Tora tara (for *to yara*) *iu geisha,*	A geisha called Tora, if I remember rightly.

Ye may be translated *to, in, into,* or *at.* Most Japanese pronounce the *y* very lightly, and sometimes omit it altogether.

Examples:—

Itsu Yoroppa ye kaerimasu ka?	When do you return to Europe?
Watakŭshi no yado ye o tomare nasare,	Stay in my lodgings for the night.

[*lit.*, my...lodging in, ...stay, do]

Doko ye irassharu?	Where are you going?

[*lit.*, where to, deign-to-go]

Kono shinshi wo kiusokujo ye go annai mōshi-ageru,	Show the gentleman into the waiting-room.

[*lit.*, this gentleman.. waiting-room into, guidance do]

N.B.—There is another *ye*(*e*), an interjection similar to the English "Eh?"

Yo accompanies nouns in the vocative case. It is emphatic, and signifies *earnest remonstrance, supplication, warning,* or *appeal.* Sometimes it stands alone as a mere exclamation having these significations. It has no exact English equivalent, the nearest being "I tell you."

Examples :—

Otottsan yo!	Father!
Kirei yo!	It is pretty, I can tell you.
O ide yo!	Do come!

Yori is almost synonymous with *kara*, meaning *from, since, than*; as

Ichi-ji yori mo, osoku natcha ikemasen,	It will not do to be later than one o'clock.

[*lit.*, one-o'clock than even, late as-for-becoming will-not-do]

Kore yori hachi ri,	Eight ri from here.
Sakunen yori,	Since last year.
Omotta yori yasui,	It is cheaper than I thought.

Zo emphasizes strongly the word it accompanies; thus,

Kita zo!	Here he comes!
Dōshite mo, shōchi shinai zo!	Do what you will, I won't consent!

[*lit.*, do-what-you-will even, consent I-do-not...]

THE PREPOSITION.

Prepositions have been fully treated in the preceding section on particles.

The English prepositions frequently require to be translated into Japanese by other parts of speech. Thus, for "over" we must use *koyete*, the past participle of *koyeru*, to cross; for "beside," *no soba ni*—literally, "at the side of"; for "between," *no aida ni*, which is really "in the space of"; &c.

THE CONJUNCTION.

Most of the conjunctions, too, have been already noticed under the head of Particles, but it must be observed that there are numerous phrases in common use in Japanese whose exact equivalents require conjunctive treatment in English. Of these the more important are :—

Da ga, or *tokoro ga*, which has at the commencement of a phrase the sense of "still," "well then," or "that being the case"; as

Tokoro ga, sono ban ni—	Well, then, on that night—

Dano, a contraction of *de aru no*, resembles very much the Alternative Form of the verb, being repeated with each noun for distinctness. Its English equivalent is the copulative "and," and its force is that of giving distinctness to objects enumerated; as

Shishi dano, tora dano, zō dano,	Lions, tigers and elephants.
Ninsoko dano, daiku dano, yaneya dano yonde, shigoto wo sasemashĭta,	He sent for coolies, carpenters, and tilers, and set them to work.

[*lit.*, coolie...carpenter...tiler having called...work caused]

Mo yahari = likewise.	*Shikashi nagara* = but.
Sonnara and *sore de wa* = then.	*Sō shite* (*lit.*, so doing) = and.
Sore de mo = though.	*Yori isso* = than, rather than.
Yue (*yuye*) *ni* = because.	*Yō ni* = that, so that.

THE INTERJECTION.

The most common interjections are:—

A!	*Ara!*	*Eh!*	*Hei!*	*Ne!*	*Ya!*
Aa!	*Dokkoi!*	*Ha!*	*Itai!*	*Oi!*	*Yaa!*
Ai!	*Dokkoisho!*	*Hai!*	*Mā!*	*Oya!*	*Yai!*
Aita!	*Domo!*	*He!*	*Naruhodo!*	*Sā!*	

NOTE.—**A!** denotes *attention*, and sometimes *acquiescence*, on the part of the listener.

Aa! expresses either *grief* or *admiration*, and when long drawn out it denotes *weariness*.

Ai! corresponds to the English "all right" in answer to a call.

Aita!—like the English "Ah!" or "Ugh!"—denotes *sudden pain* or *difficulty*.

Ara! betokens either *joy* or *fear*, and uttered quickly (usually by women) it shows *surprise* or *astonishment*.

Dokkoi! and **Dokkoisho!** are each ejaculations addressed to several persons when lifting heavy weights, &c., corresponding to the English "All together!" "Up with it!" &c.

Domo! shows *perplexity*, and is employed when the speaker does not quite know what to do, as when the English "Let me see, now," is used.

Ha! denotes *attention*, and sometimes *assent*.

Hai! and **Hei!** are indications of the listener's having heard what was said to him.

Itai! is used by a person when in *continual pain*.

Eh! is usually a listener's word introduced as an interruption to express *wonderment* or *sympathy*, though it may indicate *contempt* and *dislike*.

Ma! shows *wonder*, *surprise*, or *satisfaction*, like the English "Oh!"; sometimes *supplication*, as "Do! please do!"

Naruhodo! is used by many speakers with tedious frequency, and corresponds to the English "Really!" "Dear me!" "You don't say so," and like expressions.

Ne! occurs even more frequently than the preceding word; but whereas *naruhodo* is a listener's word, *ne* is used when addressing remarks to anybody, having somewhat the force of "Isn't it?" "Don't you think so?" &c.; as *Yorishī ne*, "It is good, isn't it?"; *Mata miōnichi o ide nasaru ne*," "You will come again to-morrow, won't you?"

Oi! is employed to call servants or intimate friends.

Oya!—usually a woman's exclamation—expresses *surprise.*

Sa! is an incitement to action—encouraging someone to do something.

Ya! denotes *pleasurable agitation* or *excitement* when witnessing anything which is taking place, and is often heard in places of amusement.

Yaa! is the opposite of the preceding word, being used to express *thorough contempt.*

Yo! mostly is a signal *to warn* a person against danger or accident.

HONORIFIC AND HUMBLE FORMS OF SPEECH.

"Honorific" and "humble" forms of expression are provided for each degree of the social scale. They consist of words and phrases set apart for the use, respectively, of an inferior addressing a superior, and *vice versâ*—also for equals when in conversation with each other. By using a "humble" form the speaker intends to humble *himself*; by using an "honorific" he intends to show respect to an equal or a superior, or to "keep at a distance" an inferior.

As a general rule, the honorific forms are limited to *Verbs, Nouns* and *Pronouns of the second person*, although they may be employed in speaking respectfully of absent persons. The polite termination *masŭ* is used with all three persons; the humble forms belong exclusively to the first person.

The student is advised to be sparing in the use of the humble forms, and to employ rather the polite and honorific expressions.

Respect and humility are indicated by means of

Honorific Prefixes and *Suffixes*.

Special *Honorific* or *Humble Nouns, Pronouns*, and *Verbs*.

1. Honorific Prefixes.

The prefixes **o** (derived from *ōki*, great) and **go** are used with *Nouns*, *Verbs*, and *Adjectives* as tokens of *respect*, and usually indicate that the words with which they are associated are in the second person or relate to the person addressed, so that the use of pronouns in this person is rendered to a considerable degree unnecessary. Thus, *o taku* (honourable house), *o mŭma* (honourable horse), may be held to signify "your house," "your horse," without the mediation of any pronoun.

In some cases the honorifics are used to show respect for the *objects* to which they are applied, and there are words with which persons of the lower classes always associate polite forms. "Food," for instance, is *go zen*; "hot water," *o yu*; "cold water," *o hiya*; &c.

NOTE.—*O* is almost exclusively affixed to Japanese words, whilst *go* is reserved for those of Chinese origin.

O is frequently used with the stems of verbs in the second person followed by the honorific verbs *nasaru* (please do, or deign) or *asobasu*; as *O machi nasai*, please wait; *o mise nasai*, please show me.

When in the Imperative mood this combination is used by contracting *nasare* into *na*, or by dropping it entirely, though in this case the honorific signification is almost absent. *O ide na*, or *o ide* (come!), would only be employed in addressing members of one's own family or servants.

O betokens respect for the person spoken to, with a humble reference to the speaker, when used before the stem followed by *mosu* in the first person. Thus,

O naoshi nasai mase,	Honourably mend condescend, i.e., please mend this (for me).

O is also employed with adjectives, as in the following phrases:

Anata wa o wakai kara,	Because you are young.
[*lit.*, you...are young because]	
O aki ni nattara watakŭshi ni kashite kureni ka?	Will you not lend it to me when you have finished with it?

[*lit.*, ...empty when became, me having lent give not]

2. Honorific Suffixes.

Sama, which indicates a similar degree of respect to that of the English *Mr.* or *Sir,* is placed after the name, description, or title in addressing superiors, especially by *employés* in speaking to their masters, and by tradesmen to their customers.

Example:—*Kanda sama,* Mr. Kanda; *danna sama,* sir; *oku sama,* the title given to the lady of the house in polite intercourse.

Sama is also used to refine phrases, with a few other words; as *O kinodoku sama,* I am sorry for you; *go taikutsu sama,* it must be tedious for you; *o sewa sama,* I am much obliged to you; *go kurō sama,* thank you for your trouble; *o machidō sama,* I have kept you waiting.

Achira sama and *kochira sama* are respectively very polite equivalents of *achira* (here) and *kochira* (there).

San, which is a contraction of *sama,* is similar to the English *Mr., Mrs.,* or *Miss,* and is employed mostly between equals, though sometimes it is used to superiors and also —somewhat patronizingly—to inferiors.

In addressing one's own relatives, or in speaking of them to others, *san* must not be used. Thus, "my father" is *oyaji,* and not *oyaji san.*

San may be used either with the surname or the personal ("christian") name, but in the latter case, when the name is that of a female, the particle *o* is ordinarily prefixed in addition; as *O Hana san,,* Miss Flower. One's own wife or servant is addressed by the personal name, with or without *o,* and in referring to her husband in the third person a woman usually employs the word *yado* (*lit.,* the house) or *teishiu* (pronounced "teishi"), husband. Instead of *san, don* should be used in addressing the servants of others.

The proper term for "Mrs. Kanda" in the third person is *Kanda san no go kanai,* or *saikun.* "Madam" is *oku san* or *o kami san,* though the latter phrase is mostly used by the very lowest classes. "Miss" is *o jō san* or *o musume go.*

In conversing with one another, children use the first part of the personal name with or without *san.* To one's own male servants the personal name is used, generally abbreviated, as *Tora* for *Torakichi.*

3. Honorific and Humble Nouns.

It must be observed that honorific and humble forms are used chiefly in referring to one's own and others' relatives—more particularly those of the person spoken to—and these relationships have imparted to them a humble or honorific force, not only by the addition of affixes and suffixes, but also by their being grouped into classes bearing distinctive names, and to which are applied the honorific prefixes already mentioned (*o*, *go*, *sama*, and *san*). For example, the ordinary name for "mother" is *haha*, my mother, but "your mother" or "his mother" requires another class-name and becomes *okkasan*; "my husband" is *danna* or *teishu*; "your" or "her husband" is *danna sama* or *go teishu*.

The most commonly used of these class-names are:—

RELATIONSHIPS.

One's own	Another's	One's own	Another's
	Grandfather.		Grandmother.
sofu,	*go sofu sama*,	*sobo*,	*go sobo*.
jiji.	*go sofu*.	*baba*.	To children:
To children:	*o jī sama*,		*o bā san*.
	o jī san.		
	Father.		Mother.
oyaji,	*go sompu*.	*haha*,	*go bokō*,
chichi.	To children:	*o fukuro*,	*haha sama*.
	ototsu san.	By children:	To children:
		okka.	*okka san*.
		When aged:	*go rōbo*.
	Son.		Daughter.
segare,	*go shikosu*,	*musŭme*.	*go sokujo*,
musŭko,	*o musuko san*.		*o musŭme go*,
kodomo (also of daughters),			*o jō san*.
sōriō,	*go sōriō* (eldest),		
jinan,	*go jinan* (second),		
sannan.	*go sannan* (third).		
	Brother.		Sister.
ani,	*o ani san* (elder),	*ane*,	*o ane san* (elder),
otōto.	*go sonkei* „	*imōto*.	*ane san*,
	go shatei sama (younger),		*o imōto go* (younger).
	go shatei „		
	otōto go „		

One's own	Another's	One's own	Another's
Husband.		Wife.	
tsure-ai (by lower class), *danna* or *teishi*, *yado*.	*danna*, *teishi* (familiar), *go teishi*.	*niōbo*, *sai*, *kanai*, *kanai*.	*o kami san* (to all persons under the rank of *samurai*), *go kanai*, *saikun* (lower rank), *oku san*, *oku sama*, *go naishitsu* (gentlemen of rank).

NOTE.—More usually the husband's surname is used in addressing the wife, and by her in referring to her husband. In the first case *san* is added. Children, and sometimes women, also add *san* when speaking of their elder relatives. Thus, a child will use the phrase *ani san* for "my elder brother," *okka san* for "my mother."

4. Honorific and Humble Verbs.

These are of two kinds: (*a*) Where an ordinary verb is replaced by an entirely different word, and (*b*) where the causative or passive (potential) verb is substituted for the verb in the simple form.

Humble verbs are confined almost exclusively to the first of these classes.

Examples:—

(*a*) *Yaru*, to give. Honorific Form, *kudasaru* or *tamau*; Humble Form, *ageru*.

Iku, to go. Hon. Form, *o ide nasaru* or *irassharu*; Humble Form, *mairu*.

Iu, to say. Hon. Form, *ossharu*; Humble Form, *mōsu*.

(*b*) *Kikashĭte kudasai*, Please tell me.
[*lit.*, causing-to-hear condescend]
Nan'to osshaimashĭta? What did you say, sir?

Syntax: Arrangement of the Words in the Sentence.

I. The normal order of the sentence in Japanese is:

1st, **the Nominative case;**

2nd, **the Indirect Object of the verb, or a Noun followed by a Postposition;**

3rd, **the Direct Object;**

4th, **the Verb, or the adjective in the Verbal Form.**

Examples:—

Watakŭshi wa suteishon de basha ni aimashĭta,	I met the carriage at the station.

[*lit.*, I (*nom.*) station at carriage (*acc.*) met]

Niwatori ni ye wo kuwasero,	Give the fowls their food.

[*lit.*, (you) fowls, food, make eat]

Ano hĭto wa Shinajin to kenkwa wo shĭta,	That man had a quarrel with a Chinaman.

[*lit.*, that man Chinaman with, quarrel did]

N.B. *An exception to this order arises in making* COMPARISONS, *when the name of the object used for the comparison is generally placed at the* BEGINNING; as

Ane hodo ōkiku wa nai,	She is not so tall as her elder sister.

[*lit.*, elder sister, big...(she) is not]

Muda na hanashi wo suru yori wa, damatte iru hō ga ii to orimasŭ,	I think that silence is better than useless talk.

[*lit.*, "useless talk ... ... than, as-for, silent being ... ... (is) good," *that* (I) think]

Itsumo yori kenkō desŭ,	He is more robust than ever.

[*lit.*, ever than, robust (he) is]

Kono yama yori are wa takai,	That mountain is higher than this.

[*lit.*, this mountain than, that...is-high(er)]

II. Qualifying words precede the words to which they relate.

Thus, the adjective or genitive precedes the noun which it modifies; the adverb precedes the verb, &c.; and dependent clauses precede the principal clause.

Examples:—

Warui onna,	A bad woman.
Kuru kojiki,	The beggar who comes.
Osoku made hataraita,	He worked until late.
Hayaku ko,	Come quickly.
Kane ga aru toki, kaimashō [*lit.*, money...is time will buy]	When I have money, I intend to buy some.

III. The signs of gender *o* and *on*, *me* and *men*, and the honorifics *o* and *go*, precede the word to which they refer. Particles showing number and case follow the noun, as do also *wa*, *ya*, *ga*, *mo*, *ka*, *to*, *nagara*; as *Tori ni*, to the bird; *futatsu nagara*, both of them; *kore ka?* is it this?

Expressions relating to Time precede those relating to Place, as

Ichi ji kara, gakkō ni iku,	I go to school at one o'clock.
Kyō no shūkwai ni wa, irasshaimasen deshĭta ka? [to-day of, meeting to..., not-going was?]	Did you not go to the meeting to-day?
Are wa mō Hiogo ni tsukimashĭtarō, [*lit.*, he already Hiogo at, has-probably-arrived]	He has probably arrived at Hiogo already.
Watakŭshi wa miōnichi Kōbe ye mairimasŭ, [*lit.*, I as-for, to-morrow, Kobe to, shall-go]	I shall go to Kobe to-morrow.

IV. Conjunctions and interrogative particles are placed at the conclusion of the sentence or clause, as

Oyaji ga naku narimashĭta kara ni san nichi o itoma wo negaimasŭ, [*lit.*, father...not became because, two or three days...leave...request]	My father is dead, so I would ask you for two or three days' leave.
Kŭtabiremashĭta kara, chotto yasumimashō, [*lit.*, (I) have-got-tired because, a-little will-probably-rest]	Let me rest a little as I am tired.
Sagashĭta keredomo, shiremasen, [*lit.*, sought although, (I) cannot-know]	Although I have looked for it, I cannot find it.
Miru mo iya desŭ, [*lit.*, seeing even disagreeable is]	I cannot bear even to see it.
Oshii koto desŭ ne! [*lit.*, regrettable thing is (eh?)]	It is a pity, isn't it?

V. Interrogation is not denoted, as in English, by inverting the usual construction. The construction remains the same, but the interrogative postposition *ka* is usually added. (See *ka*, pages 70, 71).

Conversational Sentences for Analysis,

Illustrative of the Rules, &c., contained in the Grammar.

Note.—The phrases and sentences following are not only intended to exemplify the foregoing Rules, but to offer also a variety of idiomatic constructions, differing from one another in respects which cannot be particularized in so brief a work as the present.

Watakŭshi wa Hisato Kanda de gozarimasŭ. Hajimete o me ni kakarimashĭta,	I am Hisato Kanda. I have the honour of meeting you for the first time.
[*lit.*, I... ...for the first time...eyes on have hung]	
Danna no o mŭma no shĭtaku wa yoroshiu gozarimasŭ,	Your horse is ready, sir.
[*lit.*, master's horse preparation good is]	
Kore wa Nihon go de nan' to mōshimasŭ?	What do you call this in Japanese?
[*lit.*, this...Japanese in, what call?]	
Dore wa yoroshiu gozarimasŭ?	Which do you prefer?
[*lit.*, which...good is?]	
Kono mono wa nanda?	What is this thing?
[*lit.*, this thing...what is?]	
Dō nasaimasŭ?	What do you propose to do?
[*lit.*, how do?]	
Mina san yoku irasshaimashĭta,	You are all welcome, gentlemen.
[*lit.*, all Mr. well (*hon.*) come (*past*)]	
Nan' doki desŭ? Nan' ji desŭ?	What time is it?
Nete wa imasenŭ,	He is not gone to bed.
[*lit.*, having lain down remains not]	
Dekinŭ toki wa shikata ga nai,	If it cannot be done, there is no help for it.
[*lit.*, not-can-do time...do-manner...is not]	
Arumai,	I don't think there are any.
Sugu ni kawanakŭcha narimasenŭ,	Some must be bought at once.
[*lit.*, at once...not buying does not do]	
Mitsu no uchi ni sore wa ichiban kirei de gozaimasŭ,	That is the prettiest of the three.
[*lit.*, three...among...that...number one pretty...is]	

Seiyō no hĭto demo Shinajin demo nai,	He is neither a European nor a Chinaman.
[*lit.*, west ocean...man...Chinese... ...]	
Tonari ni arimasŭ,	It is next door.
Dore ka hitotsu chōdai,	Please give me one or the other.
Sonnani o anji nasaru koto wa gozaimasenŭ,	There is no reason for your being so anxious.
[*lit.*, so much...anxious do thing...there is not]	
Konnichi dora no sōba wo kiita ka?	Have you heard what the rate of exchange for dollars is to-day?
[*lit.*, to-day dollar...rate of exchange...have heard?]	
Hei, hiaku mai ni hiaku jiu yen de gozarimasŭ.	Yes, it is 110 yen for 100 dollars.
Nan de mo yoroshii,	Anything whatever will do.
Motte kite agemashō,	I will bring it for you.
[*lit.*, having taken, having come, I will offer]	
O rusu naraba kono tegami wo motte kayere,	If he is not in, bring this letter back.
[*lit.*, absent if is, this letter...taking, come back]	
Koko ja hanasenai yo,	We cannot talk here.
[*lit.*, here...cannot talk (*emph. part.*)]	
Abunakŭ te mo kamau mono ka?	Who cares even if it be dangerous?
[*lit.*, dangerous being even care person?]	
Watakŭshi ni yoku shirareru,	He is well known to me.
Konai no d' arō,	He is probably not coming.
Kane ga aru ka? [*lit.*, money is?]	Is there any money? Have you any money?
Naoshi ni yatta ka? [*lit.*, mend...sent?]	Did you send them to mend?
Nani ni tsukai-harawareru to mo omaye no katte da,	You may spend the money on whatever you like.
[*lit.*, what for spend be paid even your...convenience is]	
Watakŭshi wa sore wo suku keredomo, dōmo watakŭshi ni wa aimasu mai.	I like them, but I fear they will not fit me.
[*lit.*, I...them...like although somehow me to...fit will not]	
Mina ureru nara hayaku kite shirasete kudasai,	If you can sell all, please come and let me know quickly.

Tenki naredo samui, [*lit.*, weather though it is, is cold]	Though the weather is fine, [it is cold.
Samukŭ te tamarimasenŭ, [*lit.*, cold...not endure]	It is so cold that I cannot [bear it.
Kono sakana wa takai ka?	Is this fish dear?
Ichi ji han ni hajimarimasu,	It begins at half-past one.
Ittaraba, kayō na koto wa dekinai hadzu de arimashĭta, [*lit.*, if had gone, this kind of thing...not become necessity...was]	Nothing like this could have occurred, if he had gone.
Taberu mono ga nai, [*lit.*, eat thing...is not]	I have nothing to eat.
Samui no ni naze atata-kai kimono ki nai ka? [*lit.*, cold...why warm clothes wear not?]	Why do you not wear warm clothing this cold weather?
Omotta yori yasŭi, [*lit.* thought...cheap]	It is cheaper than I thought.
Daremo ori wa itashimasenŭ, [*lit.*, any one remain...does not]	There is no one here.
Konnichi ame ga furazuba, Tōkyo ye o tomo itashĭtō gozaimasŭ,	I wish you to go to Tokio to-day, if it does not rain.
Medzurashi-sō ni mite oru, [*lit.*, peculiar...looking is]	He is regarding it as if it were something peculiar.
Kono shina ga makoto ni yasui, [*lit.*, this article...indeed...is cheap]	These articles are indeed [cheap.
Aru ka mo shiremasenŭ, [*lit.*, are? even cannot know]	For anything I know, there [may be some.
Watakŭshi wa ima mita no ni nani mo inai, [*lit.*, I...now looked when...something...is not]	When I looked just now, there was nothing.
Keshĭte uchi ye irete wa naranai zo, [*lit.*, really house into, admit in case not become]	Really you must not allow him into the house.
O hima no toki o hanashi ni irasshite kudasare, [*lit.*, leisure time...talk having come give]	When you have time, come (please) and have a talk.
Furuki wo tazunete, atarashĭki wo shiru,	New things are learned by studying the old.
O shidzuka ni irasshaimase!	Go in peace! (to friend departing).

Yasukŭte atatakai,	It is cheap and warm.
Mōshi-agemashĭta nedan yori shĭta de wa sashi-agerurare-masenŭ,	I cannot let you have them for less than I stated.
[*lit.*, stated price than, low with...offer can not]	
Kiō wa Kinyōbi de nai no ni dōshite o ide nasatta?	Why have you come to-day? It is not Friday.
[*lit.*, to-day...Friday...not...whilst how having done come did]	
Hana ga o suki desŭ ka?	Do you like flowers?
[*lit.*, flower...like is?]	
Anata no uwasa wo shĭte iru tokoro d'atta,	We were just speaking of you.
O hanashi wo (or *ga*) *shĭtai to omotte imasŭ,*	I have been wishing to speak to you.
[*lit.*, ...talk...wish to do thinking remain]	
Teppō wo kari ni mairi-mashĭta,	I have come to borrow a gun.
[*lit.*, gun...borrow...have come]	
Shōshō kinsu wo tsukawa-sazuba narimasŭmai,	It will be necessary to spend a little money.
[*lit.*, a little money...if not spend will not become]	
Tatte mo suwatte mo, nedan wa onaji koto,	It is as cheap sitting as standing.
[*lit.*, standing...sitting...price...same thing]	
A! sensei wa Kanda Kun de gozaimasŭ ka? Go kō-mei wa kanete uketamawatte orimasŭ,	Oh! are you Mr. Kanda? I have already heard of your high reputation.
[*lit.*, ah! elder brother Kanda Mr. are?...high name...previously having heard I remain]	
Sazo go taikutsu de' mashitarō,	You must have been bored.
Kannin shĭte kudasare,	Please have patience with me.
[*lit.*, patience having done give]	
Kono atsusa ni dōmo yowatta,	I am exhausted with this heat.
[*lit.*, this heat by somehow have become weak]	
Yō koso oide nasatta,	You are extremely welcome.
[*lit.*, well...come...]	
Kono imi ga wakarimasenŭ,	I do not understand what this means.
[*lit.*, this meaning is unintelligible]	
Rippana hĭto ni naru to iu koto wo shōchi shĭte iru,	I know that he will prove a splendid fellow.
[*lit.*, splendid...become... ...know...]	

O kayeri nasatta hō ga yoroshĭ deshō,	I think you had better go away.
[*lit.*, return did side...good will be]	
Miōnichi sono mŭma wo kaimashō,	I shall very likely buy that horse to-morrow.
[*lit.*, to-morrow...horse...will buy]	
Isshoni kitareba yok' atta,	If he had come with us, it would have been well.
[*lit.*, together if had come good was]	
Dare ka Kiōto made itte moraitai,	I want someone to go to Kioto for me.
Nan'aye mōshi-agereba-yoroshiu gozarimashĭta,	I ought to have told you my name.
Watakŭshi no sōzō ataru ka ataranai ka wa shiranŭ,	I do not know whether my idea is true or not.
[*lit.*, my idea hit ?...not hit... ...]	
Go riokwan wa dochira desŭ ?	Where are your lodgings ?
[*lit.*, travel-residence ..whereabouts is ?]	
Sore ni sōi nai,	There is no mistake about that.
[*lit.*, that about, mistake is not]	
Anata wa miōnichi iyoiyo o ide nasaru ka to kiki ni kimashĭta,	He came to ask if you had not changed your mind about going to-morrow.
[*lit.*, you...to-morrow still do you come ?...hear to, came]	
Mō chaku shimashĭta no d'arō,	He has probably arrived by now.
[*lit.*, already arrival did...will be]	
Oya mo naku kiōdai mo nai to iu mono da,	He is a man who has neither parents nor brothers or sisters.
[*lit.*, parents not brothers or sisters even not called person is]	
Tōnin wa sayō moshĭta de mo arimashō keredomo, sore wa dōmo chito shinjiraremasenŭ,	The person himself may very likely have said so, but I can scarcely believe it.
[*lit.*, person-in-question...thus said even will be although that somehow a little cannot-believe]	
Miōnichi made naorimasŭmai,	He will not have recovered by to-morrow.
[*lit.*, to-morrow till recover will not]	
Arimashō,	I believe so.
Fusoku nara, motto toraseyō,	If it is not sufficient, I will give you more.
[*lit.*, insufficient if is, more will make take]	

A Collection of Japanese Proverbs

for analysis.

Tama migakazareba, hikari nashi, A jewel unpolished will not glitter.

[*lit.*, jewel if not polished shines not]

Chiri tsumotte yama to naru, Piled-up dust becomes a mountain.

[*lit.*, dust heaping, mountain that becomes]

Okame, hachi mokŭ, A bystander sees eight moves in the game.

[*lit.*, land eyes eight checker-board squares]

Wazawai mo saiwai no hashi to naru, Even adversity becomes a bridge to prosperity.

[*lit.*, adversity also, prosperity, of bridge, that becomes]

Rei sugureba, shitsurei to naru, Too much politeness becomes rudeness.

[*lit.*, politeness, if exceed, rudeness, that becomes]

Nezumi toru, neko wa, tsume wo kakŭsŭ, The rat-catching cat hides her claws.

[*lit.*, rat-catching cat as for claws...hides]

Uri no tane ni, nasubi wa haenu, An egg-plant does not grow from a melon-seed.

[*lit.*, melon of, seed, in egg-plant as for, not produces]

Kuchi ni to wa taterarenŭ, A door cannot be made for a man's mouth.

[*lit.*, mouth to, door as for, set up cannot be]

Yasu mono kai no zeni ushinai, He who buys cheap, loses his money.

[*lit.*, cheap thing buyer of, money losing]

Kotoba ōkereba shina sŭkunashi, Many words, small matter.

[*lit.*, words abundant, if materials few]

Ichi ji, sen kin, One letter is worth a thousand dollars.

[*lit.*, one letter, a thousand pieces of gold]

Sumikaki no nakakara meiken ga deru, Famous swords sometimes are made from fire-scrapers.

[*lit.*, pokers of the middle from famous sword...comes out]

Ningen wazŭka gojū nen, Man's life is but fifty years.

[*lit.*, man's short space fifty years]

Homare aran yori, soshiri nakare, — No-blame is better than praise.
[*lit.*, praise shall be than defame be not]

Rika ni kammuri wo tadasazu, — Adjust not your cap under a plum-tree.
[*lit.*, plum-tree under, cap...not adjust]

Nusubĭto wo mite, nawa wo nau, — He makes a rope, having seen the thief.
[*lit.*, thief seeing, rope...twist]

Kashira kakŭshite, o wo kakŭsazu, — Though the head be hidden, the tail is seen.
[*lit.*, head hiding tail...not hiding]

Yome ga shūtome ni naru, — A bride becomes a mother-in-law.
[*lit.*, bride...mother-in-law to becomes]

Tsuno wo naosŭ tote, ushi wo korosŭ, — Intending to mend the horn, he kills the ox.
[*lit.*, horn...mending, that saying, ox kills]

Naki-zura wo hachi ga sasu, — Bees sting a weeping face.
[*lit.*, weeping face...bee...stings]

Rakkwa, eda ni kaerazu, — A fallen flower returns not to its branch.
[*lit.*, fallen flower, branch to, not returning]

Muri ga tōreba, dōri hikkomu, — Reason shrinks back when passion goes by.
[*lit.*, unreason...if pass by reason draws back]

Ido no naka no kawazu, daikai wo shirazu, — The frog in a well does not know the ocean.
[*lit.*, well of middle, frog great sea...knows not]

Yudan, tai teki, — Negligence is a great enemy
[*lit.*, negligence great enemy]

Gō ni itte wa, gō ni shĭtagae, — When you enter a district, conform to its customs.
[*lit.*, district into, having entered, district to, conform]

Inu ni natte mo, ō-doko, no inu ni nare, — If you become a dog, at least be the dog of a great house.
[*lit.*, dog to, becoming even large-place of, dog to, become]

Ushi wa ushi-zure, ŭma wa ŭma-zure, — Cows consort with cows, and horses with horses.
[*lit.*, cows as-for, cow-companion, horse as-for, horse-companion]

Japanese Extracts.

[The following extracts are taken from modern Japanese authors, and are intended as Reading Exercises illustrative of connected sentences and the use of honorifics.]

I.—From "Botan Dōrō," by Yenchō.

(Conversation between a gentleman of high rank and his newly-engaged servant.)

Master.—Sono hō wa shinzan mono demo kage hinata naku yoku hataraku to itte, daibu hiōban yoku mina no uke ga yoi yo. Toshigoro wa ni jiu ichi ni to miyeru ga, hito-gara to ii, otokoburi to ii, zōri-tori ni wa oshi mono da.

Servant.—Tonosama ni wa konaida-jiu go fukai de gozaimashĭta sō de o anji-mōshiagemashĭta ga; sashĭ-taru koto mo gozaimasenŭ ka.

M.—O yoku tadzunete kureta; betsu ni sashĭtaru koto mo nai ga. Shĭte—temaye wa ima made idzukata ye hōkō wo shĭta koto ga atta ka?

S.—Hei! Tadaima mada hōbō hōkō mo itashimashĭta—madzu ichi-ban saki ni Yotsuya no kanamonoya ye mairimashĭta ga, ichi nen hodo orimashĭte, kake-dashimashĭta; sore kara Shimbashi no kajiya ye mairi, mi tsŭkĭ hodo sugite kake-dashi, mata Nakadōri no Yezōshiya ye mairimashĭta ga, tōka de kake-dashimashĭta.

M.—Sono hō no yō ni sō akite wa hōkō wa dekinai yo.

S.—Watakŭshi ga akippoi no de wa gozaimasenŭ ga, watakŭshi wa dōzō shĭte buke hōkō ga itashĭtai to omoi, sono wake wo oji ni tanomimashĭtemo, oji wa buke hōkō wa mendō da kara, chōka ye ike to mōshimashite, achi kochi hōkō ni yarimasŭ kara, watakŭshi mo tsura-ate ni kake-dashĭte yarimashĭta.

Literal Translation.

Master.— ... you ... new come person even shade sunshine without-distinction well work...saying a good deal reputation well all ... reception ... is good. Age ... twenty-one or two... seem...personal appearance...say, manly bearing...say sandals take as...regrettable thing is.

Servant.—Your Lordship...for some days past...indisposition...having been appearance by feel anxious did (*humble*)—[*pause*]—important thing...is not?

M.—Oh, well, having asked gave specially important thing even it is not [*pause*]. And you now until where...service... did thing...was?

S.—Yes just now until all quarters service have done to begin with first of all ... ...ironmonger...went but one year amount having remained ran away; that after ... ... black-smith...going three months amount having passed ran away again ... ... picture-dealer ... went but ten days with ran away.

M.—You manner...so getting tired service cannot do.

S.—I...somehow or another military house service wish to do thinking, that reason...uncle having applied even uncle... ... ... trouble is because merchant's house to go (*imp.*) having said thither hither service...sends because I too face hit by-way-of having run away gave.

FREE TRANSLATION.

Master —I am told that although you are a new-comer you have met with a favourable reception, and that you have gained a reputation for working hard night and day. Your age seems to be about twenty-one or twenty-two, and with your manly bearing it is to be regretted that you are only a sandal-bearer.

Servant.—I hear that for some days past your Lordship has been indisposed, and I felt anxious about you; I hope it is nothing serious?

M.—Thank you, it is nothing of importance. And where have you been up to the present?

S.—Up to now I have been in service at several places. First I went to an ironmonger's in Yotsuya, and after remaining there one year, I ran away. Then I went to a blacksmith's in Shimbashi, but I ran away again at the end of three months and took service with a picture-dealer in Nakadori Street, but I left in ten days.

M.—If you get discontented in that manner you cannot do your duty as a servant.

S.—Oh, it is not that I am soon discontented; I wished to be employed by some military man, and for that reason I applied to my uncle to get me employment of this kind, but he said that service with a military man was very trouble-some, and that I had better go to a merchant's. So he sent me to various places, and to spite him I ran away.

II.—From "Shosei Katagi," a Japanese novel.

(*Conversation with a jinrikisha-runner.*)

Fare.—Oi! oi! Kurumaya! michi ga chigai wa shinai ka?
Coolie.—He, he, daijōbu de gozaimasŭ.
F.—Doko ye ikunda (*for* iku no da) ka shitte oru ka?
C.—He, zonjite orimasŭ: kochira kara mairimashĭta hō ga chikai no de gozaimasŭ (gara gara gara).
F.—Oi! oi! Daga, doko da ka shitteru ka?
C.—He, he, zonjite orimasŭ (gara gara).
F.—Zonjite oru ja (*for* de wa) wakaranai. Doko ye ikunda?
C.—He, he (gara gara).
F.—Kore! matte kure to iu ni (gara gara gara).

Literal Translation.

Fare.—I say jinrikisha-man road...mistake...not do?
Coolie.— ... ... quite safe...is.
F.—Where to go is? knowing remain?
C.— ... knowing remain: this way from came side...near .. ... is (rattle rattle rattle) [*of the jinrikisha*].
F.—I say! but where is? knowing remain?
C.— ... ... knowing remain (rattle rattle).
F.—Knowing remain with is-not-intelligible. Where to go is?
C.— ... ... (rattle rattle).
F.—This having-waited give that saying in (rattle rattle rattle).

Free Translation.

Fare.—I say 'rikisha-man, are you not mistaking the road?
Coolie.—Oh, it's all right, Sir.
F.—Do you know where you are going?
C.—Yes, Sir, I know; this is the shortest way (*rattle, rattle, rattle*).
F.—I say, but do you know where I am going?
C.—Yes, Sir, I know (*rattle, rattle*).
F.—I don't understand what you mean with your "I know." Where *are* you going?
C.—All right! All right! (*rattle, rattle*).
F.—Now then, wait, I tell you! (*rattle, rattle, rattle*).

THE KATAKANA AND HIRAGANA SYLLABARIES.

Rom.	Kat.	Hir.	Rom.	Kat.	Hir.	Rom.	Kat.	Hir.
a	ア	あ	ge	ゲ	げ	chi	チ	ち
i	イ	い	go	ゴ	ご	tsu	ツ	つ
u	ウ	う	sa	サ	さ	te	テ	て
e	エ	え	shi	シ	し	to	ト	と
o	オ	お	su	ス	す	da	ダ	だ
ka	カ	か	se	セ	せ	ji	ヂ	ぢ
ki	キ	き	so	ソ	そ	dzu	ヅ	づ
ku	ク	く	za	ザ	ざ	de	デ	で
ke	ケ	け	ji	ジ	じ	do	ド	ど
ko	コ	こ	zu	ズ	ず	na	ナ	な
ga	ガ	が	ze	ゼ	ぜ	ni	ニ	に
gi	ギ	ぎ	zo	ゾ	ぞ	nu	ヌ	ぬ
gu	グ	ぐ	ta	タ	た	ne	子	ね

THE SYLLABARIES (*continued*).

Rom.	Kat.	Hir.	Rom.	Kat.	Hir.	Rom.	Kat.	Hir.
no	ノ	の	pi	ピ	ぴ	yo	ヨ	よ
n(g)	ン	ん	pu	プ	ぷ	ri	リ	り
ha	ハ	は	pe	ペ	ぺ	ra	ラ	ら
hi	ヒ	ひ	po	ポ	ぽ	ru	ル	る
fu	フ	ふ	ma	マ	ま	re	レ	れ
he	ヘ	へ	mi	ミ	み	ro	ロ	ろ
ho	ホ	ほ	mu	ム	む	wa	ワ	わ
ba	バ	ば	me	メ	め	(w)i	ヰ	ゐ
bi	ビ	び	mo	モ	も	(w)u	ウ	う
bu	ブ	ぶ	ya	ヤ	や	(w)e ye	ヱ	ゑ
be	ベ	べ	(y)i	イ	い	wo	ヲ	を
bo	ボ	ぼ	yu	ユ	ゆ			
pa	パ	ぱ	ye	エ	𛀁			

The Native Syllabaries.

Rules for Transliteration.

The two syllabaries are strictly interchangeable, and whatever applies to the one applies equally to the other. Their mutual relations are similar to those of the various "founts" of type in English printing, and just as our word "grammar" may also be printed "**grammar**" or "*grammar,*" so also may the Japanese word "sayōnara" be represented in either syllabary.

The method of numbering the pages in Japanese books is exactly the reverse of that adopted in Europe; thus the title-page is situated on what would be the *last* page in an English work. The first word on each page commences at the *top right-hand* corner and the letters (syllabics) are placed under one another, column by column, proceeding to the left.

In the native syllabaries the vowel syllabics do not represent vowels in the same sense as the symbols *á*, *e*, *i*, *o*, *u* in our alphabet represent vowels. In European languages the vowel letters are mere signs of vowel sounds, and, in this capacity, enter into the formation of each syllable of words. These vowel characters, however, in the Japanese syllabaries are *independent wholes* whose sounds happen to be those of pure vowels. As will be seen on reference to the syllabaries, they do not enter into the formation of any of the consonant syllabics, that is to say, the character representing *a*, for example, forms no part of the characters representing *ka*, *ta*, *na*, &c. The consonant syllabics, of course, contain vowel elements, but these are integral parts of the syllables.

In the following pages the vowels, when forming parts of consonant syllables, are written above the line, thus k^a, w^o, &c.

The juxtaposition of the syllabics produces modifications of their individual values according to the following rules, which are numbered consecutively to facilitate reference:—

VOWEL-SYLLABIC MODIFICATIONS.

RULE 1. When a vowel syllabic is doubled, the pronunciation is that of a double long, or slow, vowel sound; thus:

aa = *ā*. ii = *ī*. uu = *ū*.

When two *different* vowel syllabics are juxtaposed, their pronunciation is modified as follows:—

2. *e* following *a* tends to become y^e; thus:

a e r^u is written *ayeru.*

3. *o* following *a* tends to become w^o; thus:

a o r^i is written *awori.*

4. Vowels preceded by *i* assume an initial *y* sound; thus:

i a t^e r^u is written *iyateru.*
i e ts^u „ „ *iyetsu.*

5. The juxtaposition of *a* and *u* and of *o* and *u* produces a double long, or slow, *o* sound; thus:

a u t^o = *ōto*. o u k^e n = *ōken*.
a u g^i = *ōgi*. o u n^a = *ōna*.

6. The juxtaposition of *e* and *u* produces *yō*. The explanation of this peculiarity is as follows:—In Japanese etymology, *e* is equivalent to *i* + *a*, so that eu = *iau*, and it has been stated that *au* is pronounced *ō*, and thus *iau* easily passes into *iō* or *yō*.

Examples:

e u g^a k^u = *yōgaku*. d^o e u b^i = *doyōbi*.
e u j^i = *yōji*. e u ch^i = *yōchi*.

7. Vowels preceded by *o* or *u* assume an initial *w* sound; thus:

o i r^u is written *owiru.*
u e r^u „ „ *uweru.*
u i u „ „ *uwiyu.*

CONSONANT-SYLLABIC MODIFICATIONS.

8. When the syllabic *n* precedes one of the B, M or P series it is pronounced *m*; thus

m^e n b^o k^u = *memboku*. e n p^i ts^u = *empitsu*.
n^e n b^u ts^u = *nembutsu*. k^a n m^u r^i = *kammuri*.

9. When at the beginning of a word, w^o drops the *u* sound except in the case of the postposition *wo* which is written in full.

Examples:

$w^o\ k^a\ m^e$ = *okame*. $w^o\ t^o\ k^o$ = *otoko*.

Vowel + Consonant Syllabics.

10. When the syllabics of the H series follow the vowel syllabics, or, what is virtually the same thing, when they follow the vowel sound of *any* syllabic, the aspirate is dropped. H^a is then sounded like *wa*, and the other syllabics of the series coalesce as pure vowels with those preceding.

Examples:

uh^a	= *uwa*.	$ih^a\ sh^i$	= *iwashi*.
oh^i	= *oi*.	$h^a\ f^u$	= *hō*.
if^u	= *iu*.	$g^o\ f^u$	= *gō*.
ih^e	= *ie*.	$n^a\ h^a$	= *nawa*.
uh^e	= *ue*.	k^o hi	= *koi*

Consonant + Vowel Syllabics.

11. The modifications produced by these combinations are practically the same as in the case of vowel-syllabics only: thus

h^o u = *hō*.	r^i u = *ryū*.
g^a u = *gō*.	t^a u m^e = *tōme*.

12. The pronunciation of *eu* as *yō* holds equally when the vowel sound *e* occurs in consonant syllabics with the same associations as the vowel *e*; thus $t^e u$ becomes *chō*, for eu = *yō*, and *t* preceding the sounds *i* and *y* is equivalent to *chi*. Thus we get *chi yō*, which is changed into *chō*.

Examples:

d^e u = ji yo = *jō*.	h^e u = hi yo = *hyō*.
k^e u = ki yo = *kyō*.	g^e u = gi yo = *gyō*.

13. When f^u, preceded by a syllabic with *a* or *o* as the vowel element, terminates a verb, the aspirate only is dropped and the result is *au* or *ou*; thus

$k^a\ f^u$ = *kau*, and not *kō*.

o $m^o\ f^u$ = *omou*, and not *omō*.

Light and Elided Sounds.

14. When the sound *u* ends a word, either as a vowel syllabic or as an element of a consonant syllabic, it is generally touched so lightly that it may be regarded as virtually silent.

Examples:

g^o z^a i m^a s^u = *gozaimasŭ.* t^a t^e r^a r^e n^u = *taterarenŭ.*

15. When a *ch* sound follows *ts*^{u} not at the beginning of a word, the u sound of *ts*^{u} is elided; thus

i ts^u ch^i = *itchi.* i ts^u t^e u = its teu = itchiyo = *itchō.*

16. When a K syllabic follows *k*^{u} not at the beginning of a word, the *u* sound is elided; thus

k^a k^u k^i = *kakki.* a u z^o k^u k^o k^u = *ōzokkoku.*

17. When ts^u, not at the beginning of a word, is followed by a syllabic of the K, S, T or P series, its sound (i.e., *ts*^{u}) is elided and the consonant following is doubled, except in the case of *sh* of which the *s* only is doubled.

Examples:

k^e ts^u k^a u = *kekkō.* m^o ts^u te = *motte.*

m^a ts^u s^u g^u = *massugu.* t^e ts^u p^a u = *teppō.*

18. When *k*^{u} or *g*^{u} precedes *w*^{a} the *u* sound is elided; thus

k^u w^a j^i = *kwaji.* g^u w^a i k^o k^u = *gwaikoku.*

19. In polysyllables the sounds *i* and *u* as elements of the K, H, S and T series tend to become silent; thus

a s^a g^i t^a = *asagĭta.* k^a sh^i r^a = *kashĭra.*

h^i k^a r^u = *hĭkaru.* i ch^i m^a n = *ichĭman.*

Coalescent Sounds.

20. When the syllabics sh^i, j^i, and ch^i are followed by the syllabics *y*^{a}, *y*^{o}, *y*^{u}, *u*, or the diphthongal syllables *yō*, &c., the first and the last sounds only of the combinations are are heard; thus:

sh^i y^o = *sho.* j^i y^a u = ji yō = *jō.*

j^i y^a = *ja.* j^i f^u = ji yū = *jū.*

MISCELLANEOUS EXAMPLES.

(*The numbers refer to the preceding Rules for Transliteration.*)

Native.	Romanized.	Native.	Romanized.
o h^a s^e r^u	*owaseru* (10)	h^i ts^u k^o m^u	*hikkomu* (17)
k^i u g^i u	*kyūgyū* (11)	b^a n m^e	*bamme* (8)
j^i ts^u p^u n	*jippun* (17)	m^o r^a f^u	*morau* (13)
s^u k^u n^a sh^i	*sŭkunashi* (19)	y^u h^i n^a f^u	*yuinō* (10)
o h^o u w^o	*ōuwo* (10)	m^o t^o m^u	*motomŭ* (14)
sh^i m^a f^u	*shimau* (13)	g^e u t^a i	*gyōtai* (12)
o o j^i	*ōji* (1)	d^e u t^e ts^u	*jōtetsu* (12)
n^i u b^o	*nyūbo* (11)	o u b^u n	*ōbun* (5)
n^i u b^a u	*nyūbō* (11)	w^o k^e	*oke* (9)
e u ch^i ye n	*yōchiyen* (6)	sh^i k^a sh^i	*shĭkashi* (19)
ch^i ts^u t^o	*chitto* (17)	ch^i y^o u b^o	*chōbo* (20, 11)
k^u s^a r^i	*kŭsari* (19)	k^u w^a i sh^i y^a	*kwaisha* (18, 20)
sh^i y^u u y^a	*shūya* (20)	sh^i f^u i	*shūi* (10, 20)
n^a n b^i k^i	*nambiki* (8)	s^u h^a u	*sūō* (10, 11)
h^o h^o d^a t^e	*hōdate* (10)	m^e u k^u w^a	*myōkwa* (12, 18)
j^i f^u k^i	*jŭki* (10)	i h^a u	*iwō* (10, 11)
w^o r^e r^u	*oreru* (9)	sh^i y^a u b^a i	*shōbai* (20, 11)
h^a h^e r^u	*haeru* (10)	r^i f^u r^o n	*ryūron* (10, 11)
r^i u k^i u	*ryūkyū* (11)	e u t^e u	*yōchō* (6, 12)
r^e u r^i	*ryōri* (12)	g^a k^u k^a u	*gakkō* (16, 11)
o u s^e ts^u	*ōsetsu* (5)	n^i f^u t^e u	*nyūchō* (10, 12)
ts^u k^e g^i	*tsŭkegi* (19)	o u m^e u	*ōmyō* (5, 12)
m^o r^a f^u	*morau* (13)	j^i y^a h^a f^u	*jahō* (20, 10)
j^i y^a k^u	*jaku* (20)	w^o h^i y^o m^e	*oiyome* (9, 10)
h^i h^a r^i	*hiwari* (10)	h^e u r^i u	*hyōryū* (12, 11)
a o r^u	*aworu* (3)	k^i u r^a f^u	*kyūrō* (11,10)
k^a k^u k^i	*kakki* (16)	o u h^o u	*ōhō* (5, 11)
f^u h^a f^u	*fuhō* (10)	e u d^o u	*yōdō* (6, 11)
e u r^a k^u	*yōraku* (6)	w^o r^i h^a	*oriwa* (9,10)
i i y^e	*īye* (1)	r^a k^u k^u w^a	*rakkwa* (16, 18)

Part II. EXERCISES.*

A. Exercises for Translation.

1.

kashi, cake, sweetmeat.
nakanaka, very.
kōen, (public) park.
mukashibanashi, story, tale.
sŭki, fond of, liking.
dōka, please (asking favour).
goro, time, about.
tori, thoroughfare, way.
matchi, match, lucifer.
hon, book.
Igirisu, England.
umareru, to be born.
taihen, very
(*o*) *taku*, (your) house.
chabon, tea-tray.
utsŭkushii, nice, beautiful.
shōchi, knowledge.
mada (with neg.), not yet.
yōji, business, something to be done.
issho ni, together.
saisho, (at) first.
shikkari, firmly.

(A) Translate into English:—

1. *Dare ga kimashĭta ka?—Okuro san ga kimashĭta.* 2. *Dare ga ikimasŭ ka?—Watakŭshi ga ikimasu.* 3. *Kanai ga orimasŭ ka?* 4. *Niwa ye ikimashō ka?* 5. *Niwa ni hana ya ki ga arimasŭ ka?* 6. *Anata no ototsan wa go sōken de gozaimasŭ ka?* 7. *Go shisoku wa o ikutsŭ desŭ ka?—Segare wa ima nanatsŭ de gozaimasŭ.* 8. *Kono o kashi wa nakanaka ii n' desu.* 9. *Ashĭta tenki ga yokereba, kōen wo mi ni ikimashō.* 10. *Nihon-go wa Eigo yori (mo) muzukashii.* 11. *Kono mukashibanashi no uchi de dore ga ichiban omoshiroi?* 12. *Sake yori mo o cha ga sŭki desŭ.* 13. *Kono fŭtatsŭ no chawan no uchi de dochira ga o ki ni irimasŭ ka?* 14. *Itsu mairimashĭta naraba o me ni kakaru koto ga dekimasŭ ka?—Dōka myōnichi gozen no shichiji goro ni oide kudasai (*or, *kite moraitai).* 15. *Yoroshiū gozaimasŭ ka?—Yō gozaimasŭ.* 16. *Kochira ye o tōri nasai.* 17. *Matchi wa doko ni arimasŭ ka?—Koko ni arimasŭ.* 18. *Sono akai hon wo koko ye kudasai.* 19. *Ano kata wa Igirisu de o umare nasaimashĭta.* 20. *Tegami no kami ga motto irimasŭ.*

* For Key see pp. 108-112.

(B) Translate into Japanese :—

1. Are you going?—Yes, I am (going). 2. Is the weather fine to-day?—It is very fine. 3. Is the garden large or small? (*translate*, Is large? is small?) 4. Do you like flowers?—I like flowers very much. 5. Is that expensive? —No, it is not expensive. 6. Is your house far?—No, it is very near. 7. If this tea-tray is not dear, I will buy it. 8. In summer the days are longer than in winter. 9. My brother is four years younger than I. 10. Of Japanese flowers the cherry-blossom is the nicest (*trans.*, number one nice). 11. Do you know that gentleman?—I have not yet had the pleasure of seeing him. 12. If you go to the bank now, I will go with you, as I also have some business to do there. 13. Will you go yourself? 14. Boil some water, please. 15. Did you call me?—No, I did not call you. 16. Please fasten the gate when you go out. 17. Will you go out with me for a while? 18. Where shall we go first? 19. Thank you for the flowers you brought the other day. 20. Take the books off the table. 21. Bring the lamp from upstairs. 22. I shall not return until seven o'clock.

2.

sensei, teacher.
hikiyaburu, to tear.
kuzu, scraps, pieces.
kamitsŭku, to bite.
sampo suru, to take a walk.
saifu, purse.
takasa, height.
bakari, only, about.
maiasa, every morning.
nan' doki, what time?
mezameru, to awake.
wasureru, to forget.
satsŭ, volume.
konaida, the other day, lately.
matsŭ, pine-tree.
gejo, (maid-) servant.

(A)

1. *Anata wa mō jinrikisha ni o mori nasatta koto ga arimasŭ ka?—Hai, watakŭshi wa Tokyō ni otta toki tabitabi notta koto ga arimasŭ.* 2. *Kore wa omae ga motte kita mono da ka?—Hai, danna san* (see p. 81) *temae ga ichi de katta yasai de gozaimasŭ.* 3. *Kore wa Nihon no fune desŭ ka?—Hai, sore wa Nihon no jokĭsen desŭ.* 4. *Anata wa tabitabi Hiogo ye oide deshĭta ka?—Ie, iku tabi mo mairimasen deshĭta.* 5. *Anata wa donata de gozaimasŭ ka.—Watakushi wa Tsune to mōsŭ mono*

de gozaimasŭ. 6. *Are wa dare no uchi desŭ ka?* 7. *Okkasama wa mō inaka kara o kaeri dė gozaimasŭ ka?* 8. *Sensei kara uketta tegami ni sugu ni kotaemashĭta.* 9. *Kore wa kodomo no hikiyabutta tegami no kuzu desŭ.* 10. *Maiasa nan' doki ni o mezame ni narimasŭ ka?—Roku-ji ka roku-ji han ni okimasŭ.* 11. *Ano hito wa inu ni ashi wo kamitsŭkaremashĭta.* 12. *Konnichi sampo shĭta toki ni hachi ni hĭtai wo sasaremashĭta.* 13. *Jū ichī ji made de yokereba o shirase itashimashō.* 14. *Watakushi wa saifu wo doko ye ka oki-wasuremashĭta.*

(B)

1. Who is the man you brought with you?—That is my teacher. 2. What is the name of the school you attend? 3. Have you many books?—No, I have only a few volumes. 4. Have you much money?—No, I have only a little. 5. The horse I have bought is good. 6. What is it you have thrown into the water? 7. The plant I bought in the market the other day has faded (*kareru*) already. 8. I have brought the books to-day which you ordered yesterday. 9. This house is small; it has only (*shĭka arimasen*) four rooms. 10. The highest mountain in (of) Japan is Fuji; its height is over 12,000 *shaku.* 11. How many trees are there in your garden?—There are only three pine-trees and one plum-tree. 12. What time is it by (as to) your watch?—Mine has stopped. 13. Tell the servant to dress (cause to, &c.) the children at once. 14. What are you looking for?—I have lost my gloves. 15. Leave this here a little longer. 16. Lift it a little higher please. 17. I have lost my penknife; lend me yours please. 18. Listen! don't you hear something? 19. I was asleep when you knocked.

3

sendatte, recently, lately.
bonyari suru, to feel dazed; to be absent-minded.
narawashi, custom.
tagai ni, mutually.
nigiru, to grasp.
himo, string, fastening.
katai, firm, secure.
heya, room, chamber.
zehi, positively.
kembutsu suru, to go to see (sights, &c.)
tsumori, intention.
asŭko, there, that place.
ijō, more than, above.
jitensha, bicycle.

(A)

1. *Koko kara Hiogo ye yı k ı no ni wa nan' jikan gurai kakarimasŭ ka?* 2. *Sendatte o taku ye agarimashĭta ga, o rusu de gozaimashĭte zannen deshĭta.* 3. *Sonna ni bonyari shĭte iru, kawa ye ochiru yo.* 4. *Bangoro wa suzushii kara, machi wo sampo suru hito ga ōi.* 5. *Taitei no kuni no narawashi wa hito ni aimashĭta toki ni tagai ni te wo nigiriaimasŭ.* 6. *Konaida no tegami wa mada yaku ga dekimasen deshō ne.* 7. *Kono tsutsumi no himo wo kataku o shime nasai.* 8. *Uchi ni haitte kimashĭta toki ni ano kata wa samukute furuete orimashĭta.* 9. *Ano kata wa toki wo machigaete o hiru sugi ni irasshaimashĭta.* 10. *O demashi ni natte kara go fun hodo tachimasŭ to ano kata ga oide ni narimashĭta.* 11. *Watakŭshi ga Nippon wo tatte kyō de chōdo shichi nen ni narimasŭ.* 12. *Sampo suru ni wa go han wo tabete kara mada jūbun toki ga tatanai.* 13. *Nihonjin no namae wa oboe-nikū gozaimasŭ.* 14. *Inaka-mono wa gwai-kokujin wo mitagarimasŭ.* 15. *Anata ga kono heya ni oide nara otonashiku shinakereba narimasen.* 16. *O sore irimasŭ ga, empitsu wo mō ichido haishaku shitō gozaimasŭ.* 17. *Kore wa machigatte-kimashita kara, hajime kara sukka ri yari-naoshimashō.* 18. *Kesa wa mizu wo tsukaimashō.*

(B)

1. Before (*made ni*) I return to Japan I intend positively to visit London. 2. This house has a garden at the front as well as at the back. 3. Are you now on the way back from school? 4. I got up at six o'clock this morning, and I took a walk on the top of that mountain. 5. Is there anyone here who can speak English? 6. Whom are you thinking about? 7. It is twenty minutes since he was here. 8. She goes every day to Tokio, Sundays excepted. 9. It is seven years to-day since I arrived in London. 10. She will not get back in time to go. 11. Please call me early to-morrow morning. 12. If you are going to Uzo, let us go together. 13. I wish we had our bicycles with us. 14. I have used nearly all the money I brought from the bank. 15. Please speak a little louder. 16. I am going to take a short walk. 17. I generally walk a little at mid-day. 18. I do wish that man would not whip his horse so much. 19. He is coming

some time to-day. 20. I hoped he would come early. 21. Cross that bridge, and you will come to the place. 22. It ought not to cost more than two yen.

4.

bungakushi, a history of literature.
hanarezashiki, summer-house.
kinodoku, I am sorry (for your sake).
mitsudan, a private conversation.
shibaraku, some time.
hirushoku, noon-meal.
banshoku, supper.
atsuraemono, things ordered.
teishu, master (of a house).
tabun, perhaps, probably.
dekiagaru, to get ready or finished.
zutsu, each, at a time.
inabikari ga suru, it lightens.
toshi, a year, age.
uekiya, gardener.
massugu, straight.
asu, to-morrow.

(A)

1. *Boku no heya de cha ippai nonde sugu dekakeyō.* 2. *Watakŭshi no hon ni wa Nihon bungakushi ga arimasen.* 3. *Ano hanarezashiki wa nani ni tsŭkaimasŭ ka?—Sore wa cha no yu mata wa mitsudan ni tsŭkaimasŭ.* 4. *O kinodoku desŭ ga, mō shibaraku o machi kudasai.* 5. *Hirushoku to banshoku no aida ni cha wo nomimasŭ.* 6. *Anata no o atsuraemono wa asu made matte kudasai.* 7. *Omae wa gakkō ye yuku mae ni itsu mo shĭtayomi wo shinakereba narimasen.* 8. *Kono tsŭtsumi wo motte-itte kudaseru koto ga dekimasŭ ka?* 9. *Mō osoi kara dare mo konai darō.* 10. *Dorobō ga jōmae wo akete miru tokoro ye ie no teishu ga haitte kita.* 11. *Kono tetsŭdō ga tabun shĭchi-gatsu nakagoro made ni dekiagarimashō.* 12. *Konnichi wa tenki ga ii kara, uchi no niwa ye ikimashō.* 13. *Kaze de kami ga chira-barani narimashĭta.* 14. *Kore wo nani-ka ni tsŭkaimasŭ kara nokoshĭte oite kudasai.* 15. *Asa-ban ni san jikan zutsu wa yōji ga arimashĭte isogashū gozaimasŭ.* 16. *Sore de wa mō ippen yoku o wakari ni naru yō ni o hanashi itashimashō.* 17. *Inabikari ga suru toki ni wa takai ki no soba ni tatte wa arimasen.* 18. *Kono kotoba wo iidasu ya ina ya, hijō ni okotte kimashĭta.*

(B)

1. What is that man doing there? 2. Such high houses as these do not exist in Japan. 3. Have you forgotten your promise? 4. You must not say such foolish (*tsumaranai*) things. 5. Have you read the telegram that was in yesterday's paper? 6. The old gardener is here with some flowers. 7. I bought a plant yesterday to send to Mrs. Oka. 8. Has the carpenter died who fell from the roof yesterday? 9. You must not enter a person's house with such dirty clothes on. 10. I will go anywhere you please. 11. Her daughter is growing to be a handsome girl. 12. I will give you leave to go if you get your lessons done. 13. She gave me another book in the place of the one she lost. 14. Hold yourself straight when you walk. 15. Please hand me my inkstand and pen. 16. When light is not needed always turn the lamps down. 17. If anyone should call and wish to see me, say I will return at four o'clock. 18. I cannot imagine why you think so. 19. It is best not to interfere in the matter. 20. I have trodden on my pencil and broken it.

Key to Exercises.

[NOTE.—Each of the following translations of the Exercises on pp. 103-108 may also be used as an Exercise in translation with the foregoing as the Key.]

1.

(A)

1. *Who has come?—Mr. Okuro has come.* 2. *Who will go?—I will go.* 3. *Is my wife here?* 4. *Shall we go into the garden?* 5. *Are there flowers and trees in the garden?* 6. *Is your father in good health?* 7. *How old is your son?* 8. *This cake is very good.* 9. *If the weather is fine to-morrow, I will go to see the park.* 10. *Japanese is more difficult than English.* 11. *Which is the most interesting of these tales?* 12. *I like tea better than "sake."* 13. *Which of these two teacups do you like best?* 14. *When may I come to see you?—Please come to-morrow morning at seven o'clock.* 15. *It is all right.* 16. *Come*

this way, please. 17. *Where are the matches?—Here they are.* 18. *Hand me that red book, please.* 19. *He was born in England.* 20. *I must buy some more writing-paper.*

(B)

1. Anata wa ikimasŭ ka?—Hai, watakushi wa ikimasŭ. 2. Konnichi wa tenki ga ii ka?—Taihen (goku) ii. 3. Niwa wa ōkii ka chiisai ka? 4. Hana ga sŭki desŭ ka?—Hana ga goku sŭki desŭ. 5. Kore wa takai ka?—Ie, takō gozaimasen. 6. O taku wa tō gozaimasŭ ka?—Ie, goku chikō gozaimasŭ. 7. Kono chabon ga takaku nakareba kaimashō. 8. Natsŭ wa fuyu yori (mo) hi ga nagai. 9. Otōto wa watakushi yori toshi ga) yotsŭ shĭta desŭ (*or*, wakai). 10. Nihon no hana no uchi de sakura ga ichiban utsŭkushii. 11. Anata wa kono o kata wo go shōchi de gozaimasŭ ka?—Mada o me ni kakarimasen. 12. Anata wa ima ginkō ye oide nasaimasŭ to, watakushi mo nani ka yōji ga arimasŭ kara, go issho ni mairimashō. 13. Anata wa go jibun de oide ni narimashō ka? 14. O yu wo wakashite o kure. 15. O yobi nasaimashĭta ka?—Ie, yobimasen. 16. Anata ga o ide nasaru toki mon wo shikkari shimete kudasaimachi. 17. Anata mo go issho ni irasshĭte kudasaimasen ka? 18. Doko ye saisho ni yukimashō ka? 19. Senjitsu wa hana wo arigatō gozaimashĭta. 20. Dai kara hon wo totte o kure. 21. Nikai kara rampu wo motte kite o kure. 22. Shichi ji made wa kaerimasumai.

2.

(A)

1. *Did you ever ride in a jinrikisha?—Yes; when I was at Tokio I often went in one.* 2. *Are these the things you brought with you?—Yes, sir; they are the vegetables I bought in the market.* 3. *Is this a Japanese ship?—Yes, it is a Japanese steamer.* 4. *Did you often go to Hiogo?—No, I only went there a few times.* 5. *Who are you?—My name is Tsune.* 6. *Whose house is that?* 7. *Has your mother already come back from the country?* 8. *I have at once answered the letter I received from my teacher.* 9. *These are the pieces of the letter which the children have torn.* 10. *At what time do you get up every morning?—I get up at six or half-past six.* 11. *He has had his leg*

bitten by a dog. 12. *I was stung* (sasu) *on the forehead by a bee when I was taking a walk to-day.* 13. *I can let you know by eleven o'clock.* 14. *I have left my purse somewhere.*

(B)

1. Anata ga tsurete kita hito wa dare desŭ ka?—Sore wa watakŭshi no sensei desŭ. 2. Nan' to iu gakkō ye ikimasŭ ka? 3. Anata wa takŭsan no shomotsu wo motte imasŭ ka?—Ie, iku satsŭ mo arimasen. 4. Kane wo takŭsan motte imasŭ ka?—Ie, ikura mo arimasen. 5. Watakushi no katta uma ga ii. 6. Omae no (*or*, ga) mizu ni nagekonda mono wa nan' da ka? 7. Konaida ichi de katta ueki wa mō karete shimaimashĭta. 8. Sakujitsŭ o atsurae nasaimashĭta hon wo konnichi motte mairimashĭta (jisan itashimashĭta). 9. Kono ie wa chiisakute yo-ma shĭka arimasen. 10. Nippon no mottome takai yama wa Fuji desŭ; sono takasa wa ichi-man ni-sen-shaku ijo desŭ. 11. Anata no o niwa ni ki wa iku hon (nambon) arimasŭ ka?—Matsu wa sambon ume wa ippon bakari arimasŭ? 12. O tokei wa nan' ji de gozaimasŭ ka?—Watakushi no wa tomatte imasŭ. 13. Sugu gejo ni kodomo no kimono wo kisesasete kure. 14. Nani wo sagashĭte irasshaimasŭ ka?—Watakushi wa tebukuro wo nakushimashĭta. 15. Ima shibaraku koko ni o oki nasaimashi. 16. Sŭkoshi takaku mochi agete kudasai. 17. Kogatana wo nakushimashĭta kara anata no wo kashĭte kudasai. 18. Chotto o kiki nasai! nani-ka kikoemasen ka? 19. O tataki nasutta toki nemutte orimashĭta.

3.

(A)

1. *About how many hours does it take to go from here to Hiogo?* 2. *I went to your house the other day, but unfortunately you were not at home (absent).* 3. *You will fall into the river if you are so absent-minded.* 4. *As it is cool about nightfall, there are many people who walk about the streets.* 5. *In most countries the usual custom is to shake hands on meeting.* 6. *I suppose you have not yet translated that letter for me.* 7. *Kindly tighten the string of this parcel.* 8. *She trembled with cold when she came into the house.* 9. *He mistook the time, and came in the afternoon instead of at night.* 10, *He came five minutes after you had gone.* 11. *It is seven years to-day since I left*

Japan. 12. *It is too soon after dinner to walk.* 13. *It is difficult for me to remember the Japanese names.* 14. *Country people like to watch foreigners.* 15. *If you stay in this room, you must be quiet.* 16. *I shall have to borrow your pencil once more.* 17. *I must begin my work over again; I did not do it right.* 18. *I will bathe in cold water this morning.*

(B)

1. Watakŭshi wa zehi Nihon ye kaeru made ni Rondon no kembutsŭ wo suru tsumori desŭ. 2. Kono ie wa omote ni mo ushiro ni mo niwa ga arimasŭ. 3. Kimi wa ima gakkō no kaerimichi desŭ ka? 4. Watakushi wa kesa roku-ji ni okite ano yama no ue wo sampo shimashĭta. 5. Dare ka Eigo no wakaru hito ga arimasŭ ka? 6. Dare no koto wo kangaete imasŭ ka? 7. Ano kata ga oide ni natte kara ni jippun tachimashĭta. 8. Nichiyōbi no hoka wa mainichi Tōkyō ye irasshimasŭ. 9. Watakŭshi ga Rondon ni kite kara kyō de shichi nen ni narimasŭ. 10. Asuko kara o kaeri nasute kara de wa osoku narimashō. 11. Myō-asa hayaku okoshĭte kudasai. 12. Anata mo Uzo ye oide desŭ nara, go issho ni negaimashō. 13. Jitensha wo motte-kureba yokatta no ni. 14. Ginkō kara motte kita kane wo taitei tsukatte shimaimashĭta. 15. Sŭkoshi koe wo takaku shĭte kudasai. 16. Sŭkoshi undō ni mairimasŭ. 17. Itsu-mo o hiru ni sŭkoshi undō wo itashimasŭ. 18. Ano hito ga ano uma wo amari muchi-utanai yō ni shitō gozaimasŭ. 19. Kyō jū ni kuru no desŭ. 20. Motto hayaku kitaraba ii no ni. 21. Ano hashi wo wataru to sugu desŭ. 22. Ni yen ijō wa kakarumai.

4.

(A)

1. *Let us take a cup of tea in my room and then go at once.* 2. *There is no history of Japanese literature amongst my books.* 3. *For what purpose do you use that summer-house?—We use it for tea-parties or private conversations.* 4. *I am sorry I cannot let you enter just yet.* 5. *Between dinner and supper one takes tea.* 6. *Kindly wait until to-morrow for the articles you ordered.* 7. *Before you go to school, you must always prepare your lessons.* 8. *Can you carry these parcels for me?* 9. *It is too late now for anyone to call.* 10. *The master (of the house) entered just*

when the thief had opened the lock. 11. *This railway will perhaps be ready by the middle of July.* 12. *As it is fine weather to-day, we will go into the garden.* 13. *The wind has disarranged my papers.* 14. *Do not let this be destroyed; I want to use it for something.* 15. *Every morning and evening I am engaged for several hours.* 16. *I will try to explain it more clearly.* 17. *When it lightens you must not stand near a high tree.* 18. *Scarcely had I uttered this word when he got extremely angry.*

(B)

1. Asŭko no hito wa nani wo shĭte imasŭ ka? 2. Kō iu yō na takai ie wa Nihon ni wa arimasen. 3. Anata wa o yakusoku shimashĭta koto wo o wasure nasaimashĭta ka? 4. Sonna tsumaranai koto wo it' cha ikemasen. 5. Sakujitsŭ no shimbun ni dete ita dempō wo mita ka? 6. Toshi totta uekiya ga hana wo motte mairimasŭ. 7. Sakujitsu Oka san ni okuru tsumori de ueki wo kaimashĭta. 8. Kinō yane no ue kara ochita daiku wa shinimashĭta ka? 9. Sonna ni yogoreta kimono wo kite hito no ie ni haitte wa naranŭ. 10. Doko ye demo anata no o nozomi no tokoro ye yukimasŭ. 11. Ano kata no musume san wa dan-dan utsukŭshiku narimasŭ. 12. Moshi anata no keiko ga yoku dekimashitara hoka ye yuku koto wo yurushimashō. 13. Ano kata no naku shita hon no kawari ni hoka no hon wo kudasaimashĭta. 14. Anata no karada wo massugu ni shite o aruki nasai. 15. Inki-tsubo to fude wo motte-kite kudasai. 16. Akari no iranai toki ni wa shin wo zutto hikkomashĭte oite o kure. 17. Dare ka tazunete mairimashĭtara yo ji ni kaeru to itte o kure. 18. Naze sonna koto wo osshaimasŭ. 19. Sono koto ni kankei shinai hō ga yō gozaimasŭ. 20. Ima bokuhitsu wo a'hi de fumi-tsubushimashita.

B. Reading Exercises.*

1.

1. *Nihon ni wa kane wo mōkeru tame gaikoku*
Nee-hohn nee wah kah-neh woh moh-keh-roo tah-meh gahee-koh-koo

ye itte kane wo jūbun ni mōketa ato de
yeh eet-teh kah-neh woh joo-boon nee moh-keh-tah ah-toh deh

kuni ye kaeru ninsoku ga ōi. 2. *Nihon wa*
koo-nee yeh kah-eh-roo neen-soh-koo gah *oh*-ee. Nee-hohn wah

chizu de mite wakaru tōri namboku ni na-
chee-dzoo deh mee-teh wah-kah-roo *toh*-ree nahm-boh-koo nee nah-

gaku arimasŭ, kara kikō no moyō mo toko-
ngah-koo ah-ree-mahs', kah-rah kee-*koh* noh moh-*yoh* moh toh-koh-

ro ni yotte taihen ni chigaimasŭ. 3. *Watakŭshi*
roh nee yoht-teh *ti*-hehn nee chee-ngah-ee-mahs'. Wah-tahk'shee

wa kon-do de, Fūji[1] *ye to-san wa san-do-me desŭ*
wah kohn-doh deh, *foo*-jee yeh toh-sahn wah sahn-doh-meh dehs'

ga,[2] *shi-awase to itsu mo tenki-tsūgō ga yō go-*
gah, shee-ah-wah-seh toh ee-tsoo moh tehn-kee-tsoo-ngoh gah *yoh* goh-

zaimasŭ. 4. *Yama-michi de hi wa kuremashĭta ga,*[2]
zi-mahs'. Yah-mah-mee-chee deh hee wah koo-reh-mahsh'tah gah,

tsure ga ozei datta kara ki-jōbu deshĭta. 5. *Ban-*
tsoo-reh gah oh-zeh-ee daht-tah kah-rah kee-*joh*-boo dehsh'tah. Bahn-

koku-kōkō ga arō ga nani ga arō ga,[2] *mada*
koh-koo-*koh*-*koh* gah ahr*oh* gah nah-nee gah ah-r*oh* gah, mah-dah

mada dōri bakari de wa katsŭ koto ga dekima-
mah-dah d*oh*-ree bah-kah-ree deh wah kahts' koh-toh gah deh-kee-mah-

sen. 6. *Nihon ni hana no shurui wa takŭsan ari-*
sen. Nee-hohn nee hah-nah noh shoo-roo-ee wah tahk'sahn ah-ree-

masŭ ga, sono uchi de mo sakura wa kana no ō
mahs' gah, soh-noh oo-chee deh moh sah-koo-rah wah kah-nah noh *oh*

tō iwareru kodo de, nakanaka migoto desŭ.
toh ee-wah-reh-roo koh-doh deh, nah-kah-nah-kah mee-ngoh-toh dehs'.

* For translation see pp. 117-118.

[1] For the pronunciation of *fu* see p. 12. [2] *Ga*, at the end of a phrase, has an adversative force, but it is usually best translated by affixing "but" or "yet" to the succeeding phrase. Often the adversative force is modified into a mere hint of discontinuity between successive actions or conditions, in which case *ga* should be rendered by "and" or "and so."

7. *Dete kita no wa sono soma no niōbō to mi-*
Dehteh kee-tah noh wah soh-noh soh-mah noh nee-*oh*-boh toh mee-

yete, toshigoro wa nijū shichi hachi de, iro
yeh-teh toh-shee-ngoh-roh wah nee-joo shee-chee hah-chee deh, ee-roh

shiroku hana suji tōri, yamaga ni wa mare
shee-roh-koo hah-nah soo-jee *toh*-ree, yah-mah-ngah nee wah mah-reh

na onna de gozaimasŭ. 8. *Mon wo waki no momi-*
nah ohn-nah deh goh-*zi*-mahs'. Mohn woh wah-kee noh moh-mee-

ji wa rippa ni kōyō shimashĭta. 9. *Yoshino wa*
jee wah reep-pah nee *koh-yoh* shee-mahsh'tah. Yoh-shee-noh wah

mukashi kara hana de yūmei de aru bakari
moo-kah-shee kah-rah hah-nah deh *yoo*-meh-ee deh ah-roo bah-kah-ree

de naku rekishi jō ni mata nadakai tokoro
deh nah-koo reh-kee-shee *joh* nee mah-tah nah-dah-ki toh-koh-roh

de arimasŭ. 10. *Hirugoro ni uchi kara motte*
deh ah-ree-mahs'. Hee-roo-ngoh-roh nee oo-chee kah-rah moht-teh

kita bentō wo toridashĭte tabete izumi kara
kee-tah behn-*toh* woh toh-ree-dahsh'teh tah-beh-teh eedzoomee kah-rah

kunda mizu ippai nonde mata dekakemashĭta.
koon-dah mee-dzoo eep-*pi* nohn-deh mah-tah dehkahkeh-mahsh'tah.

2.

1. *Mono wo uru hĭto*[1] *ga ōkŭte kau hĭto ga sŭkuna-*
Moh-noh woh oo-roo sh'toh gah *oh*k'teh kah-oo sh'toh gah s'koo-nah-

kereba, sono nedan ga yasuku naru ga, uru
keh-reh-bah, soh-noh neh-dahn gah yah-soo-koo nah-roo gah, oo-roo

hĭto ga sŭkunakŭte kau hĭto ga ōkereba nedan
sh'toh gah s'koo-nahk'teh kah-oo sh'toh gah *oh*-keh-reh-bah neh-dahn

ga kaette takaku narimasŭ. 2. *Kesa sŭkoshi*
gah kah-eht-teh tah-kah-koo nah-ree-mahs'. Keh-sah s'koh-shee

isoide yakŭsho ye itta keredomo, yōyō tō-
ee-soh-ee-deh yahk'shoh yeh eet-tah keh-reh-doh-moh *yoh-yoh toh-*

chaku shĭta tokoro de futo bentō wo wasurete
chah-koo sh'tah toh-koh-roh deh foo-toh behn-*toh* woh wah-soo-reh-teh

ita koto wo omoidashĭta. 3. *Sakuban, inu ga*
ee-tah koh-toh woh oh-moh-ee-dahsh'tah. Sah-koo-bahn ee-noo gah

hoete, sōzōshĭkute neraremasen deshĭta. 4. *Yuki*
hoh-eh-teh *soh-zoh*sh'koo-teh neh-rah-reh-mah-sehn dehsh'tah. Yoo-kee

[1] In the syllable *hi* the *h* assumes, in the mouths of many speakers, the sound of the German *ch* in *ich*; but, except in the word *hĭto*, such pronunciation is considered rather vulgar.

wa kirei desŭ ga, ato no michi ni komarimasŭ.[1]
wah kee-reh-ee dehs' gah, ah-toh noh mee-chee nee koh-mah-ree-mahs'.

5. *Nikkō kara yamamichi wo ni-san-ri noboreba*
Neek-*koh* kah-rah yah-mah-mee-chee woh nee-sahn-ree noh-boh-reh-bah

Chūsenji to iu kosui ga ari, mata sono to-
choo-sehn-jee toh ee-oo koh-soo-ee gah ah-ree, mah-tah soh-noh toh-

chū ni wā takŭsan taki ga arimasŭ kara, kono
ch*oo* nee wah tahk'sahn tah-kee gah ah-ree-mahs' kah-rah, koh-noh

hen wa mattaku natsŭshirazu[2] *de arimasŭ.* 6. *Nikkō*
hehn wah maht-tah-koo nahts'shee-rah-dzoo deh ahreemahs'. Neek-*koh*

wa Tokugawa ichi-dai shōgūn Ieyasŭ no ta-
wah toh-koo-ngah-wah ee-chee-di sh*oh*-ngoon ee-eh-yahs' noh tah-

maya no aru tokoro de, kenchiku sōshoku tō
mah-yah noh ah-roo toh-koh-roh deh, kehn-chee-koo s*oh*-shoh-koo t*oh*

subete kane wo oshimazu - Tokugawa jidai
soo-beh-teh kah-neh woh oh-shee-mah-dzoo toh-koo-ngah-wah jee-d*i*

no sui wo daidai atsumeta tokoro de ari-
noh soo-ee woh di-di ah-tsoo-meh-tah toh-koh-roh deh ah-ree-

masŭ kara, Nihonjin no kembutsŭnin mo nenjū
mahs' kah-rah, nee-hohn-jeen noh kehm-boots'neen moh nehn-j*oo*

taemasen ga, natsŭ ga koto ni ōi no desŭ. 7. *Yūbe*
tah-eh-mah-sehn gah, nahts' gah koh-toh nee *oh*-i noh dehs'. Y*oo*-beh

kuni kara no o kyaku ga kite shūya wakai
koo-nee kah-rah noh oh kee-ah-koo gah kee-teh sh*oo*-yah wah-k*i*

toki no koto wo hanashĭte otta kāra, kesa-hodo
toh-kee noh koh-toh woh hah-nahsh'teh oht-tah kah-rah, keh-sah-hoh-

nemukŭte tamarimasen.
doh neh-mook'teh tah-mah-ree-mah-sehn.

3.

1. *Futsŭka mikka bakari ame ga futte imasŭ toki*
Foots'kah meek-kah bah-kah-ree ah-meh gah foot-teh ee-mahs' toh-kee

ni inakamichi ga sukkari arukenaku nari-
nee ee-nah-kah-mee-chee gah sook-kah-ree ah-roo-keh-nah-koo nah-ree-

masŭ. 2. *Sekai no kuni-guni no uchi ni wa, sōmo-*
mahs'. Seh-k*i* noh koo-nee-goo-nee noh oo-chee nee wah, s*oh*-moh-

[1] *Lit.*, "one is troubled by the after-roads." *Lit.*, "is entirely not knowing summer."

ku mo haezu,[1] *jimbutsu mo nai tokoro ga ari-*
koo moh hah-eh-zoo, jeem-boo-tsoo moh ni toh-koh-roh gah ahree-

masŭ. 3. *Kekkon no koto wa kuniguni de iroiro*
mahs'. Kehk-kohn noh koh-toh wah koonee-ngoonee deh ee-roh-ee-roh

chigaimasŭ ga, jidai de mo, mata chigaimasŭ.[2]
chee-ngah-ee-mahs' gah, jee-*di* deh moh, mah-tah chee-ngahee-mahs'.

Ima o hanashi shiyō to iu no wa genzai ima
Ee-mah oh hah-nah-shee shee-y*oh* toh ee-oo noh wah ghehn-*zi* ee-mah

watakŭshi no kokyō de yatte iru moyō desŭ.
wah-tahk'shee noh koh-kee-*oh* deh yaht-teh ee-roo moh-y*oh* dehs'.

4. *Kono goro ni itarimashĭte, Bukkyō to mōsu*
Koh-noh goh-roh nee ee-tah-ree-mahsh'teh, book-kee-*oh* toh m*oh*-soo

mono wa, tada katō-jimmin no shinzuru tokoro
moh-noh wah, tah-dah kah-t*oh*-jeem-meen noh sheen-zoo-roo tohkoh-

to natte, chūtō ijō de wa sono dōri wo wa-
roh toh naht-teh, ch*oo*-t*oh* ee-j*oh* deh wah soh-noh d*oh*-ree woh wah-

kimaeteru hĭto ga sŭkunaku; shūmon to ieba
kee-mah-eh-teh-roo sh'toh gah s'koo-nah-koo; sh*oo*-mohn toh ee-eh-bah

sōshĭki no toki bakari ni mochiiru koto no yō
s*oh*sh'kee noh toh-kee bah-kah-ree nee moh-ch*ee*-roo koh-toh noh y*oh*

ni omoimasŭ. 5. *Ni-san-nen-zen kara hĭto ga fŭ-keiki*
nee oh-moh-ee-mahs'. Nee-sahn-nen-zen kah-rah sh'toh gah f'kay-kee

da to iimasŭ ga, hontō desŭ ka? 6. *Aru Nihon no to-*
dah toh *ee*-mahs' gah, hohn-t*oh* dehs' kah? Ah-roo nee-hohn noh toh-

modachi to miōnichi issho ni Mukōjima ye
moh-dah-chee toh mee-*oh*-nee-chee ish-shoh nee moo-k*oh*-jee-mah yeh

ikō to iu yakusoku wo itashimashĭta ga, sŭko-
ee-k*oh* toh ee-oo yah-koo-soh-koo woh ee-tah-shee-mahsh'tah gah, s'koh-

shi yondokoronai yōji ga dekimashĭte yakusoku
shee yohn-doh-koh-roh-n*i* y*oh*-jee gah deh-kee-mahsh'teh yah-koo-soh-

wo mamoru koto ga dekimasen kara, tomo-
koo woh mah-moh-roo koh-toh gah deh-kee-mah-sen kah-rah, toh-moh-

dachi ni shirasetai to omoimasŭ ga, watakŭshi
dah-chee nee shee-rah-seh-t*i* toh oh-moh-ee-mahs' gah, wahtahk'shee

wa Nihongo wa sŭkoshi hanashimasŭ ga, ji wo
wah nee-hohn-goh wah s'koh-shee hah-nah-shee-mahs' gah, jee woh

kaku no wa ikkō dekimasen kara, kotowari
kah-koo noh wah eek-k*oh* deh-kee-mah-sehn kah-rah, koh-toh-wah-ree

[1] *Haezu* is the negative gerund of *haeru* (to grow, to sprout), correlated with the present of *nai* (the negative adjective). [2] *Lit.*, "also according to the period."

no tegami wo ittsū kaite itadakitō gozaimasŭ.
noh teh-ngah-mee woh eet-tsoo ki-teh ee-tah-dah-kee-toh goh-zi-mahs'.
7. *Nani ka kaō to omotte mise ye haitta tokoro*
Nah-nee kah kah-oh toh oh-moht-teh mee-seh yeh hi-t-tah toh-koh-roh
ga, ki ni iru mono ga nakatta kara, tsui nani
gah, kee nee ee-roo moh-noh gah nah-kaht-tah kah-rah, tsoo-ee nah-nee
mo kawazu ni uchi ye kaetta.
moh kah-wah-zoo nee oo-chee yeh kah-eht-tah.

Key to Reading Exercises.

1.

1. In Japan there are many workmen who go to foreign countries to earn money, and return home after they have earned enough. 2. As one will see from looking at a map, Japan extends a long distance from south to north, and the conditions of its climate are therefore very different, according to the position. 3. This is the third time I have made the ascent of Fuji, and each time I have been fortunate enough to have fine weather. 4. It became dark while we were on the mountain-side, but as there were several of us together, we felt no alarm. 5. We may have international law, and we may have all sorts of fine things, but we are still very far from having arrived at a social state in which right always prevails. 6. There are many kinds of flowers in Japan, but amongst them the cherry-blossom is so beautiful that it might be called the queen of flowers. 7. The person who came out was apparently the wife of the woodcutter. She was twenty-seven or twenty-eight years old, with a fair complexion and a straight nose, and was a sort of woman not often found in mountain huts. 8. The leaves of the maple-tree by the gate have become beautifully red. 9. From ancient times Yoshino is not only famous for its cherry-blossoms, but is also an historically renowned place. 10. About mid-day we took our lunch, which we had brought with us from home, drank a glass of water we had drawn from the spring, and started off again.

2.

1. If the people who sell goods are many, and those who buy are few, the prices fall; but if the people who sell are few, and those who buy are many, the prices, on the contrary,

become higher. 2. This morning I went to the office a little hurriedly, but just when I arrived there at last, I suddenly remembered that I had forgotten my lunch. 3. Last night I could not sleep on account of the barking of the dogs. 4. Snow is very pretty to look at, but it makes the roads in a fearful state afterwards. 5. If one goes from Nikko as far as two or three *ri* up the mountain-way there is a lake called Chūsenji, and, as there are many waterfalls on that way, this region is "one that does not know anything of summer." 6. Nikko is the place where there is the tomb of the first *shogun** of the Tokugawa family; Ieyasu, a place where every generation has gathered, as to buildings, decorations, &c., all the elegance of the Tokugawa period, without regretting the expense. 7. A guest came from my native country last night, and, as we were talking the whole night about the incidents of our early years, I am very tired this morning.

3.

1. If it rains for two or three days only, the country roads become entirely impassable. 2. Amongst the various countries of the world there are some where no plants or trees grow, and where no human beings live. 3. The customs connected with marriage vary in all countries, and also according to the period. What I am about to relate is the manner in which marriage is performed in my native land at the present day. 4. At the present time Buddhism has sunk to being the belief of the lower classes only. Few persons in the middle and upper classes understand its principles, most of them having the idea that religion is a thing which comes into play only at funeral services. 5. For the last two or three years people have been saying that the times are bad. Is this really the case? 6. I have made an agreement with a Japanese friend to go with him to-morrow to Mukōjima, but, having some unavoidable business to do, I cannot keep my promise, and wish to let my friend know it. Now, I can speak a little Japanese, but I cannot write at all, so I wish to have a letter of refusal written for me. 7. Wishing to buy something, I entered a shop, but, as there was nothing that pleased me, I at last returned home without buying anything.

* Formerly the title of the military rulers of Japan.

C. Additional Extracts.*

1. Uguisu.

(*This Extract, which is taken from a story called "Asukagawa," is a fragment of a conversation between a young man, Takeo, and his fiancée, Shība.*)

Shība.—Ima mukō no mŭmebayashi de uguisu no hatsu ne ga shĭta yō desŭ kara, kiki ni ikimashō.

Takeo.—Sayō desŭ kara. Sore wa yukai desŭ na: sā, itte kikimashō... [*A little later*] O jō san! anata wa o damashi de wa arimasenŭ ka? Chitto mo uguisu ga nakimasenŭ ne.

Shība.—Iye, sakki yoi ne wo shĭte, futa koye bakari nakimashĭta kara anata wo o yobi mōshĭta no desŭ.

Takeo.—Sō desŭ ka? Shikashi nan' da ka ate ni naranai yō na ki ga shimasŭ ne.

Shība.—Mattaku sakki naita koto wa nakimashĭta kara sŭkoshi matte ite mimashō.

Takeo.—Sonnara kore kara mō ichiji kan hodo matte nakanakattara dō nasaimasŭ.

Shība.—Sō desŭ ne. Kō shimashō. Nan' daka hinata ye detara nodo ga kawaita yō desŭ kara, kahe wo ii-tsŭke ni iku o tsukai wo shimashō.

Takeo.—Sore wa omoshiroi. Watakŭshi mo nanda ka nomi mono ga hoshiku natta tokoro desŭ kara——

Shība.—Sore de watakŭshi no o yaku wa dekimashĭta ga; moshi naitara anata wa dō nasaimasŭ.

Takeo.—Sō desŭ ne. Naitara watakŭshi mo sono o tsukai ni ikimashō.

Shība.—Sore wa ikemasenŭ yo. Sono koto wa watakŭshi ga kangaeta no desŭ kara.

Takeo.—Sonnara nan' demo o nozomi no koto wo shimashō.

Shība.—Sakki mite o ide nasatta watashi no namaerashī mono no atta ano o tegami wo o mise nasai na.

Takeo.—Yō gozaimasŭ; moshi naitara o me ni kakemashō.

Shība.—Kitto desŭ ka?

Takeo.—Kitto o me ni kake nasŭ to mo.

* For Translation see pp. 124-128.

2. Sake To Kite Wa.

Sake-zuki ga aru hi futsŭka-yoi de zutsū ga shimasŭ kara, hachi-maki wo shi-nagara nete iru to, yume ni sake wo hĭto-taru hirotte, ō-yorokobi de, noman saki kara shĭta-uchi shĭte, "Kanro; kanro! koitsu hiroi-mono wa![1] Keisatsŭ-sho ye todokeru no ga atarimae da ga—sake to kite wa, mi-nogasenai. Mazu ip-pai yarakasō ka?—Iya! onajikuba,[2] kan wo shĭte nomu hō ga ii" to itte, kan wo tsŭkeyō to suru toki, jū-ni-ji no don no oto ni odoroite, me ga samemashĭta kara, zannen-gatte:

"Aa! hayaku hiya de nomeba yokatta!"

[1] Literally, "This fellow (as for), the pick-up-thing," which we have freely rendered by "This *is* a discovery," *wa* having an interjectional force in this instance. [2] "Sake," the national beverage, is generally warmed before being drunk.

3. Ha Bakari.

Mommō na ō-byakŭshō ga daikon wo tsŭkuraseru ni, ni-san-nen omou yō ni dekinai[1] kara, "Okata otoko-domo no sewa no warui no darō" to,[2] jibun de hatake ye dete, tsŭchi wo hotte iru tokoro ye[3]—kosaku-nin ga tōri-kakatte, "Kore wa, kore wa! Danna Sama![4] otoko-shū ni o sase nasaranai de,[5] go jishin de nasaru to wa, o habakari de gozaimasŭ" to eshaku wo suru[6] to—danna wa hara wo tatete, "Ore ga daikon wo tsŭkuru ni, ha bakari to wa fŭ-todoki da" to[7] okoru tokoro ye, mata hĭtori ki-kakatte, "Kore wa! Danna Sama no go rippuku wa go mottomo. Shĭkashi-nagara, kare wa nan no fumbetsu mo nashi ni mōshĭta no de, ne mo ha mo nai koto de gozaimasŭ."

[1] Literally, "not forthcoming according to his manner of thinking." [2] Add *omotte*. [3] *Tokoro*, in the middle of a phrase, especially when followed by *ye*, may usually be rendered by "whilst," "just as," "when," or "whereupon." [4] See p. 81. [5] *O ... de* = "not condescending honourably to cause to do." [6] *Eshaku wo suru*, which we have translated very freely by "politely," really signifies "to make excuses," "to beg pardon." [7] Add *itte* = "having said."

4. Do Iu Wake De?

Eigo no "Why" sunawachi *naze* to iu koto wa hanahada taisetsu de aru no ni shina ya Nihon no mukashi no hĭto-bito wa metta ni kono kotoba wo tsŭkawazu, "Kōshi no setsu da" to ka, "Mōshi no jiron da" to ka iu toki wa, mohaya betsu ni sono rikutsu wo sensaku suru koto mo naku, tada gaten shĭte shimau no ga tsūrei de ari; soko de motte, "Utagai wa bummei shimpo no ichi dai gen-in da" to iu ron mo dekita wake de, ima wa yaya mo sureba Seiyō-jin wa "Utagai wa taisetsu na mono da; bummei shimpo no gen-in da. Sono shōko ni wa, Shina-jin ya Nihon-jin wa, mono-goto wo utagau to iu koto wo shinai ni yotte, itsu made tatte mo shimpo shinai de wa nai ka?" to ronji-tateru kotò de aru ga—kō iu rei nado ni hĭkareru to iu wa, o tagai sama ni[1] amari zotto itasan shidai to iwanakereba narimasen.

[1] *O tagai sama ni* = "for you and me," "mutually." A semi-polite, semi-humorous turn is imparted to the phrase by the honorific *o*.

5. Shinkwa-ron.

Chikagoro Seiyō ni shinkwa-ron ga sakan ni okotte, kono tenchi bàmbutsu ga deki, kono yo naka ga deki-agattaru hō-hō wo toki-akashimasuru. Sono setsu ni yotte mireba, kono sekai ni wa hajime wa shigoku tanjun naru seibutsu shĭka arimasenanda ga—sore ga tekitō no kyōgū no hataraki wo uke, ima no fŭkuzatsu naru kono uruwashĭki sekai wo tsŭkuridashimashĭta. Kono tekitō no kyōgū to wa, sunawachi shizen-tōta to iu mono[1] ga arimasŭ. Yusho-reppai tekĭshu-seizon to iu koto ga arimasŭ. Subete kore-ra seibutsu no hattatsu, shinkwa ni tekitō naru kyōgū to iu koto wo komaka ni setsumei shitaru mono de arimasu. Ima kono kyōgū no hataraki wa, tada dō-shokubutsu[2] no nikŭtai no ue nomi narazu, mata watakŭshi-domo no chishĭki no ue ni totte kangaete mo, hanahada akiraka ni wakarimasŭ. Gakŭsha to gujin ga dekiru no mo, sono kyōgū ikan ni yotte ōi ni sadamaru koto de, ima koko ni onaji saichi onaji rikiryō wo motte oru kodomo wo totte, hĭtori wa goku inaka no shimbun wo miru koto mo nai chihō ni oki; mata hĭtori wa, kore wo totte, bummei no chushin, to iu Tōkyō ni oki, tsui ni daigaku ni irete shū-gaku seshimeta naraba, go-nen ka roku-nen no nochi ni wa, kono fŭtari no chishĭki-jō hotondo ten-chi no chigai ga dekiru koto de arimasŭ.

[1] *Mono* is here equivalent to *koto* in the following sentence. [2] An abbreviation of *dōbutsu shokubutsu*.

6. Mitsu-me Nyūdō.[1]

O tera no oshō san ga aru toki go-zuki no kyaku wo yonde, ichi-men[2] uchi-hajimemasŭ to, "sŭki koso mono no jōzu nare"[3] de, kyaku wa sumi-jimen mo doko mo kotogotoku tori-kakomimashĭta kara, oshō san ga kuyashigatte, semete ip-pō dake de mo ikasō[4] to, shĭkiri ni me wo koshiraeru koto ni kŭfū wo shĭte orimasŭ to,—atama no ue ye hai ga takatta kara, urusagatte, go-ishi wo motta te de atama wo kaki-nagara, "Kono hen ni hĭtotsu me ga dekitara, ōkata ikiru de arō."

Atama no ue ni mata hĭtotsu me ga dekitara, "mitsu-me nyūdō"[5] desŭ.

7. Gijō no Ichi-haran.

Inoue Kakugorō Kun.—Shitsumon itashimasŭ.

Gichō.—Inoue Kun no shitsumon no shui wa?

I.K.K.—Shitsumon no shushi wa kayō de arimasŭ. Kudō Kun wa, jiyū wo omonjite, kore wo o hĭki ni naru wake ni wa ikimasen ka? Kore ga shitsumon desŭ. (*Muyō! muyō!" to yobu mono ari. "Yare! yare!" to yobu mono ari.*) Sŭkoshi shizuka ni shĭte o kiki ni naranai to, wakaranai. Naruhodo, jiyū wa taisetsu na mono de aru——

Kudō Kōkan Kun.—Hĭku ka hĭkanai ka to iu nara, hĭkanai. Mata go shitsumon ga aru nara——

I.K.K.—Mizukara jihaku suru nara, nanzo aete kotoba wo tsuiyashimasen. Jiyū wo shiran hĭto to anata ga iu mono ni, tare ga shitsumon wo suru mono wa nai.

K.K.K.—Shitsumon ga nakereba, yoroshii.

Gichō.—Kinkyū-dōgi to mi-tomeru ya ina ya to iu koto ni tsuite, saiketsu shiyō to kangaemasŭ. Kudō Kun no dōgi wo kinkyū-dōgi to mi-tomuru to iu koto ni dōi no shokun no kiritsu wo motomemasŭ. (*Kiritsu-sha shōsū.*) Shōsū to mi-tomemasŭ. (*Hakushu okoru.*)

[1] This anecdote illustrates the fondness of the Japanese for puns, and to fully apprehend the *jeux-de-mots* employed, an acquaintance with the principles of the game of *go* ("go-bang" or "checkers") is necessary. In the game a board and counters are used, and the principal object is to prevent one's adversary from extending his pieces over the board, which is effected by forming "eyes" (spaces enclosed by not fewer than four of one's own checkers). [2] *Lit.*, "one surface," i.e., "one game." [3] *Lit.*, "a fond person is indeed skilful at the thing he likes." [4] *Ikasō* = Prob. Fut. of *ikasu* (trans. corresponding to intrans. *ikiru* = "to live"). It therefore means "shall perhaps make alive," hence "in order to free." [5] A bogey of Japanese children.

8 Ume no Hana.

Koko ni kanete Iijima Sama ye o de-iri no isha ni Shijō to mōsu mono ga gozaimashĭte—jitsu wa o taiko-isha no o shaberi de, shonin tasŭke no tame ni saji wo te ni toranai[1] to iu jimbutsu de gozaimasŭ kara,—nami no o isha nara, chotto kami-ire no naka ni mo gwan-yaku ka ko-gusuri de mo haitte imasŭ ga,—kono Shijō no kami-ire no naka ni wa, tezuma no tane yara, hyaku-manako nado ga irete aru gurai na mono de gozaimasŭ.

Sate kono isha no chikazuki de, Shimizu-dani ni dembata ya kashi-nagaya wo mochi, sono agari de kurashi wo tatete iru rōnin no Shinzaburō to mōsu mono ga arimashĭte, ŭmare-tsŭki kirei na otoko de,—toshi wa ni-jū-ichi de gozaimasŭ ga, mada nyōbō mo motazu, goku uchiki de gozaimasŭ kara, soto ye mo demasezu, shomotsu bakari mite orimasŭ tokoro ye,—aru hi Shijō ga tazunete mairimashĭte,—"Kyō wa, tenki ga yoroshiū gozaimasŭ kara, Kameido no Gwaryōbai[2] ye de-kakete, sono kaeri ni boku no chikazuki Iijima no bessō ye yorimashō,"—to sasoi-dashimashĭte, fŭtari-zure de Gwaryōbai ye mairi, kaeri ni Iijima no bessō ye tachi-yorimashĭte.

9. Kyū-yō.

Wakai otoko ga fŭtari Eri-zen no mise-saki de iki-aimashĭta tokoro ga, hĭtori wa awata-dashĭku te wo futte, "Kimi ni wa iro-iro o hanashi mo arimasŭ ga,—ima kyūyō ga dekite, kitaku suru tokoro desŭ[3] kara, izure kinjitsu o tazune mōshimashō," to iu to,—dōmo sono yōsu ga hen da kara, hĭtori wa odoroite, "Kyūyō to wa,[4] go byōnin de mo aru n'desŭ ka?" to kikimashĭtara,—hĭtori wa, warai-nagara: "Ie! kanai ni tanomareta hayari no han-eri wo ima kono mise de kaimashĭta ga,—tochū de temadotte iru uchi ni ryūkō-okure ni naru to, taihen desŭ kara, tachi-banashi mo o kotowari mōshimashĭta no sa!"

[1] The spoon (for mixing medicine) is the Japanese doctor's emblem, and we have used the expression "write prescriptions" as the nearest equivalent to the Japanese "handling the spoon." [2] A garden at Tokio, famous for its plum-trees. [3] *Lit.*, "I am just on my road home." [4] *Lit.*, "as for (your saying) that (there is) urgent business."

Translation of Extracts.

1. The Nightingale.

Shība.—I believe I heard the first note of the uguisu[1] in the plum grove yonder: let us go and listen to it.

Takeo.—Did you? How nice! Come along, then, we will go and hear it... [*A little later*] Young lady, have you not been deceiving me? The uguisu does not sing at all.

Shība.—Yes (it does): a short time since, it sang twice with a lovely voice; that was the reason I called you.

Takeo.—Is that so? I do not, however, quite believe it.

Shība.—Indeed it really sang a short time since, so let us wait a little and see.

Takeo.—Well, then, we will stay for an hour, and if it should not sing by then, what will you do?

Shība.—Well, we will do so, and as the heat makes me thirsty, I will go and order a cup of coffee for you.

Takeo.—That is a good idea. I feel as if I should like something to drink.

Shība.—Well, we have arranged what *I* have got to do, and what will *you* do if the uguisu does sing (after all)?

Takeo.—Yes, it is (arranged), and if it does sing I will go as your messenger.

Shība.—That will not do at all: that was my intention.

Takeo.—Very well, then, I will do anything you wish.

Shība.—A short time ago you were reading a letter with something like my name in it: show me the letter.

Takeo.—Very well; if the bird sings you shall see the letter.

Shība.—You are quite sure?

Takeo.—I will really let you see it.

[1] The "uguisu" is a bird much like the nightingale, but not, scientifically speaking, identical with it.

2. The Lost Windfall.

Once upon a time a drinker suffering from headache on the day following a carousal fell asleep with a napkin tied round his head. He dreamt that he had discovered a cask of *sake*, which pleased him so much that he smacked his lips before tasting it, and exclaimed: "How delicious! how delicious! This *is* a discovery! It should really be reported to the police, but a windfall like this *sake*—nay! I cannot allow it to go. Um! shall I have a glass?—No, no! I shall lose nothing by waiting until it is warmed." So he was about to heat it, when the noon gun[1] awoke him with a start, upon which he sorrowfully exclaimed: "Oh, what a shame that I did not at once drink it cold!"

[1] Mid-day is officially announced in Tokio by discharging a cannon.

3. Nothing but Leaves.[1]

An ignorant farmer had for two or three years grown radishes[2] with only scanty success, and, attributing the indifferent crops to the negligence of his labourers, he went out into the fields and commenced to dig himself. Whilst working, a labourer chanced to pass by, and seeing the farmer he called out politely: "Oh, master! oh, master! it is shocking to find you labouring like that yourself, instead of your men." [*Or*, "If you work like that yourself, instead of getting your men to do it, you will have only leaves." (*Ha bakari* means "only leaves"; *habakari* is a polite expression meaning "it is shocking.")]

The farmer, irritated by these words, replied: "You are an impertinent fellow for daring to say to me that when I plant radishes I shall get leaves only." Just at that moment another labourer chanced to pass, and exclaimed: "Indeed, master, you are quite right to be angry, but he did not mean what he said, so it is not worth while noticing it." [*Or*, "It is an object with neither roots nor leaves." The second man's remark would be still more irritating, since he predicts a failure, not only of roots (*ne*), but also of leaves (*ha*).]

[1] This anecdote illustrates the Japanese liking for punning expressions. It will be observed that the puns are on the word *habakari*, and on the expression *Ne mo ha mo nai* = "insignificant," but more literally, "having neither root nor leaf," as explained in the translation. [2] More literally, "having radishes grown." *Tsŭkuraseru* is the causative of *tsŭkuru* = "to make," hence "to grow" (see p. 60).

4. The Uses of Doubt.

The English term "Why?" (in our language *Naze*) is very important, although the expression was scarcely ever employed by the Chinese and Japanese in former times, and they usually acquiesced, without enquiring further into the matter, on being informed that such and such was the doctrine of Confucius or the opinion advanced by Mencius. At the present time, therefore, when the idea has been put forth that doubt is one of the most important factors towards enlightenment and progress, and when, therefore, Europeans are prone to dwell on the importance of doubt and its benefits in the cause of civilisation, and to justify this statement of theirs by referring to the Chinese and Japanese as examples of peoples for ever unprogressive, on account of their neglect to submit all matters to the scrutiny of doubt —when we hear such theories discussed, and discover ourselves alluded to as instances, we must all confess that the condition of things is undoubtedly unpalatable.

5. The Doctrine of Evolution.

During the past few years much attention has been given in European countries to the doctrine of evolution, which demonstrates the mode by which heaven and earth and all things existing therein were formed—the manner in which the world was completed. According to this doctrine, none but the most primitive forms of life existed in the world, and these, under the influence of a suitable environment, developed into the forms now exhibited by our complicated and beauteous world. This suitable environment embraces such matters as natural selection, such points as the struggle for existence and the survival of the fittest. The doctrine demonstrates minutely the conditions of environment which are beneficial to the development and evolution of living creatures. Now, this influence of environment is exerted not on the physical frames of animals and plants only, but it can also be seen in the development of our intellects. It is the environment which principally decides whether a person will be learned or ignorant. Take two children of equal intellect and capability, and place one of them in a locality where there is not even the most inferior provincial newspaper to be had. Take the other, and place him in Tokio, the centre of civilisation; let him complete his studies at the university, and after five or six years there will exist in the intellects of these two young persons a difference as great almost as that separating heaven and earth.

6. The Three-eyed Friar.

A *bonze*[1] of a Buddhist temple once invited a friend who was fond of playing *go-bang*, and they sat down to play a game. However, as the proverb says, "fondness begets skill," and to the chagrin of the *bonze* his visitor blocked every single corner of the board. "Ah! if I could only get one side free!" exclaimed the priest, and with these words he made continuous efforts to open out some spaces [*in Japanese*, "eyes"[2]]. Just then some flies alighted on the top of his head, causing him annoyance, so he scratched his head with the hand in which he held one of the counters, muttering: "If I could only get an open space [*in Japanese*, "eye"] here, very likely the corner would be liberated!"

An extra eye on the top of his head would have changed him into a "three-eyed friar"!

7. A Parliamentary Report.

Mr. Inoue Kakugorō.—I have a question.

The President.—And the purport of Mr. Inoue's question is——?

Mr. I. K.—The purport of my question is this: could not Mr. Kudō be induced to withdraw his motion, out of regard for liberty? *That* is my question. *(Voices: "No good! no good!" Other voices: Go on! go on!")* If you do not listen a little more quietly, you will not understand me. Yes, in truth liberty is an important matter——

Mr. Kudō Kōkan.—If you wish to know if I shall withdraw or not, I may tell you I shall not. If you have any other question——

Mr. I. K.—If you really admit that you despise liberty, what is the use of my wasting any more words? If you show by what you say that you are ignorant of what liberty is, who would think of putting any questions to you?

Mr. K. K.—If you have no question, well and good.

The President.—I intend taking a vote as to whether this is to be regarded as an urgency motion. I ask those gentlemen who consider that Mr. Kudō's motion should be regarded as an urgency motion to stand up. *(A minority rose.)* I find that there is a minority. *(Clapping of hands.)*

[1] *Bonze*, Buddhist priest. [2] It must be borne in mind that *me* means both "open space" and "eye."

8. The Plum-blossoms.

Now there was a man of the name of Shijō, who for a long time had been family doctor to the Iijimas. As a matter of fact, however, he was a chatterbox and a charlatan,—one of those who write no prescriptions from regard for the safety of their patients,—one who carried in his pocket-book such materials as apparatus for sleight-of-hand tricks, or paper masks for mimicry, instead of pills or powders which are usually kept by any ordinary doctor.

Well, this doctor had a friend, an unattached *samurai*[1] named Shinzaburō, living on the proceeds arising from land and house property at Shimizu-dani. He was by nature a handsome fellow, as yet a bachelor although already twenty-one years old, and so bashful that he would not go out, but spent his whole time in reading.

Shijō called upon him one day, and said: "As the weather is so fine to-day, suppose we go and view the plum-blossoms at Kameido, and on the way back call in at the villa of my friend Iijima." So saying, he led him away, and they went together to inspect the plum-blossoms, after which, on the way home, they called in at Iijima's villa.

9. A Matter of Urgency.

Two young men having met by chance near a draper's store, one of them waved his hand hastily, exclaiming: "I have a lot to talk to you about, but as I am called home on an urgent matter, our chat must be put off for a day or two, when I will look in at your house." The other, impressed by his friend's strange agitation, enquired as to the nature of this important business—whether, for instance, any of the family had fallen ill. "Oh, no!" responded the other, with a laugh. "I have just been buying here a kerchief which my wife instructed me to obtain for her, and my reason for saying that I could not stay to talk to you just now is that it would be a terrible thing if she were to fall behind the fashion whilst I was loitering on the road."

[1] *Samurai*, a gentleman of the military caste under the feudal system.

Part III. VOCABULARIES.*

Japanese-English.

NOTE.—(1) All verbs appearing in the following Vocabulary are of the First Conjugation, unless marked (2), or, *Irregular*.

(2) It has not been deemed necessary to state the part of speech in most cases, as the English words sufficiently indicate it.

ABBREVIATIONS: (*adj.*), adjective; (*intr.*), intransitive; (*irr.*), irregular; (*neg.*), negative; (*n.*), noun; (*tr.*), transitive.

Abiru (2), *to bathe.*
abumi, *stirrup.*
abunai, *perilous.*
achi *or* achira, *there.*
agaru, *to get up, to mount; to clear (of the weather).*
ageba, *wharf.*
ageru (2), *to lift up, raise.*
ago, *chin.*
ai, *deep blue, indigo.*
aida, *time, interval, while.*
aida-gara, *relationship, connection.*
aisatsu, *answer, response, acknowledgment, salutation.*
aisatsu suru, *to answer, salute.*
aisuru (*irr.*), *to love.*
aite, *companion; party (to a transaction); opponent (in a game).*
ajiwai, *flavour, taste.*
aka-daiko, *radish.*
akagane, *copper.*
akai, *red, brown.*
aka-nasu, *tomato.*
akambō, *baby.*
akari, *a light.*
akarui, *light (as opp. to dark) [adj.*
ake-gata, *day-break.*
akeru (2), *to open (tr.)*
aki, *autumn.*
akinai-suru, *to deal in.*
akinai, *commerce, trade.*
akinau, *to trade.*
akindo, *merchant, dealer.*
akippoi, *changeable, fickle.*
akiraka (na), *undoubted, evident, easily understood.*
akiraka ni, *clearly.*
akke ni torareru (2), *to be astounded.*
akkō, *abuse, reproach, insolence.*
aku, *immoral conduct, depravity.*
aku, *to open (intr.)*
akubi suru, *to yawn.*
akŭtō, *scoundrel, rogue.*
amai, *sweet.*
amari, *too, too much; (with a neg.)—not very.*
amaru, *to surpass, exceed.*
ambai ga warui, *unwell.*
ame, *rain.*
ame ga furu, *to rain.*
ame ni naru, *to begin raining.*
Amerika, *America (or U.S.A.)*
Amerika-jin, *an American.*
Amerika no, *American (adj.)*
ami, *net.*
ami wo utsu, *to catch fish (with net).*

* For rules of pronunciation and examples see pp. 11 to 15.

an, *a judgment; draft, bill.*
ana, *cavern, cavity, tunnel.*
anadoru, *to reproach, mock at.*
andon, *lamp (with paper sides).*
ane, *elder sister.*
ani (ki), *elder brother.*
anjiru (2), *to be anxious.*
annai, *guidance, a guide.*
annai suru, *to guide.*
ano, *that (adj.)*
ano hĭto, *he, she.*
anshin suru, *to be free from*
an-yo, *feet.* [*anxiety, at ease.*
anzu, *apricot.*
aoi, *blue, green.*
aomono, *greens (vegetables).*
arai, *rough.*
arare, *hail (noun).* [*gale.*
arashi, *tempest, hurricane,*
arasoi, *argument, dispute.*
arasou, *to argue, dispute.*
aratamaru, *to be mended, altered, put in order.*
aratameru (2), *to mend, re-*
arau, *to wash.* [*adjust, alter.*
arawareru (2), *to make one's self known, appear, come forth.*
arawasu, *to disclose, reveal.*
ari, *ant.* [*you!*
arigatō (gozarimasŭ), *thank*
arisama, *state (condition).*
aruji, *host, master of the house.*
aruku, *to walk.*
asa, *hemp.*
asa, *morning.*
asagi, *light green, light blue.*
asa-han, *breakfast.*
asai, *shallow.*
asatte, *the day after to-morrow.*
ase, *perspiration*
ase ga deru, *to perspire.*

ashi, *foot, leg.*
ashi no yubi, *the toes.*
ashĭta, *to-morrow.* [*ing.*
ashĭta no asa, *to-morrow morn-*
asobi, *a game* [*amuse one's self.*
asobu, asubu, *to play, to*
asŭko, *there*
asuko kara, *thence*
asŭko ye, *thither* [*grant.*
ataeru (2), *to bestow, concede,*
atai, *price, worth*
atama, *head (of body).*
atarashii, *fresh, new.*
atari, *vicinity.*
atarimae, *usually, generally.*
atarimae no, *usual; suitable, convenient, proper.*
atatameru (2), *to heat (tr.).*
ate, *trust, confidence.*
ate ni naru, *to be trustworthy.*
ate ni suru, *to confide in, rely on*
ateru (2), *to hit.* [*share.*
ate-hameru, *to portion out,*
ato, *consequence, effect; afterwards; the remainder.*
atsui, *hot; thick (in dimension).*
atsŭkau, *to manage, take upon one's self.* [*ness.*
atsŭsa, *warmth, heat; thick-*
atsŭmaru, *to gather together (intr.).* [*gether (tr.).*
atsŭmeru (2), *to gather to-*
atsuraeru (2), *to order (at shop,*
au, *to meet, agree, suit.* [*&c.).*
awaseru (2), *to cause to meet, (hence) to join.* [*ened.*
awatadashii, *excited, fright-*
awateru (2), *to get excited, frightened.* [*mistake.*
ayamatsu, *to err, make a*

Bagu-ya, *saddler.*
baishū, *a purchase, something bought.*
baishū suru, *to buy.*
baka, *a foolish person.*
baka na; baka-rashii, *foolish, ridiculous.* [*less.*
bakari, *only, about, more or*
bakageta koto, *foolishness.*
bakarashii, *foolish.*
bake (-mono), *ghost, spectre.*
bambutsu, *the established order of things, Nature.*
bam-meshi, *evening meal,* (*late*) *dinner.*
ban, *night, evening.*
ban, *sentry, watch, guard.*
banchi, *number* (*of a building*), *street-number.*
bandzuke, *playbill, programme.*
bantō, *manager, chief clerk.*
ban wo suru, *to be on guard.*
bari, *abuse, scurrilous language*
bari suru, *to abuse, slander.*
basha, *a carriage.*
bassuru, (*irr.*), *to punish.*
bata, *butter.*
bāya, *an old lady, "granny."*
bemmei, *explanation, illustration.*
bemmei suru, *to explain thoroughly, make clear.*
benjiru (2), *to argue about, discuss.*
benkō, *fluency* (*in speech*).
benkō no yoi, *fluent* (*in speech*).
benkyō, *industry, application, perseverance.*
benri, *convenience, suitableness.*
benri no yoi; benri (na), *convenient, suitable.*
benri no warui, *inconvenient, unsuitable.*
berabō (-me), *a villain, rogue.*
bessō, *villa.* [*larity.*
betsu, *a difference, dissimi-*
betsudan no, *special.*
betsu ni, *differently, especially.*
betsu no, *different, not alike.*
bettō, *groom.*
bifu-teki, *beefsteak.* ["*beer.*"
biiru, *beer* (*corruption of*
bijin, *a beauty* (*woman*).
bimbō, *indigence, want.* [*want.*
bimbō na, *needy, indigent, in*
bin, *bottle.*
birōdo, *velvet.*
bō, *a cudgel, club, stick.*
bōeki, *business, commerce.*
bōenkyō, *telescope.*
bon, *tray, salver.*
bon-yari, *weariness,* (*ennui*).
bon yari shita, *stupid* (*dazed*).
bōshi, *hat, cap.*
botan, *button.*
botan no ana, *buttonhole.*
bōtetsu, *rod-iron.*
buchi taosu, *to fell, prostrate.*
buchōhō, *clumsiness* (*gaucher-*
buchōhō na, *clumsy.* [*ie.*)
budō, *grapes.*
budō-shu, *wine.*
buki, *weapon.*
bummei, *civilisation, refinement of manners, &c.*
bummei na, *enlightened, civilised, cultured.* [*deal out.*
bumpai suru, (*irr.*) *to allot,*
bun, *a part.*
burei, *discourtesy, incivility.*
burei na, *impertinent, rude, vulgar.*

bushō, (na), *lazy, slovenly.*
buta, *pig.*
buta no niku, *pork.*
butsu, *to thrash, hit.*
byō, *tack (small nail).*
byōki, *a disease.*
byōki (na), *ill, sick.*
byōnin, *a sick person, a patient.*

Cha, *tea.*
cha-ba-take, *tea-plantation.*
chabukuro, *tea-chest.*
cha-ire, *tea-caddy.*
chakŭsuru (*irr.*), *to arrive.*
cha-nomi-jawan, *tea-cup.*
chanto, *quietly.*
chanto shĭta, *quiet.*
cha-saji, *teaspoon.*
chashi, *tea-grower.*
cha-shōnin, *tea-dealer.*
chawan, *tea-cup, basin.*
cha wo ireru, *to make tea.*
cha-ya, *tea-house.*
chi *blood.*
chi ga deru, *to bleed (intr.).*
chichi, *a father.*
chichi, *milk.*
chie, *wisdom, sagacity.*
chigai, *an error, difference.*
chigau, *to be mistaken.*
chiisai ; chiisa na, *small.*
chikagoro, *of late, recently.*
chikai, *near.*
chikai uchi, *soon.*
chikara, *strength.*
chikaro wo tsŭkusu, *to strive earnestly, try hard.*
chikazuki, *a near friend ; friendship.*
chikushō, *a (lower) animal, a brute.*
chinsen, *fare (charge).*
chiri, *dust.*
chizu, *a map.*
chō, *butterfly.*
chō, *a measure of length (about 120 yds.)*
chō, *a million.*
chōai, *love.*
chōai suru, *to love.*
chōbatsu, *punishment.*
chōbatsu suru, *to punish.*
chōchaku suru(*irr.*), *to thrash.*
chōchin, *lantern.*
chōdo, *exactly, just.*
chōhō, *usefulness, convenience.*
chōhō na, *useful, convenient.*
chokki, *waistcoat.*
chō tsugai, *a hinge, joint.*
chōzu-bachi ; chōzu-darai, *a wash-hand basin.*
chūi, *helpfulness, care.*
chūi suru, *to pay attention.*
chūmon, *a command, an order (at a shop, &c.).*
chūshi, *a discontinuance, a stoppage.*
chūshin, *centre.*

Dai (*in compounds*), *large, great, very.*
dai, *table.*
dai, *a generation, reign.*
Dai-Buritania, *Great Britain.*
daibu, *a large quantity, much.*
daichi, *the floor, ground.*
dai-chō, *ledger.*
dai-dokoro, *a kitchen.*
daidzu, *haricot-beans.*
dai-gennin, *lawyer.*
daigen-nin, *attorney.*
dai ichi ni, *firstly, in the first place.*
daiji, *importance.*
daiji na, *important, of consequence.*
daiji ni suru, *to tend carefully.*

daikai, *the open sea.*
daiku, *joiner, carpenter.*
dairi-nin, *agent.*
dai sŭki, *liking much, very fond.*
dajaku (na), *idle.*
damaru, *to be silent.*
damasu, *to cheat.*
dampan, *consultation, deliberation.*
dan, *a step, pace.*
dan-dan, *gradually.*
dangi, *oration, sermon; counsel.*
dangō, *consultation.*
dangō suru, *to take counsel.*
danjiru (2), *to consult.*
danki, *warmth, heat.*
danna, *a master.*
darake, *covered, smeared with.*
dasu, *to place outside, take out.*
de-au, *to meet, come across.*
de-guchi, *an outlet, way out.*
de kakeru, *to go forth, go out.*
de-kakeru (2), *to set out, start away.*
dempō, *telegram.*
denki, *electricity.*
denki-to, *electric light.*
denshin - kyoku, *telegraph-office.*
denwa, *telephone.*
deru (2), *to issue forth, come out.*
de shabaru, *to jut out (intr.).*
deshi, *student, pupil.*
do, *an occasion, a time, as* ichi-do, *once.*
dō, *how?*
dō de mo, *anyhow.*
dobu, *ditch.*
dōbutsu, *animal.*
dochi? *or* dochira? *where?*
dōgu, *utensil.*
dōgu-ya, *a second-hand store; a keeper of second-hand goods.*

Doitsu, *Germany.*
Doitsu-jin, *a German.*
Doitsu no, *German (adj.).*
doko? *where?*
dokoera? *whereabouts?*
doko kara? *whence?*
doko made? *how far?*
doku, *poison.*
doku ni naru, *to be unwholesome.*
domburi, *basin (small).*
donata? *who?*
dono? *which? (adj.).*
dono kurai? *how much?*
dore? *which? (pron.).*
dore-dake? *what amount?*
dorobō, *thief.*
dōsuru (*irr.*), *to be agitated.*
dote, *slope, embankment.*
doyōbi, *Saturday.*

E, *picture, sketch.*
e, *handle (of tool).*
eda, *a bough, branch.*
efu, *label (tag).*
egaku, *to paint (pictures).*
Eigo, *English (language).*
Ei (koku), *England.*
ekaki, *an artist, painter.*
eki-chō, *station-master.*
eki-fu, *railway-porter.*
empitsu, *pencil, crayon.*
empō, *at a great distance.*
empō na, *far away, distant.*
engin-mame, *French-beans.*
ennichi, *a fair; festive day.*
enryo, *bashful, diffident.*
enryo suru, *to be bashful, diffident.*
ensoku, *picnic, excursion.*
enzetsu, *oration, lecture.*
enzetsŭ suru, *to make a speech, lecture.*

erabu, *to select.*
eru, *to choose.*
eshaku, *bow ; apology.*
eshaku wo suru, *to bow ; to apologise.*
[*ignorant of.*
Fu-annai, *unacquainted with,*
fuben, *inconvenience.*
fuben na, *inconvenient.*
fuda, *ticket.* [*usual.*
fudan no, *general, common,*
fuda wo tsukeru, *to label.* [*ing.*
fude, *pen.*
fueru (2), *to increase (intr.).*
fujin, *a lady.*
fŭkai, *deep.*
fŭku, *to wipe.*
fŭkumu, *to enclose within, to include, to contain.*
fŭkuro, *a bag.*
fumi-hazusu, *to stagger, stumble.* [*ness.*
fu-mimochi, *evil, vice, wicked-*
fumi-shimeru, *to walk firmly.*
fumu, *to step on.* [*minute.*
fun, *fraction ; tenth part ; a*
funadzumi-shōsho, *bill-of-lad-*
funa-watashi, *ferry.* [*ing*
fune, *ship, boat (any kind).*
funinjō, *unkindness, harsh treatment.*
furaneru shatsŭ, *flannel-shirt.*
Fŭransu, *France.*
Fŭransu-jin, *Frenchman.*
Fŭransu no, *French (adj.).*
fureru (2), *to touch.* [*of snow.*
furi, *a downpour of rain ; fall*
furi, *demeanour ; gait.*
furo, *bath.*
furu, *to wave, brandish.*
furueru (2), *to shake, tremble.*

furui, *old (used of things only).*
furukusai, *stale.*
furute, *second-floor.*
furuu, *to shake (tr.).*
fŭsagaru, *to be full up, obstructed.* [*bed.*
fŭseru (2), *to recline, retire to*
fūsetsu, *report (rumour).*
fŭ-shi-awase na, *sad, unhappy.*
fŭshigi na, *miraculous, strange, curious.*
fŭshin, *doubt.*
fŭshin, *erection, building.*
fŭshin ni omou, *to doubt.*
fŭ-shinsetsu (na), *cruel, unkind.*
fŭshōchi, *objection, dissent.*
fŭshōchi wo iu, *to object.* [*tr.*
fŭsuru, *to submit, surrender*
fŭto, *all at once, suddenly ; accidentally.*
fŭtotta, *stout, obese.*
futsū (no), *common, general.*
fuyasu, *to augment (tr.).*
fuyu, *winter.* [*absent.*
fuzai, *away from home,*

Gakkō, *college, school.*
gakkwa, *subject of study, branch of learning pursued.*
gaku, *learning, science.*
gakumon, *study, application.*
gakumon suru, *to study.*
gakŭsha, *savant, learned man.*
gakŭtai, *band (of musicians).*
gaman, *patience.*
gaman suru, *to be patient.*
garasu, *glass.*
gehin (na), *low (vulgar).*
gejo, *a female servant.*
genan, *a male servant.*
gen-in, *origin, source.*

genkin, *cash, ready money.*
genkwa (n), *porch, entrance.*
genron, *discussion, speech.*
genzai, *now, at present.*
geppu, *monthly instalment.*
geshiku-ya, *boarding-house.*
getsuyōbi, *Monday.*
gimu, *obligation, duty.*
gin, *silver.*
ginen, *suspicion, doubt.*
ginkō, *bank (for money).*
ginkō no shinyō-hoshō-jō, *letter of credit.*
ginkō-sha, *banker.*
ginkō shihei, *bank-note.*
gin-zaiku, *silverware.*
giron, *argument.*
giyaman, *glass (noun).*
go, *five.*
gochisō, *a feast.*
gogo, *afternoon.*
go-gwatsu, *May (month).*
gohan, *food; rice.*
gōhon-ginkō, *jointstock bank.*
go-jū, *fifty.*
goke, *widow.*
goku, *extremely, very.*
gozen, *forenoon.*
gu, *stupid, dull.*
gujin, *blockhead, dull person.*
gurai, *roughly, approximately.*
gururi, *around.*
gutto, *suddenly.*
gwaikoku, *abroad, foreign parts.*
gwaikoku-jin, *foreigner.*
gwaikoku no, *foreign.*
gwaitō, *great coat, surtout.*
gyō, *occupation, work.*
gyosha, *driver of a carriage.*
gyū (-niku), *beef.*

Ha, *leaf (of plant).* [*toothache.*
ha, *tooth;* ha ga itai, *I have*
haba, *width.*
haba no hiroi, *wide.* [*fear.*
habakaru, *to be ashamed; to*
habikoru, *to spread (intr.).*
hachi, *bee; wasp.*
hachi, *eight.*
hachi-gwatsu, *August.*
hachi-jū, *eighty.*
haeru (2), *to grow (intr.).*
hagaki, *post-card.*
hagane, *steel.*
hai, *a fly (insect).*
hairi kŭchi, *entrance, way in.*
hairu, *to enter.*
haitatsu nin, *postman.*
hai-tō-kin, *dividend (on shares).*
haji, *the end, edge, ledge of any object.*
hajimari, *the commencement.*
hajimaru, *to commence (intr.).*
hajimeru (2), *to commence (tr.).*
hakujō suru, *to acknowledge (confess).*
hako, *a box.*
hakobu, *to carry, convey.*
haku, *to sweep.*
hakurai, *brought from abroad.*
hakurai-hin, *an imported*
han, *meal (food), rice.* [*article.*
hana, *flower; blossom.*
hana-fŭki, *pocket-handkerchief.*
hanahadashii, *extreme, ex-*
hana-ike, *flower-vase.* [*cessive.*
hana-muko, *bridegroom.*
hana-yome, *bride.*
hana, *nose.*
hanashi, *story, tale.*
hanasu, *to tell, say, speak.*
hane, *feather; wing.*

hara, *a moor.*
harai, *a payment.*
harai-nin, *payer (of money-order, &c.).*
hara-obi, *saddle-girth.* [*temper.*
hara wo tateru, *to get into a*
hari, *pin; needle.*
hasami, *scissors.*
hasan-nin, *a bankrupt.*
hashi, *a bridge.*
hashiru, *to run.*
hataraku, *to work.*
hateru (2), *to finish, end(intr.).*
hato, *pigeon.*
hau, *to creep.*
hayai, *early, soon; quick.*
haya-tsŭkegi, *a match (for*
hei, *hedge, fence.* [*striking.*
heishi, *soldier.*
heizei (no), *usual, common.*
hen na, *curious, strange.*
hen, *vicinity, locality.*
henji, *a reply.*
henkyaku suru, *to repay.*
hentō, *a reply.*
hentō suru, *to reply.* [*tr.*)
herasu, *to lessen, make smaller*
heru, *to lessen, grow smaller*
hi, *the sun; a day.* [*intr.*)
hi no de, *sunrise.*
hi no iri, *sunset.*
hi, *fire.*
hidoi, *severe, unkind.*
hidoi me ni awaseru, *to treat*
higashi, *east.* [*unkindly.*
hige, *the beard.*
hiji, *elbow.* [*dinary.*
hijō (na), *uncommon, extraor-*
hĭkaru, *to sparkle, shine.*
hĭki-fuda, *advertisement, notice (circular, &c.).*
hikkuri-kaesu, *to overturn, upset.*
hĭku, *to draw, pull, drag.*
hikui, *low (not lofty).*
hima, *interval, spare time.*
hima wo yaru, *to send away, dismiss.*
himo, *lace (of boot).*
hineru, *to twist (tr.).*
hinkō, *behaviour.*
hinkō no ii, *well-behaved, moral, upright.*
hinoshi, (*smoothing-*)*iron.*
hin-shitsŭ, *quality (of goods).*
hirattai, *flat.*
hira-ya, *bungalow (one storied house).*
hiroi, *broad.*
hiromaru, *to spread (intr.).*
hiromeru (2), *to spread (tr.).*
hirou, *to pick up, find.*
hiru (2), *to dry (intr.).*
hiru, *noon; daytime.*
hiru sugi, *afternoon.*
hisashii, *long (of time).*
hissori to, *tranquil; deserted.*
hisuru (irr.), *to compare.*
hĭtai, *brow, forehead.*
hĭto, *person, human being.*
hĭto me, *public notice.*
hito-sashi-yubi, *fore-finger.*
hitsuji no choppu, *mutton chop.*
hitsuji no niku, *mutton.*
hitsuyō (na), *indispensable.*
hiya, *cold.*
hiyori, *the weather.*
hiza, *knee.*
hizuke, *date (time).*
hō, *a law, custom, rule.*
hō, *cheeks.*
hōbō, *everywhere, on all sides.*

hōchō, *knife.*
hoeru (2), *to bark.*
hōken-ryō, *premium of insur-*
hoko, *fork.* [*ance.*
homae sen, *sailing-ship*
home, *praise.*
homeru (2), *to praise.*
hon, *true* ; *quite* (*generally used*
hone, *a bone.* [*with the affix* no)
honō, *a flame.*
hontō, *truth.*
hon-ya, *bookshop* ; *bookseller.*
hon-yaku, *translation.*
hon-yaku suru, *to translate.*
hori, *canal, ditch.*
horo, *hood* (*of jinrikisha*).
horobiru (2), *to be ruined.*
horobosu, *to ruin or overthrow.*
horu, *to dig* ; *to carve.*
hōru, *to throw.*
hoshii, *wishful, desirous.*
hoshō-nin, *guarantee* (*person*).
hoshō-ryō, *guarantee* (*money*).
hosoi, *fine* (*slender*).
hosoi, *narrow.*
hoso-nagai, *slim, slender.*
hossuru (*irr.*), *to wish.*
hosu, *to dry* (*tr.*).
hotondo, *almost, nearly* (*with*
hōyū, *friend.* [*neg.*), *scarcely.*
hōzu, *termination* ; *limit.*
hyakŭshō, *a farmer* ; *rustic,*
countryman.
hyōban, *report, rumour.*
hyōban wo suru, *to gossip.*

Ichiban-yoi, *first-rate.*
ichigo, *strawberry.*
ie, *house.*
ie no uchi, *indoors.*
Igirisu, *England.*
Igirisu-jin, *Englishman.*
Igirisu no, *English.*
ii-wake, *an excuse.*
ijiru, *to interfere, annoy.*
ikioi, *strength, power, force.*
ikiru (2), *to live.*
ima, *now.* [*time.*
ima ni itatte, *by now, by this*
ima-imashii, *unpleasant, dis-*
agreeable.
imashimeru (2), *to find fault*
imo, *potato.* [*with* ; *warn.*
inaka, *country* (*as opp. to*
inki-tsubo, *inkstand.* [*town.*
inochi, *life.*
inshi, *postage-stamp.*
inu, *dog.* [*versal.*
ippan (no), *widespread, uni-*
ireru (2), *to insert* ; *to make*
tea.
iri-kunda, *intricate, involved.*
iro, *colour.*
iro-iro (no), *all kinds.*
ironna, *various* ; *every kind.*
iru, *to enter.*
iru (2), *to shoot.*
irui, *clothing, apparel.*
isha, *doctor* (*medical*).
ishi, *stone* (n.).
ishi-bei, *stone wall.*
isogashii, *occupied, busy.*
isogu, *to hurry.*
issakujitsu, *the day before*
isu, *chair.* [*yesterday.*
itai, *painful* (*physically*).
itameru (2), *to cause pain, to*
hurt (*physically*).
itami, *pain* (*phys.*).
ito, *a string, thread, filament.*
itou, *to avoid, to shun.*
itsuwari, *a falsehood.*

iwashi, *sardines.*
iyagaru, *to hate, dislike.*
iye-nushi, *landlord* (*of house*).
izumi, *spring of water ; fountain.*

Jama, *hindrance, obstruction.*
jama suru, *to interfere.*
jami, *jam* (*preserves*).
ji, *earth, ground.*
ji, *hour, time.*
jibiki, *dictionary.*
jihaku suru, *to confess, to own.*
jijitsu, *a fact.*
jiki (ni), *immediately.*
jimen, *a plot of land.*
jin, *human being, person.*
jinka, *a house for human beings.*
ji-nushi, *landlord* (*ground-*).
jinryoku suru (*irr.*), *to do one's best, try earnestly.*
jisuru (*irr.*), *to refuse.*
jitensha, *bicycle.*
jitsu, *truth.*
jitsu no, *true.*
jiyū, *liberty. freedom.*
jiyū na, *free.*
jō, *a lock* (*fastening*).
jō wo orosu, *to lock.*
jōbu (na), *firm, strong ; robust.*
jōbukuro, *an envelope.*
jōdan, *droll story, joke.*
jōdan wo iu, *to joke.*
jōki, *vapour, steam.*
jōkisen, *steam-vessel.*
jōkisha, *railway.*
jōmae, *lock* (*on box, door, &c.*).
jōmae-ya, *locksmith.*
jorei ni hansoku suru, *to infringe* (*regulations*).
jōzu (na), *clever, skilful.*
juban, *shirt.*
jūbun, *quite ; ample, sufficient.*
jū-gwatsu, *October.*
jū-ichi-gwatsu, *November.*
jūkazei, *ad valorem duty.*
juku shita, *ripe* (*of fruit*).
juku tetsū, *wrought-iron.*
jumoku, *tree.*
jū-ni-gwatsu, *December.*
jungo, *order, turn, sequence.*
junsa, *policeman.*
junsui na, *pure* (*unadulterated*).
jūrai, *up to the present, hitherto.*

Kaban, *portmanteau.*
kabe, *a mud wall.*
kabeji, *cabbage.*
kabu, *turnip.*
kado, *corner ; gate.*
kado-guchi, *gateway.*
kaeru, *to return, go away* (*intr.*)
kaeru (2), *to change, exchange* (*tr.*).
kaesu, *to return, give back* (*tr.*).
kagami, *looking-glass.*
kage, *shadow, reflection ; influence.*
kagi, *key.*
kagi-hana, *keyhole.*
kahe, *coffee.*
kai, *a shell.*
kaigan-dōri, *Bund* (*street facing sea*).
kaijō-hoken, *marine insurance.*
kaijō-no, *marine* (*adj.*)
kaimono, *a purchase, something bought.*
kakamono, *hardware.*
kakaru, *to hang* (*intr.*).
kakato, *the heel.*
kake, *a portion broken off, fragment.*
kake-au, *to arrange about, bargain, discuss.*
kakeru (2), *to run ; to hang* (*tr.*) *; to put.*

kaki-tsŭke, *note, account, memorandum.*
kaku, *to write.*
kakureru (2), *to hide (intr.).*
kakŭshi, *pocket.*
kakŭsu, *to hide (tr.).*
kaku-zatō, *loaf-sugar.*
kami, *hair of head;* kami-yui, *hair-dresser.*
kami, *above, upper.*
kami, *paper.*
kami-ire, *pocket-book.*
kami-maki-tabako, *cigarette.*
kampeki, *natural disposition; temper.*
kamu, *to bite.*
kanadzuchi, *hammer.*
kanadzuchide utsu, *to hammer.*
kanarazu, *without doubt, certainly.*
kanau, *to agree, correspond with; to succeed.*
kane, *money; metal.*
kane-ire, *purse.*
kane-mochi, *a wealthy man.*
kane, *bell.*
kaneru (2), *to be unable.*
kangae, *deliberation, thought; intention.*
kangaeru (2), *to consider, deliberate upon.*
kanjō-bi, *pay-day.*
kanjō, *bill, note (account).*
kannin, *patience.*
kannin suru, *to have patience.*
kanshaku-mochi, *irritable, easily angered.*
kanshin, *amazement, wonder; admiration.*
kanshin suru, *to wonder at; admire.*
kanzashi, *hair-pin.*
kao, *the countenance, face.*

kara, *a collar.*
kara (na), *empty, void.*
karada *body (of any living being.*
karashi, *mustard.*
karasu-mugi, *oats.*
karei, *plaice (fish).*
kari-nushi, *debtor.*
kariru (2), *to hire; to borrow.*
kari suru, *to hunt; to shoot.*
karui, *light (not heavy).*
karuko, *a light porter.*
kasa, *parasol, umbrella, broad sun-hat.*
kasa, *amount, quantity.*
kasabatta, *bulky.*
kasanaru, *to be repeated; to be heaped up.*
kasaneru (2), *to repeat, heap up.*
kashi-kin, *a loan.*
kashira, *the head, chief; a superior.*
kashi (wa), *oak-tree.*
kassai, *encouragement, applause.*
kasu, *to lend, let (on hire).*
kata, *shoulder.*
katachi, *form, shape.*
kata-gata, *simultaneously, at the same time as.*
katai, *firm, stiff, hard; honest, strict, severe.*
katō, *plebeian; third class (on railway, &c.).*
katsu, *to win, vanquish.*
katte, *will, choice; convenience; kitchen.*
kau, *to buy.*
kawa, *hide (skin).*
kawa, *bark, rind, skin, peel; leather.*
kawaite iru, *to be dry.*
kawaku, *to dry, get dry.*

kawaru, *to change (intr.).*
kawase tegata, *draft, bill of exchange.*
kayou, *to go to and fro; to attend.*
kazari, *an ornament.*
kazariya, *jeweller.*
kaze, *the wind.*
kaze wo hiku, *to take cold.*
kazoeru (2), *to reckon, count.*
kazu, *a number.*
kazu-ji, *figure (number).*
ke, *a hair (human); wool.*
kega, *a cut, wound.*
kega suru, *to be wounded, to injure one's self.*
keiko, *practice.*
keiko wo suru, *to practise.*
keikwaku, *design, intention.*
keisatsŭsho, *police-station.*
keisatsŭkwan, *police-officer.*
kekkō (na), *magnificent.*
kekomi, *seat (of jinrikisha).*
kembun suru, *to inspect.*
kemmaku, *the face, features.*
kemuri, *smoke.*
kenkwa, *a dispute, quarrel.*
kenkwa suru, *to quarrel.*
kenkyū, *enquiry, research.*
kenkyū suru, *to enquire into, investigate.*
kennon, *peril, danger.*
kennon na, *perilous, dangerous.*
kenri, *privilege, right.*
kensa-nin, *inspector.*
keru (2), *to kick; to outstrip.*
kesa, *this morning.*
keshĭkaran, *ridiculous, absurd.*
kesshĭte, *undoubtedly, certainly (with neg.) never.*
kessuru (*irr.*) *to decide.*
kesu, *to extinguish.*
ketto, *rug, blanket.*
ki, *tree; wood (the substance).*
kibisho, *teapot.*
kibō, *a wish, desire.*
kibō suru, *to request, desire.*
kibun ga warui, *to feel ill.*
kido, *small door, wicket.*
ki iroi, *yellow.*
kiito, *silk (raw).*
kikai, *a machine.*
kikaseru (2), *to inform.*
kiki ni yaru, *to send to enquire.*
kiki-tsŭkeru, *to notice, observe.*
kikō, *temperature; climate.*
kiku, *to pay heed, hear.*
kiku-gurushii, *disagreeable (to hear.*
kimaru, *to be fixed.*
kimeru (2), *to decide, fix.*
kimi, *feelings.*
kimi ga warui, *to feel ill; to be frightened.*
kimono wo kiru, *to dress, put on clothes.*
kin, *gold, money.*
kin, *pound (weight.)*
kinchaku, *purse.*
kinjiru (2), *to prohibit.*
kinki, *joy.*
kinō, *yesterday.*
ki no kiita, *to be sharp-witted.*
ki no mi, *berry; a fruit.*
kinsatsu, *paper money.*
kinsen; kinsu, *money.*
kinu, *silk.*
kinu-ito, *silk thread.*
kin-yōbi, *Friday.*
ki-ō (no), *former, of old, past.*
kippu, *ticket.*
kippu no uridokoro, *booking-office.*
kirau, *to detest, have an aversion to.*

kirei (na), *clean* ; *neat* ; *pretty*.
kireru (2), *to cut, snap* (*intr.*).*
kiri, *fog*.
kiru, *to cut* ; *to kill*.
kiru (2), *to wear, to don*.
kĭseru, *pipe* (*smoking*).
kisha no ni-guruma, *luggage-van* (*on railway*).
kita, *north*.
kitai (na), *odd, curious*.
kitanai; kitanarashii, *dirty*.
kitte, *stamp, ticket*.
kitto, *without fail, positively*.
ki wo tsŭkeru, *to pay attention*.
ki-yō (na), *skilful, clever*.
kizu, *damage* (*injury*).
kizukai, *anxiety*.
kōbe, *the head*.
koboshi, *slop-basin*.
kobosu, *to spill* (*tr.*).
kobune, *boat*.
kochi; kochira, *here*.
kōdai (na), *immense, huge*.
kōdan, *a lecture*.
koe, *the voice*.
koe wo kakeru, *to cry out*.
ko gatana, *penknife*,
kogitte, *cheque*.
kogoto wo iu, *to scold*.
kōhei (na), *equitable, fair*.
koi, *firm, strong* ; *thick* (*of liquids*).
ko-ishi, *a small stone*.
kojiki, *beggar*.
koko, *here*.
kōkoku, *an advertisement*.
kokoro-mochi, *the feelings*.
kokoro-zuku, *to observe*.
kōkwai, *regret, remorse*.
kōkwai suru, *to regret*.

komakai; komaka (na), *small, minute*.
komaka ni, *in detail*.
kōman, *conceit, pride*.
kōman na, *conceited, proud*.
komaru, *to be nonplussed, in a fix*.
komban, *to-night*.
komeru (2), *to cram into*.
komori, *nurse, governess*.
komoru, *to be enclosed, shut in*.
kon, *deep blue*.
kona, *flour, fine powder*.
konaida, *a short time ago, recently*.
kondate, *menu, bill of fare*.
konnichi, *to-day*.
kono, *this* (*adj.*).
kono nochi, *henceforth, hereafter*.
konomu, *to be fond of, to like*.
koppu, *glass, tumbler*.
koraeru, *to bear, support, endure*.
kōre-furaoru, *cauliflower*.
kōri, *ice*.
korobasu, *to roll* (*tr.*),
korobu, *to roll* (*intr.*) ; *to fall down*.
korosu, *to kill*.
kōru, *to freeze* (*intr.*).
kōseki, *merit, efficiency*.
kōseki no aru, *efficient*.
koshi wo kakeru, *to sit down*.
koshiraeru (2), *to prepare*.
koshō, *pepper*.
koshō wo iū, *to object*.
kōshū, *the public*.
kosui, *a lake*.
kosuru, *to rub*.
kotae, *answer, reply*.
kotaeru (2), *to reply*.
kotoba wo kaesu, *to retort*.

* As in "this wood cuts easily." Such constructions are much more frequent in Japanese than in English.

kotogotoku, *completely, all*
kotoshi, *this year.* [*(adv.)*.
kotowari, *a denial*; *an excuse.*
kotowaru, *to refuse, make an*
kotozuke, *a message.* [*excuse.*
ko-uri, *retail.*
ko-ushi-no-niku, *veal.*
kowagaru, *to be alarmed, afraid.*
kowai, *afraid*; *frightful.*
kowareru (2), *to break (intr.).*
kowasu, *to break (tr.).*
ko-yubi, *the little finger.*
kubi, *the neck.*
kŭchi, *the mouth*; *an aperture.*
kŭchibue wo fuku, *to whistle.*
kŭchi-fŭki, *serviette, napkin.*
kŭchi-nŭki, *corkscrew.*
kŭchi-yakusoku, *a verbal*
kuchibiru, *the lips.* [*promise.*
kudaru, *to descend.*
kudoi, *dull, tedious*; *verbose.*
kugi, *a nail.*
ku-gwatsu, *September.*
kūki, *the air.*
kumo, *a cloud.*
kura, *saddle.*
kurabu, *club (society).*
kurai, *dark.*
kurasa, *darkness.*
kureru (2), *to give.*
kurō, *trouble (pains).*
kuroi, *black.*
kuru *(irreg.) to come.*
kuru, *to twist, wind up.*
kuruma-ebi, *lobster.*
kurumu, *cream.*
kurushii, *painful, in pain.*
kŭsa, *herb, plant.*
kŭsai, *evil-smelling.*
kŭsari, *a chain.*
kŭsaru, *to putrefy.*
kŭshami, *a sneeze.*
kŭshami wo suru, *to sneeze.*
kŭshi, *comb.*
kŭsuri, *medicine.*
kŭsuri-ya, *chemist (apothecary).*
kŭtabireru (2), *to become tired.*
kutsu, *boot, shoe.*
kutsu-ya, *boot-store*; *boot-,*
kuu, *to eat.* [*shoe-maker.*
kui-tsŭku, *to bite (of animals).*
kuwaeru (2), *to add.*
kuwashii, *exact, minute.*
kwai, *a society, association, assembly.*
kwaiin, *member (of club, &c.).*
kwaikei-kata, *cashier.*
kwairaku, *pleasure, joy.*
kwaisha, *Company.*
kwaiwa, *conversation.*
kwan-in, *an official.* [*cipal.*
kwanshu, *head of firm, prin-*
kwa-sai hoken, *fire insurance.*
kwayōbi, *Tuesday.* [*patron.*
kyaku, *customer*; *guest*;
kyō, *to-day.*
kyōiku, *education.* [*time to-day.*
kyō-jū, *before to-night, some-*
kyonen, *last year.* [*religion).*
kyōshi, *a teacher*; *minister (of*
kyujitsu, *a holiday.*
kyūkin, *salary, wages.*
kyū (na), *sudden.*
kyū na, *urgent.*

Ma, *interval, space*; *a room.*
mabushii, *dazzling.*
machi, *a street*; *the commercial part of a town.*
machigai, *a misunderstanding, mistake.*

machigau, *to make a mistake.*
machigatta, *incorrect.*
mada, *still (at present); (with neg.) not yet.*
mado, *window.*
mado-kake, *window-curtain.*
mado no to, *window-shutters.*
mae, *before, in front.*
mae-kake, *apron, pinafore.*
mae kara, *beforehand.*
magaru, *to bend (intr.).*
magatte iru, *to be bent, contorted.*
mageru (2), *to bend (tr.).*
mai-nen, *yearly.*
mainichi, *daily.*
majiwaru, *to mix among, associate with.*
makanai-kata, *steward (ship's).*
makeru (2), *to lose; to be vanquished; to yield.*
maki, *firewood.*
maki-tabako, *cigar.*
makoto, *truth.*
makoto no, *true.*
makoto ni, *positively, really.*
makura, *pillow.*
mama, *way, manner.*
mamoru, *to guard, keep watch.*
maneku, *to invite.*
ma ni au, *to arrive in time.*
mannaka, *the centre.*
manzoku, *satisfaction, contentment.*
manzoku suru, *to be contented.*
mare ni, *seldom.*
mari, *ball (toy).*
maru de, *quite.*
marui, *round, spherical.*
massugu (na), *straight.*
masu, *to augment (tr.).*
masu-masu, *more and more.*
mata, *again, (with neg.), no more.*
matsu, *to wait.*
mattaku, *quite.*
mawaru, *to turn (intr.).*
mawasu, *to turn (tr.).*
mazeru (2), *to mix (tr.).*
mazui, *distasteful.*
me, *the eyes; an open space.*
me ni tsŭkanai, *not to observe.*
me no chikai, *short-sighted.*
me no tama, *the eyeballs.*
me wo mawasu, *to swoon.*
megane, *spectacles.*
mei, *niece.*
meigen suru, *to state clearly.*
meijiru (2), *to order.*
meiwaku, *trouble, perplexity.*
meiwaku suru, *to be in trouble, in a quandary.*
mekata, *weight.*
mekura, *blind.*
mendō, *trouble.*
mendō na, *troublesome.*
men-sha, *muslin.*
messō (na), *extravagant.*
mezurashii, *curious, amazing.*
mi-ataru, *to find.*
mi-awaseru, *to put off.*
michi, *a way, road.*
mi-dasu, *to discover.*
mienaku naru, *to become invisible, disappear.*
mieru (2), *to appear, be visible, to seem.*
migaku, *to brush (boots); to brighten (tr.).*
migoto (na), *beautiful, superb, lovely.*
migurushii, *displeasing (to the sight).*
mi-harashi, *prospect, view.*
mijikai, *short.*
mi-komu, *to estimate.*

mimi, *ears (of the head).*
mimi no tōi, *deaf.*
minami, *south.*
minashigo, *orphan.*
minato, *port, harbour.*
mi-otosu, *to overlook.*
miru (2), *to look, regard, see.*
mise, *shop.*
mise-saki, *shop window.* [*sider.*
mi-tomeru, *to observe; to con-*
mizu, *water (fresh—not salt—and cold).*
mizu-gwashi, *fruit.*
mō, *still, yet, already, more; (with neg. verb), no more.*
mō hĭtotsu, *one more.*
mochi-ageru, *to lift.*
mochiiru (2), *to employ.*
mochimono, *possessions, effects.*
mochi-nushi, *owner, possessor.*
mochiron, *certainly (of course).*
modosu, *to give back, return.*
moegi, *deep green.*
mōke, *gains, profit.*
mokuroku, *a list, catalogue.*
mokŭteki, *an object, purpose.*
mokuyōbi, *Thursday.*
momen, *cotton.*
mommō (na), *ignorant.*
momu, *to rub; to knead.*
mon, *gate.*
mondai, *a query, problem.*
moppara, *chiefly.*
mori, *wood (forest).*
mōshi-bun, *an objection.*
mōshi-wake, *an apology, excuse.*
mōshi-ukeru, *to receive into one's keeping, to take in charge.*
mōsu, *to say.*
moto, *source, cause.*
motode, *capital (money).*
motomeru (2), *to seek, ask fo • to obtain.*
motsu, *to hold, have, possess; to last, wear (intr.).*
motte iku, *to carry off.*
motte kuru, *to bring (things).*
moya, *fog, mist.*
moyō, *a pattern.*
muda (na), *useless.*
mugaku, *ignorance.* [*rant.*
mugaku na; mugaku no, *igno-*
mukaeru (2), *to welcome; to send for; to wed.*
mukashi, *ancient times, antiquity.*
muko, *son-in-law; bridegroom.*
muku, *pure, unadulterated;*
mune, *the breast.* [*solid.*
mura, *village.*
murasaki, *purple, lilac.*
muri, *unreasonable.*
muryō, *incalculable, unbounded, infinite.*
musai (no), *unmarried man, bachelor.*
musŭko, *son, boy.*
musŭme, *daughter, girl.*
muyami (na), *hair-brained, reckless.*
muyami ni, *recklessly.*
muyō (no), *futile, useless.*
mu-zei, *duty-free.*
muzukashii, *difficult.*
myōchō, *to-morrow morning.*
myō (na), *marvellous, odd, queer.*
myō-nen, *next year.*
myōgonichi, *the day after to-morrow.*
myōnichi, *to-morrow.*

Nabe, *saucepan.*
nabe-gane, *cast-iron.*
nadakai, *noted, famous.*
nakagai, *broker.*
nadameru (2), *to pacify.*
naderu (2), *to stroke.*
nagai, *long.* [*fixedly.*
nagameru (2), *to regard*
nagasa, *length.*
nageru (2), *to cast, hurl.*
naguru, *to thrash, castigate.*
nagusameru (2), *to comfort, console.*
nai-nai, *secret, private.* [*mate.*
nakama, *companion, crony,*
naku, *to sing ; to cry.*
naku naru, *to die.*
nama, *raw ; unmanufactured.*
namae wo kaku, *to sign.*
nama-gawa, *raw-hide.*
nama-iki (na), *vain, con-*
namari, *lead (metal).* [*ceited.*
nameshi-gawa, *tanned-hide.*
naoru, *to recover, get well again ; to amend, cure, change.*
nara, *oak-tree.*
narai, *a custom, habit.*
narasu, *to ring (tr.).*
narau, *to learn.*
narete iru, *to be accustomed.*
nari-kawaru, *to replace.*
naru, *to ring (intr.) ; to become ; to ripen.*
nashi, *pear.*
nasu, *to do.*
natsu, *summer.*
nawa, *rope.*
naze ? *why ?*
ne, *cost, price.*
ne-beki, *deduction, discount.*
nebeya, *bedroom.*
ne-biki, *reduction (in price).*
nedai, *bed (European).*
nedoko, *bed (native).*
negai, *desire, request.* [*beg.*
negau, *to desire, supplicate,*
negi, *onion.*
negiru, *to bargain.*
neji, *screw.*
neji-mawashi, *screw-driver.*
nejiru, *to twist (tr.).*
neko, *cat.*
nema, *bedroom.*
nempu, *yearly instalment.*
nemui, *sleepy, weary.*
neru (2), *to sleep ; to retire,*
nete iru, *to be asleep.* [*go to bed.*
netsubyō, *fever.*
nesshin, *zeal, industry.*
ne-uchi, *cost, value.*
nezumi, *rat.*
nezumi-iro, *grey.*
nichiyōbi, *Sunday.*
nigai, *bitter.*
nigeru (2), *to escape, run away.*
nigiru, *to grasp.* [*sprightly.*
nigiyaka (na), *animated,*
ni-gwatsu, *February.*
Nihon ; Nippon, *Japan.*
Nihon-go, *the Japanese language.*
Nihon jin, *a Japanese (person).*
Nihon no, *Japanese (adj.).*
ni-kai, *first-floor.*
nikki, *journal (diary).*
niku, *meat, flesh.*
niku no shiru, *gravy.* [*with.*
nikŭ-sashi, *a fork for eating*
niku-ya, *butcher's shop ; butcher.*
nimotsŭ, *freight (goods).*

ninjin, *carrot.*
nioi, *a smell, whiff.*
niru (2), *to boil (food, not water).*
nishi, *west.*
nishin, *herring.*
niwa, *garden; courtyard.*
nobasu, *to elongate, stretch (tr.), to put off.*
noberu (2), *to relate; to give an opinion.*
nobe-tetsu, *sheet-iron.*
noboru, *to ascend, climb.*
nochi, *after, afterwards.*
nodo, *the neck, throat.*
nodo ga kawaku, *to be thirsty.*
nokosu, *to leave behind.*
nomi, *only.*
nomi narazu, *not only.*
nomu, *to drink.*
nori, *starch.*
nori-ai basha, *omnibus.*
noru, *to ride (on horseback, &c.); to drive (in vehicle); to be conveyed (by water).*
nozomi, *a desire, wish.*
nozomu, *to expect, look forward to.*
nuguu, *to wipe.*
nuibari, *needle.*
nuimono, *needlework.*
nuku, *to extract, withdraw.*
nusumu, *to rob.*
nuu, *to sew.*
nozoku, *to peep.*

Oba, *aunt.*
obāsan, *old lady; grandma.*
obi, *belt, sash, girdle.*
oboe-gaki, *memorandum.*
oboeru (2), *to learn; to remember; to feel.*
odayaka (na), *tranquil, calm.*
odokasu, *to terrify.*
odoru, *to caper, dance.*
ōfŭku-gippu, *return-ticket.*
ō-hei, *impertinence, insolence, haughtiness.*
ōi, *numerous, plentiful.*
oi, *nephew.*
oi-oi, *gradually, little by little.*
oishii, *pleasant to eat, tasty.*
oi-yaru, *to drive away, repel.*
oji, *uncle.*
ojiisan, *old gentleman; grandpa.*
ōjiru, *to correspond, to answer; to suit.*
oka, *land (as opp. to water).*
okashii; okashi na, *foolish, laughable.*
okiru (2), *to get up, rise.*
ōkisa, *size.*
okkakeru (2), *to chase.*
okonai, *personal demeanour, behaviour.*
okoru, *to become angry.*
oku, *to place; to lay aside.*
okuri-kin, *remittance.*
okuri-mono, *a gift (to an inferior).*
okuru, *to give; despatch; accompany: see off; spend time.*
omocha, *toy.*
omoi, *weighty; important.*
omoi, *thought; affection.*
omoi no hoka, *unexpectedly.*
omoi-gake-nai, *unexpected.*
omonjiru (3), *to hold in great honour.*
omoshiroi, *entertaining, interesting.*
omoshirosa, *amusement, interest, jollity.*
omotai, *weighty, ponderous.*
omou, *to think.*

omoi-dasu, *to call to mind, recollect.*
omoi-kiru, *to make up one's mind.*
omoi-tatsu, *to purpose, resolve.*
omoi-yaru, *to sympathise.*
on, *kindness.*
on wo shiranai, *to show ingratitude.*
ōrai-dome, "*no thoroughfare.*"
oreru (2), *to break (intr.).*
ori-ori, *from time to time.*
oriru (2), *to descend.*
oroshi, *wholesale.*
orishi-ya, *wholesale-dealer.*
orosu, *to lower, let down.*
oru, *to break (tr.).*
osameru (2), *to pacify; to govern, guide; to put on one side.*
oshieru (2), *to instruct, show how.*
oshi-gami, *blotting-paper.*
oshimu, *to grudge; to regret.*
osoi, *late.*
osoreru (2), *to fear.*
osoroshii, *horrible, terrible.*
osu, *to push.*
oto, *sound, noise.*
otona, *an adult (person).*
otoroeru, *to become weak and feeble.*
otosu, *to omit.*
otosu, *to let fall.*
ototoi, *the day before yesterday.*
ototoshi, *the year before last.*
ou, *to chase.*
owaru, *to finish, terminate (tr. and intr.).*
oyobu, *to reach (intr.).*
oyogu, *to swim.*
ōzei, *a crowd.*

Pan, *bread.*
pay-ya, *a bakery, baker's shop; baker.*
penshiru, *pencil.*

Raida (na), *idle.*
rampu, *lamp.*
rampŭ no shin, *lamp-wick.*
rasha, *woollen cloth.*
reisŭ, *lace (needlework).*
renga, *brick.*
ressha, *railway-train.*
rettasŭ, *lettuce.*
rieki, *gain, advantage.*
ringo, *apple.*
rinjin, *neighbour.*
rippa (na), *superb, magnificent.*
rippuku, *temper (anger).*
rippuku suru, *to get into a temper.*
ri-soku, *interest (on money).*
rōka, *passage, corridor.*
roku-gwatsu, *June.*
ron, *argument, opinion.*
ronjiru (2), *to argue.*
rōseki, *marble (the stone).*
rōsoku, *candle.*
ryōgae-ya, *a money-changer's shop; a money-changer.*
ryōji, *consul.*
ryokō, *journey.*
ryokō-hi, *travelling-expenses.*
ryokō suru, *to travel.*
ryōri-nin, *a cook.*
ryōri wo suru, *to cook.*
ryōri-ya, *restaurant.*

Saba, *mackerel.*
sabishii, *dull, lonely.*
sadamaru, *to be settled, fixed.*
sadameru (2), *to settle, to fix.*
sagaru, *to descend, to go away.*
sagasu, *to seek.*
sai-chi, *intelligence; wisdom.*
saiku, *workmanship.*
sainyū, *income.*

saisho, *the commencement, beginning.*
saisoku suru, *to urge on, incite.*
saiwai, *prosperity, good luck.*
saji, *spoon.*
sakan (na), *prosperity.*
sakan (ni), *greatly.*
sakana-ya, *fishmonger.*
sakarau, *to resist.*
sakasama, *inverted, upside down.*
sakate, *tip (fee).*
sakazuki, *wineglass.*
sake, *rice-beer, alcoholic liquors in general.*
sake, *salmon.*
sakebu, *to scream out, yell.*
saki, *in front, ahead; before (of place); further.*
saki-hodo, *a short time ago; previously.*
saku, *to bloom.*
saku, *to tear, rend (tr.).*
sakura, *cherry-tree.*
samasu, *to cool (tr.).*
samatage, *an impediment, obstruction.*
samatage wo suru, *to impede, hinder.*
sameru (2), *to cool (intr.); to fade.*
samui, *cold (weather, or one's own feelings).*
samusa, *coldness (degree of).*
samushii, *dull, solitary.*
san-gwatsu, *March.*
san-kai, *second-floor.*
sao-tetsu, *bar-iron.*
sappari, *quite; (with neg.), not at all.*
sara, *plate (dish).*
saradō, *salad.*
saru, *to leave (a place).*
sasai, *a trifle.*
sasai na: sasai no, *trifling, insignificant.*
sasayaku, *to whisper.*
sashi-hiku, *to deduct.*
sashimono-ya, *joiner (carpenter).*
sasshiru (2), *to guess.*
sassoku, *immediately.*
sato, *village.*
satō, *sugar.*
satsu, *a volume; paper money.*
satsu-ire, *pocket-book.*
sawagasu, *to stir up, disturb.*
sawagi, *a commotion, row.*
sawaru, *to touch; to strike or collide with.*
sazo, *doubtless, indeed, surely.*
sebone, *backbone, spine.*
sei, *stature.*
sei no hikui, *short (in stature).*
sei no takai, *tall.*
sei, *manufacture, make (noun).*
seibutsu, *a living creature.*
seigen, *a boundary, limit.*
seigen suru, *to limit.*
seiryoku, *strength.*
sei-shitsu, *character, disposition, nature, bearing.*
seisuru, *to fabricate, manufacture.*
sei-tetsu-jo, *iron-foundry.*
seizō-ba, *manufactory.*
seizon, *existence.*
seizon suru, *to exist.*
seizō-nin, *manufacturer.*
seji, *flattery.*
seki, *cough.*
seki ga deru, *to cough.*
sekitan, *coal.*
sekinin, *liability.*
sekken, *thrift, economy.*
semai, *narrow; limited; small.*
senaka, *back (of body).*
sendō, *boatman.*

senjitsu, *the other day.*
senkoku, *a short time ago.*
senro, *a line of railway.*
sentaku suru, *to wash (garments).*
seri, *parsley.*
seri-uri, *auction.*
setsu, *a time, an occasion.*
setsu, *an opinion.*
setsumei, *an explanation.*
setsumei suru, *to explain.*
sha, *a society, company, firm.*
shaberi, *prattle, a prattler, chatterer.*
shaberu, *to prattle, chatter.*
shabon, *soap.*
sha-chō, *guard (on train).*
shain, *partner (in a firm); member (of a society).*
shakkin, *a debt.*
shaku, *a foot (measure).*
shakuba-ya, *livery-stable.*
shakuri, *hiccough.*
shakuya-nin, *tenant.*
shakuyō-oboe, *I.O.U.*
shappo, *hat, cap.*
sharei, *a fee, wages.*
shashin, *a photograph.*
shashin-kyō, *photographic instruments.*
shashin-ya, *photographer.*
shatsu, *shirt.*
shiba, *grass, turf.*
shiba-ebi, *shrimps.*
shibaru, *to tie, fasten.*
shĭchi-gwatsu, *July.*
shidzuka ni, *slowly.*
shiga, *the teeth.*
shigoku, *extremely, very.*
shi-gwatsu, *April.*
shihon, *capital (funds).*
shiite, *violently, urgently.*
shiiru, *to incite; endeavour; compel.*
shijū, *continually.*
shĭkaru, *to reprove.*
shĭkashi-nagara, *but, nevertheless.*
shikkari, *tight, firm.*
shikkari shĭta, *firm, immovable.*
shikkei, *rudeness, discourtesy.*
shikkei na, *discourteous, rude.*
shimbun, *newspaper; news.*
shimbun-ya, *newspaper shop; newsman.*
shimeppoi, *moist, damp.*
shimeru (2), *to close, fasten.*
shimo, *below.*
shimpai, *anxiety, sorrow.*
shimpai suru, *to be in suspense, to be troubled.*
shimpo, *progress.*
shimpo suru, *to progress.*
shin, *the heart; wick.*
shin (no), *true, real, not artificial.*
shin ni, *really.*
Shina, *China.*
Shina-jin, *Chinaman.*
shina-gaki, *list (catalogue).*
shinchū, *brass.*
shindai, *an estate, possession (property).*
shindai-kagiri ni naru, *to become bankrupt.*
shinjiru (2), *to believe.*
shinki (na), *new.*
shinri, *truth.*
shinrui, *relative, kinsman.*
shinsetsu, *kindness.*
shinsetsu na, *kind.*
shiraberu (2), *to enquire into, examine.*
shirase, *an announcement, notice.*
shiraseru (2), *to inform.*

shireta, *self-evident.*
shiroi, *white.*
shiroi-jiban, *white shirt.*
shiromono, *merchandise.*
shirosa, *whiteness.*
shiro-uri, *vegetable-marrow.*
shiru, *to know.*
shirushi, *a symbol, sign, mark.*
shishō, *a teacher.*
shĭta, *the tongue.*
shita, *below.*
shĭtagau, *to obey, follow.*
shita-jiban, *under-shirt.*
shĭtaku wo suru, *to prepare.*
shĭtashii, *friendly, intimate.*
shĭtate-ya, *tailor.*
shĭta-zara, *saucer.*
shitsumon, *a question.*
shitsurei, *impertinence, insolence.*
shitsurei na, *impertinent, rude.*
shiwaketchō, *journal* (*office account-book.*
shiwo-ire, *salt-cellar.*
shizuka (na), *quiet.*
shizumu, *to sink* (*intr*).
shōbai, *business, trade.*
shobun, *punishment, treatment.*
shōchi, *assent, consent, comprehension.*
shōchi suru, *to consent.*
shōchū, *spirits* (*liquor*).
shō-gwatsu, *January.*
shōjiki, *honesty, integrity.*
shōjiki na, *honest, upright.*
shoji suru, (*irr.*) *to possess.*
shōken-inchi, *revenue-stamp.*
shoken suru, *to read.*
shōkin, *indemnity.*
shōko, *a proof, testimony.*
shōko-nin, *a witness.*
shokubutsu, *a plant.*
shokuma, *dining-room.*
shokumotsu, *food.*
shokunin, *an artificer, workman.*
shomotsu, *a book.*
shōnin, *merchant, dealer.*
shosei, *student.*
shōsen, *merchant-vessel.*
shōsho, *certificate.*
shote, *the beginning.*
shotoku-zei, *income-tax.*
shōyu, *sauce.*
shui, *meaning, intention, tenour.*
shūkan, *a week.*
shūki, *a bad odour.*
shūsen, *help, aid.*
shūsen wo suru, *to help, aid.*
shushi, *intention, aim.*
shusu, *satin.* [*ture.*
shuttatsu, *setting out, depar-*
shuttatsu suru, *to set out.*
soba, *alongside.* [*rate.*
sōba, *the market price, current*
sochi; sochira, *there.*
sōda-mizu, *soda-water.*
sode, *sleeve.*
sōdō, *a tumult, uproar.*
sō-kei, *gross amount.*
sōken (na), *robust, stalwart, sturdy.*
sokonau, *to ruin; to fail.*
sō-mekata, *gross weight.*
someru (2), *to dye.*
sonaeru (2), *to provide.*
soppu, *soup.*
sora, *the sky, the heavens.*
sora-iro, *azure blue.*
sora-mame, *broad-beans.*
soroeru (2), *to arrange, set in order.* [*without hurry.*
soro-soro, *slowly, leisurely,*

soru, *to shave.*
sōshi, *magazine, journal.*
sōtai (no), *whole.*
soto, *the outside, out of doors.*
sōtō (na), *fit, suitable.*
sōzen, *tumult, row, uproar.*
sōzōshii, *riotous, noisy.*
su, *vinegar.*
suberu, *to slide, slip.*
sube-sube shĭta, *smooth, even.*
subete, *all, altogether.*
sue, *the tip, end.*
sueru (2), *to place, set.*
sugi, *past, after.*
sugiru (2), *to exceed.*
sugu ni; sugu to, *immediately.*
suifu, *sailor, seaman.*
suiyōbi, *Wednesday.*
sukkari, *completely, quite; (with neg.), not at all.*
sŭkoshi, *a piece, a little.*
sumai, *a residence.*
sumau, *to dwell, reside.*
sumasu, *to finish, (tr).*
sumi-kitta, *pure (clear).*
sumpō, *dimensions.*
sumu, *to reside, live.*
sumu, *to conclude.*
sŭna, *sand.*
suppai, *sour.*
surıbi, *match, lucifer.*
suru, *to do; to make; to rub.*
surudoi, *sharp.*
susugu, *to cleanse.*
susumeru (2), *to incite; recommend; offer.*
susumu, *to go forward, advance (intr.).*
sŭtensho, *railway station.*
sŭteru (2), *to throw away.*
suu, *to suck.*
suzu, *tin.*
suzume, *sparrow.*
suzushii, *fresh, cool.*

Tabako, *tobacco.*
tabako-ire, *tobacco-pouch.*
tabako wo nomu, *to smoke (tr.)*
tabemono, *food.*
taberu (2), *to eat.*
tabe ye deru, *to go on a journey.*
tabi, *journey.*
tabi-bito, *traveller.*
tabi-tabi, *frequently, often.*
tachi-kaeru, *to go back.*
tada, *only, simply.*
tadaima, *immediately.*
tadashii, *just, exact, correct.*
tadasu, *to investigate; warn; correct.*
taeru (2), *to suffer, support, bear.*
taira (na), *flat.*
taisetsu, *importance.*
taisetsu na, *important.*
taisō, *greatly, much, very.*
taitei, *generally, for the most part.*
taiyō, *the sun.*
takai, *high; loud; costly, dear.*
take, *length, stature.*
taku, *to cook (rice); to light (a fire).*
tama, *jewel, bead, ball.*
tamago, *egg.*
tamesu, *to taste; to try.*
tam-mono, *piece-goods.*
tamotsu, *to keep (tr.).*
tana, *a shelf.*
tana-oroshi hyo, *inventory.*
tana-ukesho, *lease.*
tanomu, *to trust to, rely on; apply to, ask; hire; engage.*
tanoshimi, *pleasure, joy.*
tara, *cod.*
tarai, *wash-basin.*

taru, *barrel, cask.*
tashĭka (na), *sure, positive.*
tashĭka ni, *certainly.*
tashĭkameru (2), *to verify; ascertain.*
tassha na, *healthy.*
tasshiru (2), *to reach, attain.*
tasŭkeru (2), *to aid; to save.*
tataku, *to knock.*
tatamu, *to heap up.*
tate-fuda, *notice-board.*
tateru (2), *to build; set up.*
tatoeru (2), *to compare.*
tatsu, *to rise, stand up; to depart.*
tazuneru (2), *to enquire, ask; to visit.*
te, *handle (of teapot, basket, &c).*
te, *hand; arm; handwriting.*
te-arai, *rough, violent.*
teberu kake, *tablecloth.*
tebukuro, *glove.*
tegami, *letter (correspondence).*
tegami-no-kami, *letter-paper.*
tegarui, *easy; slight.*
teinei (na), *courteous.*
tekitō (na), *suitable, fit.*
ten, *sky, heaven.*
tenjō, *ceiling.*
tenki, *the weather.*
tenugui, *towel.*
teppō, *gun.*
teppō-kaji, *gunsmith.*
teppō no tsutsu, *gun-barrel.*
teppō wo utsu, *to discharge (a weapon).*
teru, *to shine.*
te-shoku, *candlestick.*
tetsu, *iron.*
tetsubin, *kettle.*
tetsudō, *railway.*
tetsudau, *to assist.*
tetsudō-basha, *tram, street-car.*
tetsudō no ren-raku-eki, *junction (railway).*
to, *door.*
tobu, *to fly; to jump.*
tōchaku, *arrival.*
tōchaku suru, *to arrive.*
todana, *cupboard.*
todoku, *to reach (intr.).*
todomaru, *to stop, stay (intr.).*
todomeru (2), *to stop (tr.).*
toga, *fault, blame.*
togameru (2), *to blame.*
togatta, *pointed (sharp).*
togi-kawa, *razor-strop.*
tohōmonai, *unreasonable, extortionate.*
tōi, *far, distant.*
tojiru (2), *to bind (books); to close (tr.).*
tokei, *clock, watch.*
tokeiya, *watch-maker.*
tokeru (2), *to melt (intr).*
toki, *time.*
toki-doki, *often.*
toki-ori, *occasionally.*
toki suru, *to speculate (in stocks, &c).*
toki to shĭte, *sometimes.*
tokoro-gaki, *a written address.*
toku, *to loosen; to explain.*
toku, *advantage, profit.*
toku, *to melt (tr.).*
tokui, *customer.*
tombi, *a low Yokohama broker.*
tome-bari, *pin (for fastening dress, &c.).*
tō-megane, *telescope.*
tomeru (2), *to stop (tr).*
tomodachi, *friend, companion.*
tōnen, *this year.*

toraeru (2), *to arrest, seize.*
toru, *to take.*
tori ni iku, *to go for.*
tori ni kuru, *to come for.*
tori ni yaru, *to send for.*
tori-chigaeru, *to confuse.*
tori-isogu, *to be in a hurry.*
torikaeru, *to exchange.*
tori-motsu, *to arrange.*
tori-shiraberu, *to enquire into.*
tōtō, *at last.*
totte, *handle (of a drawer).*
tou, *to ask.*
tōzen, *fit, proper.*
tsubo, *a jar.*
tsŭchi yaki, *earthenware.*
tsue, *stick, staff.*
tsugu, *to join (tr).; to follow.*
tsuiyasu, *to spend extravagantly.*
tsūjiru (2), *to comprehend; to speak (a language).*
tsŭkaeru (2), *to serve.*
tsŭkai, *message; messenger.*
tsŭkamaeru (2), *to catch.*
tsŭkasadoru, *to direct, control.*
tsŭkau, *to employ, use.*
tsŭkawasu, *to send; to give.*
tsŭkegi, *a match (for striking).*
tsŭke-mono, *pickles.*
tsŭkeru (2), *to fix, affix; add; set down in writing.*
tsŭki, *the moon; a month.*
tsŭkiru (2), *to come to an end, to be exhausted.*
tsŭku, *to push, shove.*
tsŭku-zŭku, *attentively.* [*less.*
tsumaran (ai), *trifling, worth-*
tsumari, *at last, in the long run.*
tsumazuku, *to trip, stumble.*
tsumbō (no), *deaf.*

tsumeru (2), *to cram, stuff into.*
tsumetai, *cold (to the touch).*
tsume-yoru, *to draw near.*
tsumi no nai, *innocent.*
tsumi suru, *to punish.*
tsumoru, *to be piled up.*
tsumu, *to pick.*
tsumuri, *the head.*
tsunagu, *to fasten, tie up.*
tsunoru, *to collect (tr.).*
tsuri-ito, *fishing-line.*
tsuri-bari, *fish-hook.*
tsuri-zao, *fishing-rod.*
tsutsumi (-mono), *parcel.*
tsutsumu, *to wrap up.*
tsuyoi, *strong.*

Ubau, *to rob, take by force.*
uchi, *the inside; a house.*
uchi-guruma no jōkisen, *screw-steamer.*
ude, *the arm.*
udonko, *meal, flour.*
ueki, *a (garden) plant.*
ueki-bachi, *flower-pot.*
ueki-ya, *gardener.*
ueru (2), *to plant.*
ugokasu, *to move (tr).*
ugoku, *to move (intr.).*
ukagau, *to ask, enquire; visit; listen to.*
ukeru (2), *to receive.*
uketori, *a receipt.*
uketori-chō, *receipt-book.*
uketori-kata, *payee.*
ŭma (*pronounced* 'm-ma), *a horse.*
ŭmai (*pron.* 'm-mai), *tasty,*
ŭmaya, *stable.* [*agreeable.*
ŭme (*pron.* 'm-meh), *plum-*
umi, *the sea.* [*tree.*

umi-be, *the beach ; sea-shore.*
umi-tate, *fresh (of eggs).* [*office.*
un, *luck.*
un no yoi, *lucky.*
un no warui, *unlucky.*
unjō, *a tax, tariff.*
unsō-ten, (*parcels*) *express*
uragaeshi, *inside-out.*
uragaki, *endorsement.*
uragaki wo suru, *to endorse.*
ureshii, *joyful.*
uru, *to sell.* [*beautiful.*
uruwashii, *lovely, charming,*
ushi, *bull, cow ; beef.*
ushinau, *to lose.*
uso, *falsehood, lie.*
uso-tsŭki, *a liar.*
uso wo iu, *to lie, tell lies.*
usu-akai, *pink (colour).*
usu-gurai, *dusk.*
usui, *light (in colour); thin (of liquids) ; insufficient.*
utau, *to sing.*
utsu, *to hit, strike.*
uttōshii, *dull, overcast, cloudy.*
uwa-gaki, *address (on letter,*
uwagi, *coat, overcoat.* [*&c.*).
uwagutsu, *a slipper.*
uwo, *a fish.*
uwo wo tsuru, *to angle.*

Wa, *wheel.*
wabi, *apology.* [*lament.*
wabiru (2), *to apologise ;*
wakai, *young.*
wakari, *understanding.*
wakari no hayai, *sharp, quick-witted.*
wakari-nikui, *difficult to comprehend.* [*hend.*
wakari-yasui, *easy to compre-*
wakaru, *to comprehend.*
wakasu, *to boil (water).*
wake, *cause, reason.* [*out.*
wakeru (2), *to share, portion*
wakete, *specially.*
waku, *to boil (intr.).*
wan, *bowl.*
wara, *straw.*
warai, *laughter.*
warau, *to laugh.*
wari-barai, *instalment.*
wari-bike wo suru, *to discount.*
warui, *bad ; ugly.*
waruku iu, *to blame.*
wasureru (2), *to forget.* [*pose.*
waza to ; waza-waza, *on pur-*

Yabuku, *to tear, rend (tr.).*
yado, *dwelling-place, hotel.*
yagu, *bedclothes.*
yahari, *also.*
yakedo, *a burn.*
yakeru (2), *to burn (intr).*
yakimochi, *jealously.*
yaki-mono, *earthenware.*
yaki-pan, *toast.*
yaku, *to burn (tr) ; to bake, roast, toast.*
yaku, *usefulness ; service.*
yakujō, *a contract.*
yakujō suru, *to make a contract.*
yakunin, *an official.*
yakŭsha, *actor.* [*promise.*
yakŭsoku, *an agreement ; a*
yakŭsoku suru, *to agree ; to promise.*
yakwai, *an evening party.*
yama, *hill, mountain.*
yameru (2), *to put an end to.*
yamome, *widow.*
yaoya, *green-grocer.*

yaru, *to give ; to send.*
yasai (-mono), *vegetables.*
yasashii, *gentle ; easy.*
yaseru (2), *to grow thin.*
yaseta, *thin.*
yasete iru, *to be thin.*
yashoku (*late*) *dinner ; supper.*
yasui, *easy ; cheap.*
yasumi-bi, *a holiday.*
yatoi-nin, *employee.*
yatou, *to engage, hire.*
yatte shimau, *to give away.*
yawarakai ; yawaraka na, *soft.*
yo, *the night; the world.*
yo-ake, *day-break.*
yobi dasu, *to summon.*
yobi-kaesu, *to recall.*
yobō, *precaution.*
yobu, *to call.*
yohodo, *a lot, plenty, very.*
yoi, *good ; handsome.*
yōi (na), *easy.*
yōji, *tooth-brush.*
yokei, *superfluity,* (*with neg.*) *not very, not much.*
yōki, *the weather.*
yomeru (2), *to read* (*intr.*).*
yomi-yasui, *legible.*
yomu, *to read* (*tr.*).
yo-naka, *midnight.*
yo ni iru, *to become dark.*
yoppite, *all night long.*
yorokobi, *pleasure, joy.*
yorokobu, *to rejoice.*
Yōroppa, *Europe.*
yoroshii, *good.*
yoru, *the night.*
yoru, *to rely; lean on; depend.*
yoru, *to select ; to assemble.*
yoseru (2), *to collect* (*tr*).
yoso, *elsewhere.*
yosu, *to abstain from ; leave off ; omit ; put an end to.*
yotte, *for that reason, owing to that.*
yowai, *weak.*
yōyaku ; yōyō, *at last ; with difficulty ; barely.*
yu, *hot water : a bath.*
yūbe, *yesterday evening.*
yubi, *toe ; finger.*
yūbin, *the post* (*for letters &c.*).
yūbin kaiite, *postage-stamp.*
yūbin-kawase, *post-office-order.*
yūbin-kyoku, *post office.*
yubi-nuki, *thimble.*
yūbin-zei, *postage.*
yue ni, *therefore.*
yūgata, *dusk ; evening.*
yuge, *steam.*
yūgen-sekinin-kwaisha, *Limited Company.*
yuka, *the floor.*
yuki, *snow.*
yukkuri, *slowly ; leisurely*
yūkyō, *pleasure.*
yume, *dream.*
yume wo miru, *to dream.*
yūmeshi, (*late*) *dinner ; supper.*
yunyū shoshiki, *import forms.*
yureru (2), *to shake* (*intr*).
yurui, *loose.*
yurusu, *to grant ; permit.*
yushutsu, *export* (*noun*).
yushutsu menjō, *export permit.*
yushutsu shoshiki, *export form* or *blank.*

* As in "this poem reads well" (v. footnote, p. 141).

yushutsu suru, *to export.*
yuu, *to do (bind up) the hair.*
yuzu, *lemon.*

Zannen, *regret (for own sake).*
zannen-garu, *to regret.*
zappi, *petty expenses.*
zashĭki, *a room.*
zasshi, *magazine; review.*
zei, *impost, tariff.*
zeikwan, *custom-house.*
zen, *virtue.*
zeni, *coppers; coin.*
zenryō (na), *good, moral, virtuous.*
zōkin, *a duster.*
zoku na, *low, vulgar.*
zonjiru (2), *to know.*
zonji-yori, *an opinion.*
zubon, *trousers.*
zuibun, *much, a great deal; very; pretty (adv).*
zutsū, *headache.*
zutsū ga suru, *to have headache.*
zutto, *quite; straight; much, a great deal.*

English-Japanese.

NOTE.—Even in so short a Vocabulary as the following it has occasionally been found impossible to supply *exact* equivalents for the English words; but those given will prove to be generally intelligible throughout Japan.

Able (can), *dekiru.*
about (approximately), *kurai* [(*gurai*) *hodo.*
above, *no ue.*
absence, *rusu.*
absent, to be, *rusu da ; inai.*
absurd, *bakarashii ; tonde-monai.*
accept, to, *ukeru.*
according to, *ni yotte.*
account (invoice, &c.), *kanjō.*
acknowledge (admit), to, *shōchi suru.*
acknowledge (confess), to, *hakujo suru.*
acquire (obtain), to, *eru.*
across, *no mukō ni.*
add to, *kuwaeru ; awaseru.*
address (written), *tokoro-gaki ;* (on envelope, &c.), *uwa-gaki.*
admit(allow to enter), to, *ireru.*
advance (go forward), to, *susumu.*
advance (progress), to, *shimpo* [*suru.*
advantage, *toku ; rieki.*
advertisement, *kōkoku ;* (in newspaper) *hĭki-fuda.*
afraid, *kowai.*
after, *no nochi ni.*
afternoon, *hiru-sugi.*
afterwards, *nochi ni.*
again, *mata.*
agent, *dairi-nin.*
ago, *mae.*
air (atmosphere), *kūki.*
alive, to be, *ikite iru.*
all, *nokorazu ; mina.*
allow, to, *yurusu.*
almost, *hotondo.*
alone, *hĭtori.*
already, *mohaya ; sude ni.*
also, *mo, yahari.*
always, *itsudemo.*
America, *America.*
among, *no uchi ni.*
amuse one's-self, to, *asobu.*
amusing, *omoshiroi.*
ancestor, *senzo.*
angry, to be, *hara wo tateru ; rippuku suru.*
another, *hoka no ; mō hĭtotsŭ.*
answer (noun), *henji ; hentō.*
answer, to, *hentō suru; kotaeru.*
anxious, to be, *shimpai suru.*
anybody, *dare de mo.*
anyhow, *dō de mo.*
anything, *nan de mo.*
any time, *itsu de mo.*
anywhere, *doko de mo.*
apple, *ringo.*
April, *shi-gwatsu.*
arm (of body), *ude ; te.*
around, *no mawari ni.*
arrange (put in order), to, [*soroeru.*
arrival, *tōchaku.*
arrive, to, *tōchaku suru.*

article (object), *shinamono.*
artizan, *shokunin.*
ashamed, to be, *haji wo kaku.*
ashes, *hai.*
ask, to, *kiku ; tou.*
assist, to, *tetsudau.*
assistance, *shūsen.*
at, *ni.*
attention, to pay, *ki wo tsŭkeru.*
attorney (lawyer), *daigen-nin.*
attorney, "power of," *dairi-nin-jō.*
auction, *seri-uri.*
August, *hachi-gwatsu.*
aunt, *oba.*
autumn, *aki.*
awkward, *heta (na).*

Baby, *akambo.*
back (of body), *senaka.*
bad, *warui.*
bag, *fŭkuro.*
baggage, *nimotsu.*
bake, to, *yaku.*
baker, *pan-ya.*
ball (toy), *mari ; tama.*
bamboo, *take.*
band (musicians), *gakŭtai.*
bank (establishment), *ginkō.*
banker, *ginkō-sha.*
bank-note, *ginkō-shihei.*
bankrupt, a, *hasan-nin.*
bankrupt, to become, *shindai-kagiri ni naru.*
barber, *kami-yui.*
bargain, to, *negiru.*
bark (of tree), *kawa.*
bark, to, *hoeru.*
barrel (cask), *taru.*
barrel (gun), *teppō no tsutsu.*
basin (small), *domburi.*
basin (slop-), *koboshi.*
basin (wash-), *tarai.*
bath *furo.*
bath-room, *furo-ba.*
bath-tub, *furo-oke.*
beach (sea), *umibe ; hamabe.*
beans, *mame.*
beans (broad), *sora-mame.*
beans (haricot), *daidzu.*
beans (French), *engin-mame.*
beard, *hige.*
beat, to, *butsu* (more polite, *utsu*).
beautiful, *kirei (na); utsŭkushii; migoto (na).*
because, *kara.*
become, to, *naru.*
bed, *nedai ; nedoko.*
bed-clothes, *fŭton ; yagu.*
bedroom, *nema ; nebeya.*
bee, *hachi.*
beef, *ushi ; gyūniku.*
beefsteak, *bifu-teki.*
beer, *biiru.*
before, *saki ; no mae ni.*
beggar. *kojiki.*
begin, to (*tr.*), *hajimeru.*
begin, to (*intr.*), *hajimaru.*
behind, *no ura ni ; no ushiro ni.*
believe, to, *shinjiru ; omou.*
bell, *kane.*
below, *shita.*
belt (girdle), *obi.*
bend, to (*tr.*), *mageru.*
bend, to (*intr.*), *magaru.*
beneath, *no shĭta ni.*
berth (on ship), *ne-doko.*
besides, *no hoka ni.*
between, *o aida ni.*
beyond, *no mukō ni ; no saki ni.*
big, *ōkii ; ōki (na).*
bill (account), *kanjō.*
bill of exchange, *kawase-tegata.*
bill of fare, *kondate.*

bill-of-lading, *funadzumi-*
bird, *tori*. [*shōsho*.
bit (small quantity), *kire*; *sŭkoshi*; *kake*.
bite, to, *kui-tsŭku*; *kamu*.
bitter, *nigai*.
black, *kuroi*.
blind, *mekura* (*no*).
blood, *chi*.
blotting-paper, *oshi-gami*.
blow, to, *fūku*. [(*no*).
blue, *ai*; *aoi*; *asagi*; *sora-iro*
boarding-house, *geshiku-ya*.
boat, *fune*, *kobune*.
body, *karada*.
boil, to, (water), *wakasu*.
boil, to, (food), *niru*.
boiling water, *ni-tatta yu*.
bone, *hone*.
book, *hon*; *shomotsu*.
booking-office, *kippu no uridokoro*.
bookseller, *hon-ya*.
boot, *kutsu*.
borrow, to, *kariru*.
both, *dore mo*; *ryōhō*.
bottle, *tokkuri*.
bottom, *shĭta* (*no hō*).
bow, to, *o jigi wo suru*.
box, *hako*.
boy, *musŭko*; *otoko no ko*.
branch, *eda*.
brass, *shinchū*.
bread, *pan*.
break, to (*tr.*), *kowasu*; *oru*.
break, to (*intr.*), *kowareru*;
breakfast, *asa-han*. [*oreru*.
brick, *renga*.
bride, (*hana-*) *yome*.
bridegroom, (*hana-*) *muko*.
bridge, *hashi*.

bridle, *tazuna*. [*kuru*.
bring, to, (an object), *motte*
bring, to (a person), *tsurete*
broad, *hiroi*. [*kuru*.
broker, *nakagai*; (low Yokohama broker, *tombi*).
bronze, *karakane*.
brother (elder), *ani*.
brother (younger), *otōto*.
brown, *akai*; *kuri-iro* (*no*).
build, to, *tateru*.
building (edifice), *tate-mono*.
bulky, *kasabatta*.
Bund (street facing sea), *kaigan-dōri*. [*hira-ya*.
bungalow,(one-storied house),
business, *shōbai*; *yō*; *yōmuki*.
busy, *isogashii*.
butcher, *niku-ya*.
butter, *bata*.
button, *botan*.
button-hole, *botan no ana*.
buy, to, *kau*.
by, *ni*; *de*.

Cabbage, *kabeji*.
cake, *kwashi*.
calculate, to, *kanjō suru*.
call, to, *yobu*.
call, to, (waken), *okosu*.
can (able), *dekiru*.
canal, *hori*.
candle, *rōsoku*.
candlestick, *te-shoku*.
capital (funds), *shihon*; *motode*.
capital (city), *miyako*.
card playing), *karuta*.
card (visiting), *nafuda*; *meishi*.
care, to take, *ki wo tsŭkeru*.
carpenter, *daiku*.
carpet, *shĭki-mono*.

carriage, *basha.*
carry, to, *hakobu.*
carve, to, (meat), *niku wo* [*kiri-dasu.*
cash (money), *genkin.*
cashier, *kwaikei-kata.*
cat, *neko.*
catch, to, *tsŭkamaeru.*
cauliflower, *kōre-furaoru.*
cause, *gen-in ; wake.*
ceiling, *tenjō.*
certain, *tashĭka* (*na*).
certainly (without doubt), [*mochiron.*
certificate, *shōsho.*
Chamber-of-Commerce, *Shōgyō-kwaigi-sho.*
chain, *kŭsari.*
chair, *isu.*
change, to, (*tr.*), *kaeru ; tori-* [*kaeru.*
change, to, (*intr.*), *kawaru.*
change, (a), *henkwa ; kawari* ; (money) *tsuri.*
character (nature), *seishitsu.*
charge (price), *nedan.*
cheap, *yasui.*
cheat, to, *damasu.*
cheeks, *hōpeta ; hō.*
chemist (apothecary), *kusuri-* [*ya.*
cheque (bank-), *kogitte.*
cherry-tree, *sakura.*
chest (of body), *mune.*
chicken, *niwa-tori.*
child, *ko ; kodomo.*
chin, *ago.*
China, *Shina ; Kara.*
choose, to, *erabu.*
cigar, *ha-maki* (*tabako*).
cigarette, *kami-maki-tabako.*
circumstance, *koto ; baai ; kotogara.*
civilisation, *bummei; kaikwa.*
class (first), *jōtō.*
class (second), *chūtō.*
class (third), *katō.*
clean, *kirei* (*na*).
clever, *rikō* (*na*).
climb, to, *noboru.*
clock, *tokei.*
cloth (woollen), *rasha.*
clothes, *kimono ; ifŭku.*
cloud, *kumo.*
club (association), *kurabu.*
coal, *sekitan.*
coat, *uwagi.*
cod (-fish), *tara.*
coffee, *kahe ; kōhi.*
cold (of weather), *samui ;* (to the touch), *tsumetai.*
cold, to catch, *kaze wo hĭku.*
collar, *eri ;* (dog-), *kubi-wa.*
collect (*tr.*), *yoseru ; atsumeru.*
collect (*intr.*), *tamaru ;* [*atsumaru.*
college, *gakkō.*
colour, *iro.*
comb, *kŭshi.*
come, to, *kuru.*
come in, to, *hairu.*
common (ordinary), *nami no.*
company (firm), *kwaisha ; shōkwai.*
company (visitors), *o-kyaku.*
confusion, *ō-sawagi; konzatsu.*
consent, to, *shōchi suru.*
consul, *ryōji.*
consulate, *ryōji-kwan.*
consult, to, *sōdan suru.*
contained, to be, *haitte iru.*
contented, to be, *manzoku suru.*
contract, to make a, *yakujō* [*suru.*
contract, a, *yakujō.*
convenient, *tsugō no yoi ; benri* (*na*).
cool, *suzushii.*

copper, *akagane.*
corkscrew, *sen-nuki.*
corn, *mugi ; ko-mugi.*
corner, *kado.*
cotton, *momen.*
cough, to, *seki ga deru.*
count, to, *kazoeru.* [*inaka.*
country (as opp. to town),
course, of, *mochiron; moto yori.*
cow, (*me-*)*ushi.*
cream, *kuriimu.*
creditor, *kashi-nushi.*
crooked, to be, *magatte iru.*
crowd, *ōzei.*
cry, to, *naku.*
cucumber, *ki-uri.*
cup, *chawan.*
cupboard, *todana.*
curtain, *mado-kake.*
cushion, *zabuton.*
custom, *shĭ-kitari ; fūkoku.*
customer, *tokui ; kyaku.*
custom-house, *zeikwan.*
cut, to, *kiru.*

Daily, *mainichi.*
damage (injury), *kizu.*
damage (loss), *son.*
damp, *shimeppoi.*
dance, to, *odoru.* [*abunai.*
dangerous, *kennon* (*na*) ;
dark, *kurai.*
date, *gwappi; hizuke; tsŭki-hi.*
daughter, *mŭsume.*
dawn, *yo-ake.*
day, *hi.*
day after to-morrow, *myōgo-nichi;* (less polite), *asatte.*
day before yesterday, *issakujitsu ;* (less polite), *ototoi.*
day-time, *hiru.*

dead, to be, *shinde iru.*
deaf, *tsunbō* (*no*).
deal in, to, *akinai suru.*
dear (expensive), *takai.*
debt, *shakkin.*
debtor, *kari-nushi.*
December, *jū-ni-gwatsu.*
decide, to, *kimeru; kettei suru.*
deduct, to, *sashi-hiku.*
deduction (price), *ne-beki.*
deep, *fūkai.*
dentist, *ha-isha.*
depend, to, *yoru; kwankei suru.*
dictionary, *jibiki ; jisho.*
die, to, *shinuru.*
different, *chigatta ; betsu* (*no*).
difficult, *muzukashii.*
dig, to, *horu.*
dining-room, *shokudō ; shokuma.* [*meshi.*
dinner (late), *yūshoku ; bam-*
dirty, *kitanai ; kitanarashii.*
dirty, to, *yosogu ; dainashi ni suru.*
disappear, to, *mienaku naru.*
discount, *wari-bike.*
discount, to, *wari-biki wo suru.*
discount (*noun*), *wari-biki.*
dish, *ōzara.*
dislike, to, *kirau.*
dismiss, to, *hima wo yaru.*
dispose of (sell), to, *uru.*
distance, *michi-nori ; risū.*
distant, *empō* (*na*) ; *tōi.*
dividend (on shares), *hai-tō-kin.*
do, to, *suru ; nasu ; itasu.*
doctor, *isha.*
document, *kaki-tsŭke.*
dog, *inu.*
door, *to.*

doubt (a), *utagai ; ginen.*
doubt, to, *fŭshin ni omou ; utagau.*
down, *shĭta (ye).*
downstairs, *shĭta.*
draft (bill), *kawase-tegata.*
draught (current of air), *sŭkima-kaze.*
drawer, *hĭki-dashi.*
drawing-room, *kyakuma.*
dream, to, *yume wo miru.*
drink, to, *nomu.*
drive (in a vehicle), *noru.*
driver, *gyosha.*
drop (globule), *shizuku; teki.*
drop, to, (*tr.*), *otosu.*
drop, to, (*intr.*), *ochiru.*
dry, to, (*tr.*), *hosu.*
dry, to be, *kawaite iru.*
duck, *ahiru.*
dull (of weather), *kumotta ; uttōshii.*
dust (which settles), *gomi.*
dust (raised by wind), *hokori.*
duster, *zōkin.*
duty, (impost), *zei.*
duty, (obligation), *gimu.*
duty (ad valorem), *jūkazei.*
duty-free, *mu-zei.*
dye, to, *someru.*

Ear, *mimi.*
early, *hayai.*
earth, *tsŭchi.*
earthenware, *yaki-mono.*
east, *higashi.*
easy, *yasashii ; zōsa mo nai.*
eat, to, *taberu.*
egg, *tamago.*
elbow, *hiji.*
electricity, *denki.*
electric-light, *denki-tō.*
employ (hire), to, *yatou.*
employee, *yatoi-nin.*
empty, *kara (na).*
end, *owari ; shimai.*
endorse, to, *uragaki wo suru.*
endorsement, *uragaki.*
engage, to, *tanomu ;* (less polite), *yatou.*
England, *Igirisu ; Eikoku.*
English (language), *Igirisu no kotoba ; Eigo.*
enough, to be, *tariru.*
envelope, *jō-bukuro.*
Europe, *Yōroppa ; Seiyō.*
even (*adv.*), *sura ; sae ; de mo*
even (smooth), *taira (na).*
evening, *yūgata ; ban.*
everybody, *dare de mo.*
every day, *mainichi.*
every time, *maido.*
everywhere, *doko de mo ; hōbō.*
examine (enquire into), *tadasu ; aratameru ; shiraberu.*
except, *no hoka ni.*
exchange, to, *tori-kaeru.*
exchange money, to, *ryōgae suru.*
expense, *nyūhi.*
expense, *uyūyō ; nyūhi.*
expenses, petty, *zappi.*
expenses, travelling, *ryokō-hı.*
explain, to, *toki-akasu.*
export (*n.*), *yushutsu.*
export form (blank), *yushutsu shoshiki.*
export permit, *yushutsu menjō.*
export, to, *yushutsu suru.*
express office (parcels), *unsō-ten.*
express (train), *kyūkō resha.*
eye (organ of sight), *me.*
eye (of needle), *medo.*

Face, *kao*.
fail, to, *sokonau; hazureru*.
fail, without, *kitto; machigai naku*.
faint, to, *me wo mawasu; [kizetzu suru*.
fair, a, *ichi; ennichi*.
fall, to, *ochiru*.
false, *hontō de nai; uso (no)*.
famous, *nadakai*.
far, *tōi; empō (na)*.
fare (charge), *chinsen*.
farmer, *hyakŭshō*.
fashion, *hayari; ryōkō*.
fast (speedy), *hayai*.
fat, to be, *fŭtotte iru*.
feast, *gochisō*.
feather, *hane*.
February, *ni-gwatsu*.
feel, to, *kanjiru; oboeru*.
female, *mesu*.
festival, *matsuri*.
fetch, to, *totte kuru*.
fever, *netsubyo*.
figure (number), *kazu-ji*.
figure (form), *katachi*.
fill, to, *ippai ni suru*.
find, to, *mi-ataru; mi-dasu; mi-tsŭkeru*.
fine (in quality), *yoi; rippa [na)*.
fine (slender), *hosoi*.
fine (minute), *komaki*.
fine (beautiful, etc.), *kirei na*.
finger, *yubi*.
finger (fore-), *hito-sashi-yubi*.
finger (middle-), *naka-yubi*.
finger (ring-), *kusuri-yubi*.
finger (little-), *ko-yubi*.
finish, to, *shimau*.
fire (flame), *hi*.
fire (conflagration), *kwaji*.
fire insurance, *kwa-sai hoken*.
firewood, *maki*.
first-rate, *ichiban yoi*.
fish [for food (dead)], *sakana*.
fish (alive), *uwo*.
fish-hook, *tsuri-bari*.
fishing-line, *tsuri-ito*.
fishing-rod, *tsuri-zao*.
fishmonger, *sakana-ya*.
fish, to, *uwo wo tsuru*; (with net), *ami wo utsu*.
flame, *hi; honō*.
flat, *taira (na); hirattai*.
flesh, *niku*.
floor, *yuka*.
floor (first-), *ni-kai*.
floor (second-), *san-kai*.
floor (ground-), *shita*.
flour, *kona; udonko*.
flow, to, *nagareru*.
flower, *hana*.
flower-pot, *ueki-bachi*.
flower-vase, *hana-ike*.
fly, to, *tobu*.
fly (insect), *hai*.
follow, to, *tsuite iku*.
food, *tabemono; shokumotsu*.
foolish, *bakarashii*.
foolishness, *bakageta koto*.
foot, *ashi*.
for, *no tame ni*.
forbid, to, *kinjiru*.
forehead, *hĭtai*.
foreign, *gwaikoku (no)*.
foreigner, *ijin; gwaikokujin*.
forget, to, *wasureru*.
forgive, to, *yurusu*.
fork (for eating), *nikŭ-sashi*.
fowl, *tori*.
France, *Fŭransu; Futsŭkoku*.
free, *jiyū (na)*.
freight (goods), *nimotsŭ*.

Frenchman, *Furansu-jin.*
frequently, *tabi-tabi.*
fresh (of eggs), *umi-tate.*
fresh (new), *atarashii ; shinki* [*na.*
fresh (cool), *suzushii.*
Friday, *kin-yobi.*
friend, *hōyū ; tomodachi.*
frightful, *osoroshii.*
from, *yori ; kara.*
front, *omote.*
fruit (growing), (*ki no*) *mi.*
fruit (for eating), *mizu-gwashi.*
fry, to, *ageru.*
full, *ippai* (*na*)
funny, *omoshiroi ; okashii.*
furniture, *kazai ; dōgu.*

Gain, to, *mōkeru.*
gain (*noun*), *mōke.*
game, a, *asobi.*
garden, *niwa.*
gardener, *ueki-ya.*
gate, *mon.*
gateway, *kado-guchi.*
general (customary), *ippan no ; futsū no.*
Germany, *Doitsu.*
get (receive), to, *morau.*
get in, to, *hairu.*
get out, to, *deru.*
get up, to, (rise), *okiru.*
girl, *mŭsume ; onna no ko.*
give, to, *yaru.*
give away, to, *yatte shimau.*
give back, to, *kaesu.*
give in, to, *makeru.*
give up, to, (cease), *yosu.*
glad, *ureshii.*
glass (the substance), *giyaman.*
glass (a), *koppu.*
glove, *te-bukuro.*
go, to, *iku.*
go away, to, *itte shimau ; kaeru.*
go down, to, *kudaru ; oriru.*
go in, to, *hairu.*
go out, to, *deru.*
go up, to, *noboru.*
gold, *kin.*
good, *yoroshii ; ii ; yoi.*
good (to eat), *ŭmai.*
goodbye, *sayōnara.*
goods, *shina-mono.*
gradually, *dan-dan.*
grand (splendid), *rippa* (*na*).
grandchild, *mago.*
grandfather, *ojiisan.*
grandmother, *obāsan.*
grass (turf), *shiba.*
gravy, *niku no shiru.*
grease, *abura.*
Great Britain, *Dai-Buritania.*
green, *midori ; aoi ; moegi.*
green-grocer, *yaoya.*
greens (vegetables), *aomono.*
grey, *hai-iro* (*no*) ; *nezumi-iro* (*no*).
grocer, *tōbutsu-ya.*
groom, *bettō.*
gross amount, *sō-kei.*
gross-weight, *sō-mekata.*
guarantee (person), *hoshō-nin.*
guarantee (money), *hoshō-ryō.*
guard, to, *mamoru.*
guard (of train), *sha-chō.*
guest, *kyaku.*
guide, *annai* (*no mono*).
gun, *teppō.*
gunpowder, *kwayaku.*
gunsmith, *teppō-kaji.*

Hair, *ke*; (of the head), *kami*; *kami no ke*.
hairdresser, *kami-yui*.
hairpin, *kanzashi*.
half, *han*; *hambun*.
hammer, *kanadzuchi*.
hammer, to, *kanadzuchi de utsu*.
hand, *te*.
handkerchief, *hankechi*; *hanafŭki*.
handle (of tool), *e*.
handle, (of teapot, basket, &c.), *te*.
handle (of a drawer), *totte*.
hang, to (*tr.*), *tsuru*; *kakeru*; *tsuri-ageru*.
hang, to (*intr.*), *kakaru*.
hard (solid), *katai*.
hard (difficult), *mudzukashii*.
hardware, *kanamono*.
hat, *bōshi*; *shappo*.
have, to, *motsu*; *motte iru*.
he, *ano otoko*; *ano hĭto*.
head, *atama*.
head (manager of a Company), *shihai-nin*.
head (principal of firm), *kwanshu*.
headache, *zutsū*.
healthy, *tassha na*.
hear, to, *kiku*.
heart, *kokoro*.
heat, *danki*; *atsŭsa*.
heat, to, *atatameru*.
heavy, *omoi*, *omotai*.
heel, *kakato*.
help, to, *sewa wo suru*; *tetsudau*.
hemp, *asa*.
hen, *mendori*.
here, *koko*; *kochi* (*ra*).
herring, *nishin*.
hesitate, to, *chū-chū suru*.
hiccough, *shakuri*.
hide, to, *kakusu*.
hide, to, one's-self, *kakureru*.
hide (skin), *kawa*.
hide (raw-), *nama-gawa*.
hide (tanned-), *nameshi-gawa*.
high (of both height and price), *takai*.
high, *takai*.
hill, *yama*; (rise in road), *saka*.
hinge, *chō-tsugai*.
hire, to (a servant), *yatou*.
hire, to (a house, &c.), *kariru*.
hit, to, *butsŭ*.
hitherto, *kore made*; *ima made*.
hold, to, (retain, possess) *motsu*; *te ni motsu*.
hold, to, (contain), *hairu*.
hole, *ana*.
holiday, *kyūjitsu*; *yasumi-bi*.
home, *uchi* (dwelling); *kuni*, country.
honest, *shōjiki* (*na*).
horse, *ŭma* (pron., *'m-ma*).
hospital, *byōin*.
host (master), *aruji*.
hot (as mustard), *karai*.
hot (not cold), *atsui*.
hotel, *yadoya*.
hotel-keeper, *yadoya no teishu*.
hour, *jikan*; *toki*.
house-rent, *ya-chin*.
house, *uchi*; *ie*; *taku*.
how? *ikaga?* *dō?* *dō shĭte?*
how long? *itsu made?*
how many? *iku mai?* *ikutsu?*
how often? *iku tabi?*
hungry, to be, *haraga heru*; *o naka ga sŭku*.
hurry, to be in a, *isogu*.
hurt, to (*intr.*), *itamu*.
hurt one's-self, to, *kega wo suru*.

Ice, *kōri*.
idle, to be, *namakete iru*.
ignorant of (unacquainted with), *fu-annai*.
ignorant (not learned), *muyaku na*.
ill (in bad health), *byōki* (*na*).
illness, *yamai; byōki*.
immediately, *sassoku; sugu* [*ni*.
impertinence, *burei; shitsurei*.
import, to, *yunyū suru*.
import forms, *yunyū shoshiki*.
impossible, *dekinai*.
in, *ni*.
included, to be, *haitte iru*.
income, *sainyū*.
income-tax, *shotoku-zei*.
inconvenient, *futsugō* (*na*.); *fuben* (*na*.); *tsugō no*.
incorrect, *machigatta*.
indemnity, *shōkin*.
India, *Indo; Tenjiku*.
indeed, *jitsu ni*.
indeed! *naruhodo!*
indoors, *ie no uchi*.
infringe (regulations), to, *jōrei ni hansoku suru*.
ink (Indian), *sumi*.
ink-stand, *inki-tsubo*.
inn, *yadoya*.
insect, *mushi*.
inside, *ni; no naka*.
inside-out, *uragaeshi*.
inspect, to, *kensu suru; kembun suru*.
inspector, *kensa-nin*.
instalment, *wari-barai*.
instalment (yearly), *nempu*.
instalment (monthly), *geppu*.
instead, *no kawari ni*.
interest (on money), *ri-soku*.
interesting, *omoshiroi*.
interfere, to, *jama suru*.
interpret, to, *tsūben wo suru*.
interpreter, *tsūben; tsūji*.
into, *ni; no naka ye*.
introduction, letter of, *shōkwai-jō*.
invalid, *byōnin*.
inventory, *tana-oroshi-hyō*.
investigate, to, *tori-shiraberu*.
invite, to, *maneku*.
invoice, *okuri-jō*.
I.O.U., *shakuyō-oboe*.
iron, *tetsu*.
iron (bar-), *sao-tetsu*.
iron (cast-), *nabe-gane*.
iron (rod-), *bōtetsu*.
iron (sheet-), *nobe-tetsu*.
iron (smoothing-), *hinoshi*.
iron (wrought), *juku tetsū*.
iron-foundry, *sei-tetsu-jo*.

Jam (preserves), *jami*.
January, *shō-gwatsu*.
Japan, *Nippon; Nihon* [(*politer*).
jar, a, *tsubo*.
jealousy, *netami; yakimochi*.
jeweller, *kazariya*.
jinrikisha-apron, *mae-kake*.
jinrikisha-hood, *horo*.
jinrikisha-seat, *kekomi*.
join, to (*tr*.), *tsugu; awaseru*.
joiner, *sashimono-ya*.
Jointstock Bank, *gōhon-ginkō*.
Jointstock Company, *gōhon-kwaisha*.
joke, *jōdan*.
journal (office account book), *shiwaketchō*.
journal (diary), *nikki*.
journey, *ryokō*.
journey, to, *ryokō suru*.

jug, *mizu-tsugi.*
July, *shĭchi-gwatsu.*
junction (railway), *tetsudō no ren-raku-eki.*
June, *roku-gwatsu.*
just (exactly), *chōdo.*
just (equitable), *tadashii* ; *kōhei na.*

Keep, to, (things), *tamotsu ; motte iru.*
keep, to (animals as pets), [*katte oku.*
kettle, *tetsubin.*
key, *kagi.*
key-hole, *kagi-hana.*
kick, to, *keru.*
kill, to, *korosu.*
kind (species), *yō ; shurui.*
kind (good-natured), *shinsetsu* [*na*).
kitchen, *dai-dokoro ; katte.*
knee, *hiza.*
knife, *hōchō.*
knock, to, *tataku.*
knock down, to, *buchi-taosu.*
know, to, *shiru ; shitte iru.*

Label (tag), *efu.*
label, to, *fuda wo tsukeru.*
lace (of boot), *himo.*
lace (needlework), *reisŭ.*
lacquer, *urushi.*
lacquer-ware, *nuri-mono.*
lady, *okŭsan.*
lame, *chimba ; bikko.*
lamp, *rampu.*
lamp-wick, *rampu no shin.*
land, *riku ; oka.*
land, to (*tr.*), *riku-age suru.*
land, to (*intr.*), *jōriku suru.*
landlord (of ground), *ji-nushi.*
landlord (of hotel, inn), *teishiŭ.*
landlord (of house), *iye-nushi.*
language, *kotoba.*
lantern, *chōchin.*
last, at, *yōyaku ; tsui ni.*
last, the, *ato-no ; sue no.**
last, to, *motsu.*
late, *osoi.*
laugh, to, *warau.*
law, *hōritsu ; kisoku.*
lawyer, *daigen-nin.*
lazy, to be, *namakeru.*
lead, to, *hĭku ; annai suru.*
lead (metal), *namari.*
lead-pencil, *empitsu.*
leaf (of plant), *ha.*
learn, to, *manabu ; narau.*
lease, *tana-ukesho.*
least, at, *sŭkunakute mo.*
leather, *kawa.*
leave off, to, (cease), *yosu ; yameru.*
leave (departure), *tatsu.*
leave (of absence), *hima.*
leave out, to, *habuku ; yosu.*
ledger, *dai-chō.*
lecture, *enzetsu.*
left (-hand), *hidari.*
leg, *ashi.*
legible, *yomi-yasui.*
lemon, *yuzu.*
lemonade, *ramune.*
lend, to, *kasu.*
length, *take ; nagasa.*
let, to, (house), *kasu.*
let, to, (permit), *saseru ; yurusu.*
letter (missive), *tegami.*
letter (of alphabet), *moji.*
letter of credit, *ginkō no shinyō-hoshō-jō.*

* Both approximate only.

letter-paper, *tegami-no-kami.*
lettuce, *rettasŭ.*
liability, *sekinin.*
license (permit), *menjo.*
lid, *fūta.*
lie down, to, *neru.*
lie, to (tell falsehoods), *uso wo iu.*
life, *inochi.*
lift, to, *mochi-ageru.*
light, a, *hĭkari; akari.*
light (colour), *usui-iro.*
light (in weight), *karui.*
light (not dark), *akarui.*
lightning, *inabikari.*
light, to, (a fire), *hi wo taku.*
light, to, (a lamp), *rampu wo tsŭkeru.*
like, to, *konomu; sŭki.*
lilac, *murasaki (no).*
lily, *yuri.*
lime, *ishi-bai.*
Limited Company, *yūgen-sekinin-kwaisha.*
line, *suji.*
lion, *shishi.*
lips, *kuchibiru.*
list, *mokuroku.*
list (catalogue), *shina-gaki.*
little, a, *sŭkoshi.*
little (small), *chiisa (na); chiisai.*
live, to, (reside), *sumau.*
lively, *nigiyaka (na).*
loan, a, *kashi-kin.*
lobster, *kuruma-ebi.*
lock, to, *jō wo orosu.*
lock (on box, door, &c.), *jōmae.*
locksmith, *jōmae-ya.*
lonely, *sabishii.*
long, *nagai.*
look at, to, *miru.*
look for, to, *sagasu.*
looking-glass, *kagami.*
loose, *yurui.*
lose, to, (an article), *nakusu; ushinau.*
lose, to (not to win), *makeru.*
loss (money), *son; sonshitsu.*
loud, *takai; ōki (na).*
low, *hĭkui.*
lucky, *un no yoi.*
luggage, *nimotsu.*
luggage-van (on railway), *kisha no ni-guruma.*
luncheon, *hiru-gozen.*

Mackerel, *saba.*
maid-servant, *gejo;* (more polite), *jochū.*
make, to, *koshiraeru.*
male, *osu.*
man, *otoko.*
manage, to, *tori-atsŭkau.*
manager (chief clerk), *bantō.*
manager (of an establishment), *shihai-nin.*
manufactory, *seizo-ba.*
manufacture, to, *seizō-suru.*
manufacturer, *seizō-nin.*
many, *ōku no; ōi.*
marble (*noun*), *rōseki.*
March, *san-gwatsu.*
mark, *shirushi; ato.*
market, *ichiba.*
market-price, *sōba.*
marine (*adj.*), *kaijō-no.*
marine insurance, *kaijō-hoken.*
master (of the house), *aruji.*
mat, *tatami.*
match (for striking), *haya-tsŭkegi.*
May (the month), *go-gwatsu.*
meaning, *imi.*

meanwhile, *sono uchi.*
measure, to, *sumpō wo toru.*
meat, *niku.*
mechanic, *shoku-nin.*
medicine, *kŭsuri.*
meet, to, *au.*
meeting, a, *kwai*; *shūkwai.*
member (of an association), *kwai-in.*
memorandum, *oboe gaki.*
mend, to, *naosu*; *tsŭkurou.*
merchant, *akindo*; *shōnin.*
message, *kotozuke.*
messenger, *tsŭkai no mono.*
middle, *mannaka.*
midnight, *yonaka.*
milk, *chichi.*
mirror, *kagami.*
mist, *moya*; *kiri.*
mistake, *machigai.*
mix, to (*tr.*), *mazeru.*
mix, to (*intr.*), *mazaru.*
Monday, *getsuyōbi.*
money, *kane*; *kinsu.*
money (paper-), *shihei.*
money-changer, *ryō-gae-ya.*
month, *tsŭki.*
moon, *tsŭki.*
more, *motto.*
morning, *asa.*
mountain, *yama.*
mouth, *kŭchi.*
move, to (*tr.*), *ugokasu.*
move, to (*intr.*), *ugoku.*
much, *takŭsan.*
mud, *doro.*
muslin (*noun*), *men-sha.*
mustard, *karashi.*
mutton, *hitsuji-no-niku.*
mutton-chop, *hitsuji-no-choppu.*

Nail (of metal, &c.), *kugi.*
nail (finger-), *tsume.*
naked, *hadaka.*
napkin (serviette), *kŭchi-fuki.*
narrow, *semai.*
nasty (to taste), *mazui.*
near, *chikai.*
nearly, *mo sŭkoshi de.*
necessary, *hitsuyō na.*
neck, *nodo.*
needle, *hari*; *nui-bari.*
needlework, *nuimono.*
neighbour, *kinjo no hĭto.*
neighbourhood, *kimpen*; *kinjo.*
nephew, *oi.*
new, *atarashii*; *shinki* (*na*).
news, *shimbun.*
newspaper, *shimbunshi.*
next, *tsugi no.*
niece, *mei.*
night, *ban*; *yoru.*
noise, *oto.*
noisy, *sōzōshii.*
noon, *hiru.*
north, *kita.*
nose, *hana.*
notwithstanding, *ni kamawazu.*
November, *jū-ichi-gwatsu.*
number, *kazu.*
numerous, *ōi.*

Oak, *kashiwa*; *nara.*
object (aim), *mokuteki.*
object, to, *koshō wo iū.*
oblige (compel), to, *shiite saseru.*
obscure, *bon-yari shĭto.*
observe, to, *mi-ukeru*; *ki ga tsŭku.*
October, *jū-gwatsu.*
of, *no.*
offer, to, *susumeru.*
office, *jimusho*; *yakŭsho.*

official, *shikwan ; yakunin*
often, *tabi-tabi.*
oil, *abura.*
old (of things), *furui.*
old (of persons), *toshiyori* (*no*).
omit, to, *otosu.*
omnibus, *nori-ai basha.*
onion, *negi.*
only (*adv.*), *tada ; bakari.*
open, to (*tr.*), *akeru*
open, to be, *aite iru.*
opinion, *ryōken ; zonjiyori.*
opposite, *no mukō ni.*
order (arrangement), *jun ; junjo.*
order, to, *ii-tsŭkeru ; meijiru.*
other, *ato no ; hoka no.*
out, to go, *deru.*
out-of-doors; outside, *omote ; soto.*
over, *no ue ni.*
overcoat, *gwaitō.*
owner, *mochi-nushi.*

Pack, to, *ni-zukuri wo suru.*
package, *tsutsumi.*
pain, *itami.*
painful, *itai.*
paint, *penki.*
paint, to, (pictures), *egaku.*
painter, *ekaki.*
pale, *ao-zameta.*
paper, *kami.*
parasol, *higasa.*
parcel, *ko-zutsumi.*
parent, *oya.*
parsley, *seri.*
particulars, *kuwashii.*
partner (in a firm), *shain.*
party (pleasure), *kyakurai.*
passage (corridor), *rōka.*
passenger, *noi-kyaku.*
passport (*ryokō-*), *menjō.*
patient (invalid), *byōnin.*
patient, to be, *gaman suru.*
pattern, *moyō.*
pay, to, *harau.*
pay-day, *kanjō-bi.*
payee, *uketori-kata.*
payer, *harai-nin.*
payment, *harai.*
pear, *nashi.*
peas, *endō-mame.*
pen, *fude.*
pencil, *empitsu.*
penknife, *ko-gatana.*
pepper, *koshō.*
permit, to, *shōchi suru.*
person, *hĭto ; jin.*
perspiration, *ase.*
photograph, *shashin.*
photographic instruments, *shashin-kyō.*
photographer, *sha-shin-ya.*
physician, *isha.*
pick, to, *tsumu.*
pick up, to, *hirou.*
pickles, *tsŭke-mono.*
piece-goods, *tam-mono.*
pierce, to, *tsūki-tōsu.*
pig, *buta.*
pigeon, *hato.*
pill, *gwan-yaku.*
pillow, *makura.*
pin, *tome-bari ; hari.*
pink, *momo-iro no.*
pipe (for smoking), *kĭseru.*
place, *basho ; tokoro.*
plaice (fish), *karei.*
plank, *ita.*
plant, to, *ueru.*
plant (in general), *kŭsa.*
plant (in garden), *ueki.*
plate (dish), *sara.*

play, to, *asobu.*
play-bill, *bandzuke.*
pleasure, *tanoshimi.*
plenty, *jūbun.*
pocket, *kakŭshi; fŭtokoro.*
pocket-book, *kami-ire.*
pointed (sharp), *togatta.*
policeman, *junsa.*
police-station, *keisatsŭ-sho.*
polish, to, *migaku.*
polite, *teinei (na).*
poor, *bimbō (na).*
pork, *buta no niku.*
porter (railway-), *eki-fu.*
porter (light), *karuko.*
portmanteau, *kaban.*
post (letter), *yūbin.*
postage, *yūbin-zei.*
postage-stamp, *yūbin-gitte;*
post-card, *hagaki.* [*inshi.*
postman, *haitatsu-nin.*
post-office, *yūbin-kyoku.*
post-office-order, *yūbin-kawase.*
potato, *imo;* (sweet), *Satsuma-*
pour, to, *tsugu.* [*imo.*
powder, *ko; kona.*
praise, to, *homeru.*
premium (of insurance),
hōken-ryō. [*wo suru.*
prepare, to, *koshiraeru; shĭtaku*
present (gift), *shinjō-mono;*
okuri-mono; miyage.
pretty, *kirei (na); utsŭkushii.*
prevent, to, *samatageru;*
sasenai. [*atai; ne.*
price (cost, value), *nedan;*
prison, *rōya.*
probably, *tabun.*
profit, *rieki; mōke.*
programme (concert, &c.),
ban-dzuke.

promise, a, *yakusoku.*
promise, to, *yakŭsoku suru.*
proper, *sōtō (na); sōō (na).*
property, *mochimono; fudōsan.*
proportion, *wari-ai.*
provide, to, *sonaeru.*
pudding, *(o)kwashi.*
pull, to, *hĭku.* [*suru.*
punish, to, *bassuru; tsumi*
pupil, *deshi.*
purchase, *motomeru.*
pure (clear), *sumi-kitta.* [*na.*
pure (unadulterated), *junsui*
purple, *murasaki.*
purpose, on, *waza-waza.*
purse, *kane-ire; kinchaku.*
push, to, *osu.*
put, to, *oku; sueru.*
put away, to, *katazukeru.*
put in, to, *ireru.*
put off, to, *nobasu.*
put on, to (don), *kiru.*
put out, to (extinguish), *kesu.*
put up with, to, *koraeru.*

Quality (of goods), *hin-shitsŭ.*
quantity, *taka; kasa.*
quarrel, *kenkwa.*
queer, *kitai (na).*
question, *gimon; toi.*
quick, *hayai.*
quiet, *shizuka (na).*
quilt, *futon.*
quire (of paper), *jō.*
quite, *jūbun; mattaku.*

Rabbit, *usagi.*
radish, *aka-daiko.*
railroad, *tetsŭdō.*
railway carriage, *kisha.*
rain, *ame.*

raise, to, *ageru.*
rare, *mare (na).*
rascal, *berabō; waru-mono.*
rat, *nezumi.*
rather (otherwise), *kaette;*
(somewhat), *zuibun.*
raw, *nama (na).*
razor, *kamisuri.*
razor-strop, *togi-kawa.*
reach, to (*intr.*), *oyobu;*
read, to, *yomu.* [*todoku.*
ready, to be, *shĭtaku shĭte oru.*
ready money, *genkin.*
real, *hontō (no); makoto (no).*
reason (explanation), *wake;*
receipt, *uke-tori.* [*dōri.*
receipt-book, *uketori-chō.*
receive, to, *uke-toru.*
recently, *konaida.*
recommend, to, *susumeru.*
red, *akai.*
reduce in price, to, *makeru.*
reduction (in price), *ne-biki.*
refuse, to, *kotowaru.*
register (a letter), to, *kaki-tomeru.*
registered letter, *kaki-tomi tegami.*
relations (kinsmen), *shinrui.*
remain, to, *nokoru; amaru.*
remainder, *nokori.*
remember, to, *oboeru.*
remittance, *okuri-kin.*
repay, to, *henkyaku suru.*
rest, to, *yasumu.*
retail, *ko-uri.*
restaurant, *ryōri-ya.*
return, to (*tr.*), *kaesu.*
return, to (*intr.*), *kaeru.*
rice (boiled), *gozen; meshi; o mamma; gohan.*

rice (growing), *ine.*
rich, *kane-mochi (no).*
ride, to, *noru.*
ridiculous, *okashii.*
right (proper), *honto (no); ii.*
right (hand), *migi.*
ring, to (*tr.*), *narasu.*
ring, to (*intr.*), *naru.*
ring (finger), *yubi-wa.*
ripe (of fruit), *juku shita.*
river, *kawa.*
road, *michi.*
roast, to, *yaku.*
rock, *iwa.*
roll, to (*tr.*), *korobasu.*
roll, to (*intr.*), *korobu.*
roof, *yane.*
room, a, *heya; zashĭki.*
root (*ki no*), *ne.*
rope, *nawa.*
rough, *arai.*
round, *marui.*
rub, to, *kosuru.*
rub out, to, *kesu.* [(*na*).
rude, *shitsurei (na); shikkei*
rug, *ketto.* [*fūsetsu.*
rumour, *hyōban; uwasa;*
run, to, *kakeru; hashiru.*
run away, to, *nigeru.*
rust, to, *sabiru.*

Sad, to be, *kanashimu.*
saddle, *kura.*
saddlegirth, *hara-obi.*
saddler, *bagu-ya.*
safe, *daijōbu (na).* [*bako.*
safe (for money, &c.), *kane-*
salad, *saradō.*
salary, *gekkyū.*
salt, *shio.*
salt-cellar, *shiwo-ire.*

same, *onaji*.
sample, *mihon*
sand, *sŭna*.
sardine, *iwashi*.
sash (girdle), *obi*.
satin, *shusu*.
Saturday, *Doyōbi*.
sauce, *shōyu*.
saucepan, *nabe*.
saucer, *shĭta-zara*.
save, to, *tasŭkeru*.
say, to, *hanasu*; *iu*.
school, *gakkō*.
scissors, *hasami*.
screw, *neji*.
screw-driver, *neji-mawashi*.
sea, *umi*.
second-hand, *furute*. [(*no*).
secret, *himitsu* (*na*); *naisho*
see, to, *miru*.
seed, *tane*.
seem, to, *mieru*.
seldom, *mare ni*.
self, *onore*; *jibun*; *jishin*.
sell, to, *uru*.
send, to, *yaru*; *tsŭkawasu*.
separately, *hanarete*; *betsu-betsu-ni*.
September, *ku-gwatsu*.
servant, *hōkōnin*; *meshi-*
sew, to, *nuu*. [*tsŭkai*.
shade (shadow), *kage*.
shape, *katachi*. [*suru*.
share, to, *wakeru*; *bumpai*
shave, to, *hige wo suru*; *hige wo soru*.
she, *ano hĭto*; *ano onna*.
shelf, *tana*.
shine, to, *teru*.
ship, *fune*.
ship (merchant-), *shōsen*.
ship (sailing-), *homae-sen*.
ship (screw-), *uchi-guruma no*
ship (steam-), *jōkisen*. [*jokisen*.
shirt, *shatsu*.
shirt (flannel), *furaneru shatsŭ*.
shirt (under-), *shita-jiban*.
shirt (white), *shiroi jiban*.
shoe, *kutsu*; *han-gutsu*.
shoe-brush, *kutsŭ-bake*.
shoemaker, *kutsu-ya*.
shoot, to (with firearm), *teppō*
shop, *mise*. [*wo utsu*.
shopkeeper, *akindo*. [*hĭkui*.
short (of stature), *sei no*
short (in length), *mijikai*.
shoulder, *kata*.
show, to, *miseru*.
shower (of rain), *yūdachi*.
shrimps, *shiba-ebi*.
shut, to (*tr.*), *shimeru*.
sick, to feel, *mune ga warui*.
side, *hō*; *kata*.
sign, *shirushi*.
sign, to, *namae wo kaku*.
sign (board), *kamban*.
silent, to be, *damaru*.
silk, *kinu*.
silk (raw), *kiito*.
silk-thread, *kinu-ito*.
silly, *baka* (*ni*).
silver, *gin*.
silver-ware, *gin-zaiku*.
simple, *wakari-yasui*; *tegarui*.
since, *kara*. [birds), *naku*.
sing, to (of persons), *utau*; (of
sister (elder), *ane*.
sister (younger), *imōto*.
sit, to, (as Europeans), *koshi wo kakeru*.
sit, to, (as Japanese), *suwaru*.

size, *ōkisa.*
skin, *kawa.*
sky, *sora.*
sleep, to, *neru.*
sleepy, *nemui.*
sleeve, *sode.*
slide, to, *suberu.*
slipper, *uwa-gutsu.*
slow, *osoi.*
slowly, *shidzuka ni.*
small, *chiisai ; chiisa (na).*
smell, a, *nioi.*
smoke, to, *tabako wo nomu.*
smoke, *kemuri.*
sneeze, to, *kŭshami wo suru.*
snow, *yuki.*
so, *sonna ni ; sō.*
soap, *shabon.*
soda-water, *sōda-mizu.* [*ni*).
soft, *yawarakai ; yawaraka*
soil (earth), *tsuchi.* [*su.*
soldier, *heitai ; heishi ; heisot-*
solid (*adj.*), *katai.*
somebody, *dare ka.*
something, *nani ka.*
sometimes, *toki-ori ; ori-fŭshi.*
somewhere, *doko ka.*
son, *musŭko.*
son-in-law, *muko.*
song, *uta.*
soon, *jiki ni.* [*zannen.*
sorry (for one's own sake),
sorry (for another), *kinodoku.*
sound (*noun*), *oto.*
soup, *soppu.*
sour, *suppai.*
south, *minami.*
sow, to, *maku.*
sparrow, *suzume.*
spectacles, *megane.* [*tōki suru.*
speculate, to (in stocks, &c.),
speech, to make a, *enzetsŭ suru.*
spend, to, *tsuiyasu ; tsŭkau.*
spider, *kumo.*
spirits (liquor), *shōchū.*
spoil, to, *sonjiru.*
spoon, *saji.*
spoon (tea-), *cha-saji.*
spring, to (leap), *tobu.*
spring (-time), *haru.*
spring (water), *izumi.*
springs (of a vehicle), *bane.*
square, *shĭkaku (na).*
stable, *ŭmaya.*
stable (livery-), *shakuba-ya.*
staircase, *hashigo-dan.*
stale, *furukusai.*
stamp (postage-), *yūbin-kiite.*
stamp (revenue), *shōken-inshi.*
stand, to (*intr.*), *tatsu.*
star, *hoshi.*
starch, *nori.* [*suru ; tatsu.*
start, to (set out), *shuttatsu*
state (condition), *yōsu ; ari-*
station, *teisha-ba.* [*sama.*
station-master, *eki-chō.*
steal, to, *nusumu.*
steam, *yuge ; jōki.*
steamer, *jōkĭsen.*
steel, *hagane.* [*kata.*
steward (on ship), *makanai-*
stick, to (adhere), *kuttsŭku.*
stiff, *katai.*
still (yet more), *motto.*
still (tranquil), *shizuka (na).*
still (yet), *nao ; mada.*
stirrup, *abumi.*
stone, *ishi.*
stop, to (*tr.*), *tomeru.*
stop, to (*intr.*), *tomaru.*
store (shop), *mise.*

story (tale), *hanashi.*
straight, *massugu* (*na*).
strange, *fŭshigi* (*na*).
stranger, *shiranai hĭto.*
straw, *wara.*
strawberry, *ichigo.*
street, *tōri* ; *machi.*
strength, *chikara.*
string, *ito.*
strong, *tsuyoi.*
student, *shosei.* [*ji.*
stuff (for garments, &c.), *kire-*
stumble, to, *tsumazuku* ; *fumi-*
stupid, *baka* (*ni*). [*hazusu.*
suck, to, *suu.*
sugar, *satō.*
suit, to, *kanau* ; *ki ni iru.*
sum (total), *shime-daka.*
summer, *natsu.*
sun, *hi* ; *taiyō.*
Sunday, *dontaku* ; *nichiyōbi.*
sunrise, *hi no de.*
sunset, *hi no iri.*
supper, *yūmeshi.*
sweep, to, *haku.*
sweet, *amai.*
swim, to, *oyogu.*

Table, *dai* ; *tsŭkue* ; *teifuru.*
table (writing-), *kaku-dai.*
table-cloth, *teberu-kake.*
tack (small nail), *byō.*
tail, *shippo.*
tailor, *shĭtate-ya.*
take, to, *toru.*
take time, to, *tema-doru.*
talk, to, *hanasu* ; *hanashi wo*
tall, *sei no takai.* [*suru.*
taste, *ajiwai.*
tax, *nengu* ; *zei.*
tea, *cha.*
tea-caddy, *cha-ire.*
tea-chest, *chabukuro.*
tea-cup, *cha-nomi-jawan.*
tea-dealer, *cha-shōnin.*
tea-grower, *chashi.*
tea-house, *chaya.*
tea-kettle, *tetsŭ-bin.*
tea-plantation, *cha-ba-take.*
tea-pot, *kibisho.*
tea-spoon, *cha-saji.*
teach, to, *oshieru.*
teacher, *kyōshi* ; *sensei* ; *shishō.*
tear, to (*tr.*), *saku* ; *yabuku.*
tears, *namida.*
telegram, *dempō.*
telegraph-form, *rai-shin-shi.*
telegraph-office, *denshin-*
telephone, *denwa.* [*kyoku.*
telescope, *bōenkyō* ; *tō-megane.*
tell, to, *hanasu* ; *iu* ; *kataru.*
tenant, *shakuya-nin.*
than, *yori.*
thank, to, *rei wo iu.*
then, *sono toki.*
there, *asŭko* ; *soko* ; *achira.*
therefore, *da kara* ; *desŭ kara* (politer).
they, *ano hĭto-tachi* ; *kare-ra.*
thick (in consistency), *koi.*
thick (dimension), *atsui.*
thief, *dorobō.*
thigh, *momo.*
thimble, *yubi-nuki.*
thin, to be, *yasete iru.*
think, to, *omou* ; *zonjiru.*
thirsty, to be, *nodo ga*
throat, *nodo.* [*kawaku.*
through, *tōshĭte* ; *tōtte.*
throw, to, *nageru*, *hōru.*
Thursday, *mokuyōbi.*
ticket, *kippu.*

ticket (return), *ōfuku-gippu.*
tie, to, *shibaru.*
tight, *katai.*
till, *made.*
time, *toki.*
time-table, *jikan-hyō.*
time, to take, *tema-doru*
tin, a, *burikki.*
tin (metal), *suzu.*
tip (fee), *sakate.*
tired, to get, *kŭtabireru.*
to, *ni ; ye.*
toast (bread), *yaki-pan.*
tobacco, *tabako.*
tobacco-pipe, *kiseru.*
tobacco-pouch, *tabako-ire.*
to-day, *konnichi ; kyō* (less
toe (*ashi no*) *yubi.* [polite).
together, *issho ni.*
tomato, *aka-nasu.* [(less polite).
to-morrow, *myōnichi; ashĭta*
tongs (fire), *hibashi.*
tongue, *shita.*
to-night, *komban ; kon-ya.*
too (excess), *amari.*
too (as well), *mo ; yahari.*
tool, *dōgu.*
tooth, *ha.* [*itai.*
toothache (to have), *ha ga*
tooth-brush, *yōji.*
tooth-powder, *ha-migaki.*
top, *ue* (*no hō*).
touch, to, *sawaru ; fureru.*
towards, *no hō ye.*
towel, *te-nugui.*
town (capital), *miyako.*
town (port), *minato.*
town (post), *shŭku.*
trade, *bōeki ; akinai.*
trade-mark, *shōhyō.*
tradesman, *akindo.*
train (railway), *kisha ; ressha.*
tram, *tetsŭdō-basha.*
translate, to, *hon-yaku suru.*
travel, to, *ryokō suru.*
traveller, *tabi-bito.*
tray, *bon.*
tread, to, *fumu.*
treat, to, *tori-atsŭkau.*
tree, *ki.*
tremble, to, *furueru.*
trick (manner), *kŭse.*
trouble, to be in, *komaru.*
trouble, *tekazu.* [(*na*).
troublesome, *urusai ; mendō*
trousers, *zubon.*
true, *hōnto* (*no*) ; *makoto* (*no*).
trunk (receptacle), *kaban.*
trust, to, *shin-yō suru ; shinjiru.*
try, to, *yatte miru ; tamesu.*
Tuesday, *kwayōbi.* [*goppu.*
tumbler (glass), *mizu-nomi-*
tunnel, *ana.*
turn, to (*tr.*), *mawasu.*
turn, to (*intr.*) *mawaru.*
turnip, *kabu.*
twilight, *kure-gata.*
twine, to (*intr.*), *karamu*
twist, to, *hineru ; nejiru*

Ugly (to the sight), *migu-*
umbrella, *kōmori-gasa.* [*rushii.*
unable, to be, *dekinai.*
unavoidable, *yondokoronai.*
uncle, *oji.*
uncomfortable, *fujiyū* (*na*).
under, *no shĭta ni.*
understand, to, *wakaru; shōchi suru.*
undress, to, *kimono wo nugu.*
unfortunately, *ai-niku.*

unhappy, *fu-shiawase.* [*na*).
unkind, *funinjō; fūshinsetsu*
unwell, *ambai ga warui.*
unwholesome, to be, *doku ni*
upon, *no ue ni.* [*naru.*
upright (erect), *massugu* (*na*).
upset, to (*tr.*), *hikkuri-kaesu.*
upside down, *sakasama.*
upstairs, *nikai.*
urgent, *kyū na.*
use, to, *mochiiru; tsŭkau.*
useful, *chōhō* (*na*); *yaku ni tatsu.*
useless, *yaku ni tatanai.*
usual, *tsune* (*no*); *heizei* (*no*).

Vain, *nama-iki* (*na*); *kōman*
value, *atai*; *ne-uchi.* [(*na*).
various, *iro-iro* (*no*); *ironna.*
veal, *ko-ushi-no-niku.*
vegetables, *yasai* (*mono*).
vegetable-marrow, *shiro-uri.*
velvet, *birōdo.*
vice, *fu-mimochi; akuhei.*
view, (prospect), *mi-harashi;*
village, *sato; mura.* [*keshĭki.*
vinegar, *su.*
violent, *te-arai.*
virtue (goodness), *zen.*
visit, to pay a, *tazunete kuru.*
visitor, *kyaku.*
voice, *koe.*
volume (book), *satsu.*
vulgar, *gehin* (*na*).

Wages, *kyūkin.*
waistcoat, *chokki.*
wait, to, *matsu.*
waiter, *kyūji.*
waiting-room, *machi-ai-ba.*
walk, to, *aruku.*
wall (stone), *ishibei;* (mud), [*kabe.*
want, to, *hoshii.*
warehouse, *dozō; kura.*
warm, *atatakai; atataka* (*na*).
warn, to, *imashimeru.*
wash, to, *arau.*
wash-hand bowl, *chōzu-darai.*
waste, to (*tr.*), *tsuiyasu muda ni tsŭkau.* [*ban wo suru.*
watch, to, *ki wo tsŭkeru;*
watch (timepiece), *tokei.*
watch-maker, *tokeiya.* [*yu.*
water (cold), *mizu;* (hot), (*o*)
way (road), *michi.* [*ambai.*
way (manner), *shĭkata; yō;*
weak, *yowai.*
wear, to (*tr.*), *kiru.*
wear, to (*intr.*), *motsu.*
weather, *yōki; tenki.*
Wednesday, *suiyōbi.*
week, *shūkan.*
weigh, to (*tr.*), *hakaru.*
weight, *mekata.*
well (in health), *jōbu* (*na*).
well, to get, *naoru.*
west, *nishi.*
wet, to be, *nurete iru.*
wheel, *kuruma; wa.*
when? *itsu?*
where, *tokoro;* where? *doko?*
which? *dore?*
white, *shiroi.*
who? *dare? donata?*
whole, *mina; sōtai* (*no*).
wholesale, *oroshi.*
wholesale-dealer, *oroshi-ya.*
wholesome, to be, *kŭsuri ni naru.*
why? *naze? dō iu wake de.*
wide (*haba no*), *hiroi.*
width, *haba.*

win, to, *katsu*.
wind, to, *kuru*; *maku*.
wind, the, *kaze*.
window, *mado*.
window-shutters, *mado no to*.
wine, *sake*; *budōshu*.
wine-glass, *sakazuki*.
wing, *hane*.
winter, *fuyu*.
wipe, to, *nuguu*; *fūku*.
wire, *harigane*.
wish, to, *hoshii* (*adj.*).
with (together), *to issho ni*.
with (by means of), *de*; *de motte*.
withdraw, to (*intr.*), *shirizoku*.
witness, *shōko-nin*.
woman, *onna*; *fujin* (more polite).
wonderful, *mezurashii*; *myō* (*na*); *fūshigi* (*na*).
wood (trees), *mori*.
wood (fire-), *ki*.
wool, *rasha*; *ke*.
woollen-cloth, *rasha*.
word, *kotoba*.
work, to, *hataraku*.
work (*noun*), *shigoto*.
workman, *shokunin*.
world, *sekai*.
worth, *atai*; *ne-uchi*.
worthless, *tsumaranai*.
wound, *kizu*; *kega*.
wrap up, to, *tsutsumu*.
wrist, *te-kubi*.
write, to, *kaku*.
wrong (*adj.*), *warui*; *machigatta*.

Yawn, to, *akubi suru*.
year, *toshi*.
year, this, *kotoshi*.
year, last, *saku-nen*.
year, next, *myō-nen*.
yearly, *mai-nen*.
yellow, *ki-iroi*.
yesterday, *kinō*; *sakujitsu* (more polite).
yolk (of egg), *ki-mi*.
young, *wakai*.

Zeal, *nesshin*.
zinc, *totan*.

Money, Weights and Measures.

NOTE.—With the exception of the *hiro* and the *tsubo*, all the names of the measures, weights, &c., given in the following tables are of Chinese origin, and are accompanied by the Chinese numerals only.

1. MONEY.

The CURRENCY IS DECIMAL; the unit is the *yen*, a silver coin equivalent to about two English shillings (50 cents. American), which has taken the place of the Mexican dollar, formerly used in Japan but now obsolete. One yen = 100 sen; one sen = 10 rin.

GOLD PIECES of 2, 5, 10 and 20 yen are also coined.

COPPER COINS vary from $\frac{1}{10}$ of a sen (1 rin) to 2 sen.

There is also a PAPER CURRENCY, consisting of notes of from 5 *sen* up to 10 and 20 *yen*. Not only in the towns, but throughout Japan generally, paper money, and especially that of the Bank of Japan, is regarded with more favour than gold or silver coin.

BANKING TRANSACTIONS, and indeed commercial transactions in general are framed on English models. Thus, ordinary and telegraphic money orders are issued; there is a Post Office Savings Bank; and Letters of Credit, Bills of Exchange and Bankers' Orders are all in constant use.

2. WEIGHTS.

10 rin	=	1 fun	=	5.8 grs.
10 fun	=	1 momme	=	58 ,,
100 momme	=	1 hyaku-me	=	about $\frac{3}{4}$ lb. (av.)
160 ,,	=	1 kin	=	1.325 lbs.*
1000 ,,	=	1 kamme	=	8.28 ,,

* Usually reckoned $1\frac{1}{3}$ lb. avoirdupois in transacting business with foreigners.

3. Long Measure.

10 rin	= 1 bu	...	= .1193 in.	($\frac{1}{8}$ in.)
10 bu	= 1 sun	...	= 1.193 ,,	($1\frac{1}{5}$ in.)
10 sun	= { 1 shaku *or* kaneshaku }		= 11.93 in.	(nearly 1 foot)
6 shaku	= 1 ken	...	= 71.58 ,,	(nearly 2 yds.)
10 ,,	= 1 jō	...	=119.3 ,,	(nearly 10 ft.)
60 ken	= 1 chō (*nearly*)		=119.3 yds.	(about 120 yds.)
36 chō	= 1 ri	...	= 2.44 miles.	

For nautical measurements the *kai-ri* which equals the European geographical mile, is now in general use; whilst for indicating the depth of water, the *hiro* (about 5 feet) is employed.

4. Superficial or Land Measure.

30 tsubo	= 1 se	= 118.6 sq. yds.	
10 se	= 1 tan	= 1186 ,,	(over $\frac{1}{4}$ acre)
10 tan	= 1 chō	= 2.45 acres	(2 a. 1 r. 32 p.)

The *tsubo*, the common unit of measurement, is 6 *kaneshaku* square, i.e., about 3.95 square yards.

5. Dry Goods Measure.

In measuring dry goods a *shaku* (termed *kujiraku*) of 14.913 inches is employed. Silk and cotton goods are generally made up into pieces measuring a little more than $10\frac{3}{4}$ yards (*tan*) and also into pieces of double that length (*hiki*).

The English yard is now becoming generally known in the towns.

6. Measure of Capacity.

10 sai	= 1 shaku	=	$\frac{1}{31}$ pint
10 shaku	= 1 gō	=	about $\frac{1}{3}$ pint
10 gō	= 1 shō	=	,, $3\frac{1}{5}$ pints
10 shō	= 1 to	=	,, 4 gals.
10 to	= 1 koku	=	,, 39.7 ,,

This measure is employed for grain and liquids. The *shō* equals .397 (about two-fifths) of a gallon. The *koku* is employed for measuring junks, and is equal to about 4-27ths of a ton (nearly 3 cwt.), or $2\frac{1}{2}$ piculs. (1 picul = 100 kin.)

INDEX TO PART I.

A

B

C

N

O

P

MARLBOROUGH, PEWTRESS & Co., 52, Old Bailey, London, E.C.